Executive Editor: Krishna Bista

Guest Editor: Osman Gültekin

Vol. **14** No **5** **(2024)**

JOURNAL OF INTERNATIONAL STUDENTS

A Flagship Publication on International Education

Access this journal online at jistudents.org

Editorial Office:
PO BOX 374
Baltimore, Maryland (US)

Print ISSN 2162-3104
Online ISSN 2166-3750

ISBN: 9798230207412

Cover Design: Nabi Saribaş

Disclaimer

Facts and opinions published in the *Journal of International Students* (JIS) express solely the opinions of the respective authors. Authors are responsible for citing sources and ensuring the accuracy of their references and bibliographies. The editors cannot be held responsible for any lack or possible violations of third parties' rights.

Subject Area: International Education

At JIS, we prioritize submissions that present significant advancements on under-researched aspects of international education, especially those focusing on underrepresented regions, populations, and contexts. We emphasize scholarship that centers perspectives of women, people of color, and Global South communities, spans boundaries, and utilizes diverse theories and methodologies.

Research Focus Areas:

- AI and technology in international education
- Global competence and intercultural communication
- Cross-cultural emotional wellness
- Decolonization and the politics of belonging
- Employability and multinational careers
- Ethical internationalization
- Immigration politics and human rights
- Intersectional studies of language and identity
- New geographies of student mobility
- STEM and culturally relevant pedagogies
- Sustainability and ecological consciousness
- Racial justice and systemic reforms
- Transnational identities and communities
- Virtual mobility and online learning
- Technology-enabled language immersion

More at *jistudents.org*

Global Essay Project

Call for Essays

Everyone has a memorable story of studying or working outside the country of birth. What is your story about studying overseas? What are your cross-cultural experiences from exchange programs or study abroad? Are you a current or former international student? Tell your stories of exploring the words, the world, and the wonders.

Essay Categories
International Student Experience
Study Abroad / Exchange Program Experience
Faculty/ Staff Experience

Languages
You can write your story/essay in any of the following eight languages: Arabic, Chinese, English, French, German, Hindi, Russian, Spanish

Essay Writing Suggestions
Share a story: Focus on moments, encounters, and experiences that shaped your journey as an international student. Tell a story that no one else could tell. Your story can be about friendship, service, freedom, discrimination, injustice, activism, belonging, family, courage, resilience, citizenship, academics, spirituality, parenthood, discovery, inclusion, self-discovery, growth, etc.

Tell your challenges and lessons. Flavor your writing with idioms and figures of speech from your language. Paint the picture. Be concrete about what you have seen in your travels, academic encounters, woes, and wows!

Format Requirements
A story or essay of 1000-1,500 words; Typed in 12-pt size, Times Roman font; double-spaced; 1-inch margins on all sides; includes page numbers. We accept Microsoft Word files only.

See guidelines and sample essays:
https://starscholars.org/lanterns-across-the-sky/

ISSN: 2162-3104 Print/ ISSN: 2166-3750 Online
© *Journal of International Students*
Jistudents.or

Editorial Team

Barry Fass-Holmes, San Diego State University (US)
Benjamin Nam, SHISU (CN)
Benu Prasad Dahal, Royal Government of Bhutan (BT)
Bernardo Sfredo Miorando, Universidade Federal de Ciências da Saúde (BR) ★
Bettina Teegen, University of Surrey (UK) ★
Bich Tran, Dartmouth College (US)
Blair Matthews, University of St Andrews (UK)
Bo Chang, Ball State University (US)
Bowen Zhang, Manchester University (UK)
Bruna Navarone Santos, Oswaldo Cruz Foundation/Oswaldo Cruz Institute (BR)
Caroline Wekullo, Texas A&M University (US)
Catherine Hartman, University of South Carolina (US)
Charles R Harris, Arkansas State University (US)
Chenyang Lin, University of California, Los Angeles (CN)
Chetanath Gautam, Delaware State University (US)
Chih-Hsin Hsu, university of arkansas tech (US)
Christine Cress, Portland State University (US)
Christine Fiorite, University of Chicago (US)
Congcong Xing, Queensland University of Technology (AU)
Conor Nolan, National College of Ireland (IE) ★
Cosmin Ionut Nada, CIIE-FPCEUP (PT)
Dae Seok Chai, Colorado State University (US)
Dan Dickman, Ivy Tech Community College of Indiana (US)
Dana Van De Walker, Sam Houston State University (US)
Daniel Adrian Doss Doss, Jackson State University (US)
Danielle Geary, Georgia Tech (US)
David Austin Willis, University of Tennessee, Knoxville (US) ◊
David Vargas, Masarykova Univerzita (CZ)
Deborah Okin, Fielding Graduate University (US)
Dong Chen, University of Arizona (US)
Dorothy Mayne, University of Illinois (US)
Elena K. Taborda, University of Massachusetts Boston (US) ◊
Eman Elturki, Washington State University (US)
Emma Sabzalieva, UNESCO IESALC (CA)
Eric Terzuolo, Stanford University (US)
Erika Saito, National University, College of Education (US)
Fan Fang, Shantou University (CN)
Fikri Yanda, Universitas Pendidikan Indonesia (ID) ★
Galicia Blackman, University of Calgary (CA) ★
Garth Stahl, University of Queensland (AU)
Gene Vasilopoulos, University of Ottawa (CA)
Genevieve Hiltebrand, San Juan College (US)
Giorgio Di Pietro, University of Westminster (UK)
Gloria Wong, Hong Kong University (HK)
Gul Rind, Miami University/ Sukkur IBA University, Pakistan (PK)
Guoqin Gong, University of Hong Kong (HK)
Hany Zaky, Union County College, UCC, NJ, USA (US)
Hélène Syed Zwick, ESLSCA University Egypt (EG) ★
Hyejin Yoon, University of Wisconsin-Milwaukee (US)
Ibrahim Bicak, University of Chicago (US)
Icy Anabo, University of Deusto (ES)

Intan Pradita, UII Yogyakarta (ID)
Ireena Nasiha Ibnu, Universiti Teknologi MARA (MY)
James Burford, La Trobe University (AU)
James Elwood, Meiji University (JP)
Jami Leibowitz, East Carolina University (US)
Jana Jaffa, Penn State (US)
Jason Li, Wichita State University (US)
Jasvir Kaur, La Trobe University (AU) ★
Jayme Scally, West Virginia University (US)
Jeanne-Marie Viljoen, University of South Aastralia (AU)
Jennifer Majorana, Central Michigan University (US)
Jeongwoon Jeong, The University of New Mexico (US)
Jia Li, Yunnan University (CN)
Jingran Yu, Southern University of Science and Technology (CN)
Jinqi Xu, University of Sydney (AU)
Jon Woodend, University of Victoria (CA) ◊
Judith Borràs, Universitat Pompeu Fabra (ES)
Juhee Kim, Eastern Kentucky University (US)
Jungyeol Park, University of Minnesota (US)
Kalypso Filippou, University of Turku (FI) ★
Kandy K. Turner, Widener University (US)
Karlo Avenido, Simon Fraser University (CA)
Kat Stephens, University of Massachusetts Amherst (US)
Kate Maloney Williams, University of Maryland, College Park (US)
Kati Bell, University of California, Irvine (US)
Keenan Daniel Manning, University of Hong Kong (HK) ★
Kelly A. Pengelly, American University (US)
Kenichi Doi, Peking University (CN)
Keri Freeman, Griffith University (AU)
Kim Bullington, Old Dominion University (US)
Kimberley Daly, George Mason University (US)
Kyunghee Ma, University of South Carolina (KR) ★
Laura Engel, The George Washington University (US)
Laura Soledad Norton, Sapienza University of Rome (IT) ★
Laura Vaughn, Florida State University (US)
Lilik Istiqomah, Universitas Islam Negeri Raden Mas Said Surakarta (ID)
Lin Ma, University of Bristol (UK)
Lisa Unangst, SUNY Empire State College (US)
Malin Glimäng, Malmö University (SE)
Manca Sustarsic, University of Hawaii at Manoa (US) ◊
Mardene Carr, Grand Canyon University (US) ◊
María Cruz Cuevas Álvarez, Universidad Juárez Autónoma de Tabasco (MX) ★
Marthy Watson, University Of Southern Queensland (AU)
Mary Ann Bodine Al-Sharif, University of Alabama at Birmingham (US) ◊
Mary Jacinta Nekesa, Makerere University (UG)
Max Crumley-Effinger, Loyola University Chicago (US)
Melissa Baralt, Florida International University (US)
Melissa Yeung, University of Houston (US) ◊
Mengwei Su, Ohio University (US)
Mengwei Tu, East China University of Science and Technology (CN)
Michael Salmon, University of Bath (UK)

Michał Wilczewski, University of Economics & Human Sciences (PL) ★
Milad Mohebali, University of Iowa (US)
Ming Xie, West Texas A&M University (US)
Minghui Hou, Old Dominion University (US)
Mohd Muzhafar Idrus, Universiti Sains Islam Malaysia (MY) ★
Mudithani Maheshika Hettiarachchi, University of Houston (US) ◊
Namrata Rao, Liverpool Hope UNiversity (UK) ★
Nara M. Martirosyan, Sam Houston State University (US)
Nina Marijanovic, University of Kentucky (US)
Ning Guo, Saint Louis University (US)
Nizamuddin Sadiq, Universitas islam Indonesia (ID)
Nora Isacoff, Columbia University (US)
Norihito Taniguchi, Nagoya University (JP)
Oluwasegun Oladipo, Peking University (CN)
Omolabake Fakunle, University of Edinburgh (UK)
Oumaima Elghazali, Mohammed V University in Rabat (MA)
Paul Garton, University of South Carolina (US)
Peggy Gesing, Eastern Virginia Medical School (US)
Pengfei Pan, Queensland University of Technology (AU)
Per A. Nilsson, Umeå University (SE) ★
Peter G. Ghazarian, Ashland University (US)
Prabin Shrestha, Tri Chandra Multiple Campus (NP)
Pratik Ambani, Consulting & Implementation Services (AU) ◊
Qianqian Zhang-Wu, Northeastern University (US)
Reyhan Aslan, Middle East Technical University (TR)
Rong Wang, Xi'an Jiaotong Liverpool University (CN)
Rosalind Latiner Raby, California State University Northridge (US)
Ruijin Yang, Queensland University of Technology (AU)
Ryan Allen, Chapman University (US)
Ryan Deuel, St. Lawrence University (US) ◊
Sami B Mejri, Northcentral University (US)
Sara Bano, North Dakota State University (US)
Sarah Asada, Kyoritsu Women's University (JP)
Sehyun Yun, Ball State University (US)
Shanshan Jiang, University of Wisconsin-Madison (US)
Shanton Chang, University of Melbourne, Australia (AU)
Shasha Cui, University of Rochester (US)
Shihua Brazill, Montana State University (US) ◊
Shingo Hanada, Toyo University (JP) ★
Siqi Tu, NYU Shanghai (CN) ★
Siti Masrifatul Fitriyah, Jember University (ID)
Sophia Glenyse Rahming, Florida State University (US)
Steven Jones, The University of Alabama (US)
Tamara M Chung Constant, University of Massachusetts Amherst (US) ◊
Tang Tang Heng, National Institute of Education--Singapore (SG)
Tara Nicola, Harvard University (US)
Taryn Devereux, University of Maryland (US)
Terra Gargano, American University (US)
Thi Kim Thu Le, University of Windsor (CA)
Tiberio Garza, Florida International University (US)

Tiffany Viggiano, Oregon Health and Science University (US) ◊
Tran Le Huu Nghia, Australian National University (AU) ◊
Vander Tavares, York University (CA)
Wan Chi Leung, University of Canterbury (NZ) ★
Wauseca Briscoe, Morgan State University (US) ◊
Wei Liu, University of Alberta (CA)
Wonsun Ryu, University of Texas at Austin (US) ◊
Xiao Hu, Beijing Normal University (CN)
Xiaoqiao Zhang, Massachusetts General Hospital (US)
Xinxin Wang, UNC at Chapel Hill (US)
Xuewei He, The George Washington University (US)
Yan Gao, University of Victoria (CA)
Yi'En Cheng, National University of Singapore (SG)
Yifei Liang, University of Queensland (AU)
Yingling Lou, University of Calgary (CA) ◊
Yingxin Liu, The Chinese University of Hong Kong, Shenzhen (CN)
Yingyi Ma, Syracuse University (US)
Yiying Xiong, Johns Hopkins University (US)
Yolanda Palmer-Clarke, University of Saskatchewan (CA)
Yun Yu, East China Normal University (CN)
Zhenjie Weng, Ohio State University (US)
Helen Liu, York University (CN)
Dadhi Ram Panthi, Pashupati Campus (NP)
Elizabeth Margarita Hernández López, University of Guadalajara, (MX) ◊
Zoey Roosevelt, University of San Diego (US)
Thai Vu, Curtin University (AU)
Seyma Inan, Mercyhurst University (US)
Quyet Thi Nguyen, Ho Chi Minh City University of Technology and Education (VN)
Suhao Peng, University of Eastern Finland (Finland)
Sahizer Samuk, Wilfried Laurier University (Canada)
Chet Narayan Acharya, Pokhara University (Nepal)
Abdullah Al Mahmud, University of Liberal Arts Bangladesh (Bangladesh)
Yang Li, Saint Louis University (USA)
Hadi Jalabi, Student, Üsküdar University (Turkey)
Tina Renier, Global Sustainable Futures Network (International)
Maikel Pons-Giralt, University of Santa Cruz do Sul (Brazil)
Praveen Kumar Rudra, Immigreat Lancaster (UK)
Aanchal Arora, Chandigarh University (India)
Kalpesh Kamble, Sindhudurg Shikshan Prasarak Mandal (India)
Nilo Castulo, Beijing Normal University (China)
Mehradad Falavarjani, University of Saskatchewan (Canada)
Alex Erickson, George Washington University (US)
Ishwar Koirala, University of New England (Australia)
Xuechen Yuan, University of Windsor (Canada)
Nguyen B. Ngoc, Yuan Ze University (Taiwan)
Faruq Ubaidillah, Universitas Islam Malang (Indonesia)
Rakshya Baral, Morgan State University (US)
Sarah Carrica-Ochoa, University of Navarra
Frida Jaime Franco, Durham University
Hissah Alzahrani, University of North Carolina Wilmington

Hissah Alzahrani, UNCW
Bruna Navarone, Oswaldo Cruz Foundation
Candice Seale, University of the Western Cape
Justin Weller, Michigan State University
Lili/ Eika Jiang, Technische Universität Braunschweig, Germany
Jennifer Park, University of North Carolina Wilmington
Siu-Man Ting, North Carolina State University
María Cruz Cuevas Álvarez, Universidad Juárez Autónoma de Tabasco
Rully Damayanti, Petra Christian University, INDONESIA
Jihene Ftouh, Istanbul Aydin University
Lucy Lee Allen, Lancaster University
Maikel Pons-Giralt, University of Santa Cruz do Sul, Brazil
Oksana Beregovaya, Siberian Institute of Management
Praveen Kumar Rudra, Capella University
Petrit Duraj, University of Gjakova
Hyangeun Ji, Temple University
Farah Deeba, Bahauddin Zakariya Universitty
Ran Jiao, Ritsumeikan University
Muzaffar Hussain, University of Essex, UK

Indexing

ISSN: 2162-3104 Print/ ISSN: 2166-3750 Online
Journal of International Students

SUBJECT: Education- Higher Education/ DEWEY #378

Directory of Open Access Journals, 2011-
EBSCOhost, Education Source, 03/01/2012-
Gale

- Academic OneFile, 09/01/2011-
- Contemporary Women's Issues, 09/01/2011-
- Educator's Reference Complete, 09/01/2011-
- Expanded Academic ASAP, 09/01/2011-
- InfoTrac Custom, 09/01/2011-

ProQuest

- Education Collection, 10/01/2011-
- Education Database, 10/01/2011-
- Education Database (Alumni Edition), 10/01/2011-
- ProQuest Central, 10/01/2011-
- ProQuest Central - UK Customers, 10/01/2011-
- ProQuest Central (Alumni Edition), 10/01/2011-
- ProQuest Central (Corporate), 10/01/2011-
- ProQuest Central (US Academic Subscription), 10/01/2011-
- ProQuest Central China, 10/01/2011-
- ProQuest Central Essentials, 10/01/2011-
- ProQuest Central Korea, 10/01/2011-
- ProQuest Central Student, 10/01/2011-
- ProQuest Research Library, 10/01/2011-
- ProQuest Research Library (Corporate), 10/01/2011-
- ProQuest Social Sciences Premium Collection, 10/01/2011-
- Research Library (Alumni Edition), 10/01/2011-
- Social Science Premium Collection, 10/01/2011-

Clarivate Analytics

- Web of Science
- Emering Sciences Citation Index
- Higher Education Abstracts

Source: Ulrichsweb Global Serials Directory

You may access the print and/or digital copies of the Journal of International Students from **700 libraries worldwide**

Table of Contents

Vol. 14 No. 5 (2024): Journal of International Students
Published: November 15, 2024

Articles

This edition was published in collaboration with

Guest Editorial:

Journal of International Students
Volume 14, Issue 5 (2024), pp. i-ii
ISSN: 2162-3104 (Print), 2166-3750 (Online)
jistudents.org

Navigating Challenges and Enriching Perspectives: Insights into the Experiences and Success of International Students

Osman Gultekin
Istanbul Aydin University, Turkey

I have greatly enjoyed reading and editing the insightful articles for this edition, each of which contributes to shaping policy and practice for a global audience. In this volume of the *Journal of International Students*, the diverse challenges, motivations, and experiences of international students are examined through a lens that reflects the evolving global landscape of higher education. The featured articles address critical themes including mental health, cultural adaptation, professional aspirations, and educational strategies that support international student success across various contexts.

Esther Son and Kristen Cvancara's investigation into "Zoom fatigue" offers timely insights into the toll of virtual learning environments on international students in the U.S., emphasizing the need for adaptive teaching strategies to mitigate fatigue and enhance engagement. Bing Gao and Pamela M. Wesely's work on acculturation sheds light on the complexities faced by international graduate students as they navigate academic and social integration within U.S. institutions.

The empowerment of students in research, as discussed by Lillian Hung and colleagues through "appreciative inquiry," provides an inspiring model for fostering resilience and confidence. Meanwhile, Trung Tu Nguyen and Manu Sharma highlight the obstacles that international graduates encounter in the Canadian labor market, calling for reforms to create equitable opportunities for skilled international students.

This volume also explores cultural and emotional dimensions, as seen in Sarah Carrica-Ochoa and Eleanor Joanne Brown's study on intercultural sensitivity among Latin American exchange students, and Justin Weller's examination of college transitions for third-culture individuals. Rawan Alzukari and Tianlan Wei's meta-analysis on gender differences in acculturative stress further underscores the importance of tailored support strategies.

Additionally, articles by Fihris Fihris and colleagues on the motivations of Southeast Asian students in teacher education, and Siu-Man Raymond Ting and

Zhiqi Angel Liu on the impact of COVID-19 stressors on Chinese students, reveal the personal and external factors influencing students' educational journeys.

Collectively, this volume contributes valuable knowledge to international education research, offering actionable insights for policymakers, educators, and administrators to better support the academic and personal well-being of international students globally.

The *Journal of International Students* has positioned itself as a leading, peer-reviewed publication dedicated to advancing knowledge in international education. As a quarterly flagship journal based in Maryland, United States, JIS serves as a multilingual platform that fosters critical dialogue on pressing issues in global education, drawing contributions from researchers, educators, and policymakers worldwide. The journal's inclusive approach prioritizes research that centers voices from the Global South, highlights underrepresented populations, and challenges conventional frameworks through innovative theories and methodologies. By promoting multi-authored, collaborative work that spans borders, JIS remains at the forefront of scholarship in international education, shaping policy and practice for a global audience.

I am deeply grateful for the opportunity to work alongside our esteemed senior editors and the dedicated editorial team whose expertise and guidance have been instrumental in bringing this volume to life. My heartfelt thanks go out to each reviewer who generously gave their time and insights to ensure the quality and rigor of every manuscript selected for this edition. I also extend my sincere appreciation to the editorial office staff, whose unwavering support and commitment have been invaluable throughout the process. Together, this collaborative effort has made this publication a true testament to the dedication and passion that drive our shared mission in international education.

Bio:

Osman Gültekin holds the prestigious UNESCO Chair on Cultural Diplomacy, Governance, and Education, and is an Assistant Professor in Political Science and International Relations at Istanbul Aydin University. He serves as the Assistant Director of Academic International Relations at Istanbul Aydin University. Dr. Gültekin is also the STAR Scholars Country Director for Turkey. His work focuses on fostering international collaboration and advancing cultural diplomacy through academic initiatives and research.

Article

Journal of International Students
Volume 14, Issue 5 (2024), pp. 1-20
ISSN: 2162-3104 (Print), 2166-3750 (Online)
jistudents.org

Exploring Zoom Fatigue among International Students in U.S. Virtual Classes

Esther Son
University of Maryland, College Park, USA

Kristen Cvancara
Minnesota State University, Mankato, USA

ABSTRACT

Online video conferencing platforms, such as Zoom, are widely used for virtual classes. Zoom platforms bring flexibility and convenience but also contribute to fatigue, which is called "Zoom fatigue." The purpose of this study is to investigate Zoom fatigue among international students at U.S. universities and its links to virtual classroom communication in the field of education. The study investigated how English competency and course engagement affected Zoom fatigue in virtual classes experienced by 152 international students. The results showed that English competency and course engagement had a negative relationship with Zoom fatigue. The study implied that when international students had high English competency, they had less Zoom fatigue experience. In addition, international students had less Zoom fatigue experience when they engaged in virtual classes. The study suggested future directions for decreasing Zoom fatigue and increasing course engagement among international students in virtual classes.

Keywords: computer-mediated communication, course engagement, English competency, international students, virtual classes, Zoom fatigue

In the digital age, technology is a pivotal resource for communicating with others. Instead of meeting in person, people communicate with each other through phone or online video conferencing platforms. Online platforms are convenient and flexible so that people can communicate from any place at any coordinated time. These conveniences and flexibilities impact our interpersonal communication in the workplace and in school. In other words, people have started to replace in-person meetings or classes with video conferencing platforms. While offering convenience and flexibility, one drawback is that whenever the usage time increases, people start to express negative feelings regarding how these platforms leave them exhausted and burned out. Zoom Video Communications, Inc., is a U.S.-based company that provided one of the most common video conferencing platforms used when the COVID-19 pandemic swept the world in 2019; thus, this phenomenon has been referred to as "Zoom fatigue" (McCabe et al., 2023; Nesher Shoshan & Wehrt, 2022; Riedl, 2022).

"Zoom fatigue" emerged as a newly coined word from the workplace when people started relying on online video conferencing platforms. Many studies have shown that zoom fatigue occurs because of cognitive load (Lee, 2020; McCabe et al., 2023). The concept of cognitive load is that an individual has a limited capacity for working memory to interact with unlimited long-term memory for thinking and learning (McCabe et al., 2023). People feel fatigued in virtual meetings because they invest extra cognitive effort in computer-mediated communication (CMC) to acquire, store, produce, and interpret knowledge. Thus, CMC focuses on cognitive processes because meanings can be interpreted differently, formed or comprehended depending on communication media (Yao & Ling, 2020).

As video conferencing platforms have become embedded in our workplace and school, computer-mediated communication has become common in our lives. Current studies investigate how people use video conferencing platforms in workplaces and education and why people feel fatigued from these platforms (Epstein-Shuman & Kushlev, 2022; McCabe et al., 2023; Nesher Shoshan & Wehrt, 2022; Riedl, 2022). People tend to feel more fatigued in these platforms because more nonverbal cues are provided (e.g., viewing others/own screen, icons, chatting) than face-to-face communication media. Similarly, video conferencing platforms require more cognitive effort to interpret and produce information because of extra nonverbal cues (Bailenson, 2021; McCabe et al., 2023).

As the number of virtual classes has increased, especially since the pandemic, more studies on Zoom fatigue in virtual classes are needed. Specifically, studies should consider individual characteristics in computer-mediated communication to distinguish international students from domestic students because nonnative English-speaking students experience more language barriers than native speakers do. In this sense, international students may be especially prone to experience fatigue if English competency exacerbates Zoom fatigue because of increased cognitive load. In addition, studies should consider how course engagement is related to Zoom fatigue in virtual classes among international students. Thus, the current study provides theoretical explanations of media richness theory to explore how international students' English competency and course engagement affect Zoom fatigue. This study utilizes a quantitative survey design to establish a baseline understanding of Zoom fatigue among a sample population of international students studying at a mid-sized state university in the U.S. The ultimate goal of the current research is to investigate Zoom-mediated communication to suggest future directions for decreasing Zoom fatigue and increasing course engagement among international students attending virtual classes at U.S. universities.

LITERATURE REVIEW

International students abroad

Many U.S. colleges or universities accept international students because they bring mutual benefits to students and institutions. First, international students can extend their perspective and enrich the learning environment by sharing their different views and cultures. International and domestic students can develop a deeper understanding by exchanging information, ideas, and support (Andrade, 2006; Grayson, 2008), which brings educational benefits to each other. Second, international students contribute to revenue because they pay full tuition fees. When domestic students take federal student loans to cover their tuition fees, the universities do not fully gain money because the federal student loan funds are disbursed to the U.S. Department of Education. Specifically, the U.S. Department of Education has the authority to regulate federal student loan funds to the university, and the funds can be used for only intended purposes (e.g., faculty salaries, campus maintenance, and academic programs). Thus, international students' tuition fees directly help the university support operations without any restrictions from the federal state or U.S. Department of Education. Third, international students earn personal development, such as improving foreign language skills, engaging in career development, and building networks (Costello, 2015).

The Institute of International Education indicates that total international enrollment reached 1,057,188, an increase of over 100,000 students compared to the 2021-22 figures (Nietzel, 2023). Since the number of international students has increased in U.S. colleges and universities, it is important to study their virtual learning experiences and course engagement related to Zoom fatigue. Zoom fatigue negatively affects mental health and well-being (Nesher Shoshan & Wehrt, 2022), which could jeopardize students' academic success and prompt them to question whether to continue their studies. Thus, exploring Zoom fatigue among international students to retain international students is important.

Zoom fatigue

Virtual classrooms are facilitated via online video conferencing platforms, also known as online education platforms (Zoom is an example of a commonly used platform), in which the person does not have to be physically present on campus to learn or teach (Minhas et al., 2021). Many educators use the Zoom platform for their virtual classes because of high-quality audio and video. Zoom platforms assist people in maintaining their careers and relationships without physically being in the same space. Instead of going to classes, many students can take the course remotely (e.g., at home or in a coffee shop), which provides them with a comfortable atmosphere and convenience by saving commuting time.

Despite convenience, students who use Zoom platforms feel fatigued during virtual classes (Epstein-Shuman & Kushlev, 2022; McCabe et al., 2023). The fatigue that people experienced with the Zoom platform was first shown in the workplace. People reported feeling anxious, mentally or emotionally drained, or socially isolated as the duration of the video conference increased, prompting the label "Zoom fatigue" (Nesher Shoshan & Wehrt, 2022; Riedl, 2022). Zoom fatigue has been widely shown in video conferences because most employees feel physically trapped by staring at the screen for long periods, and women feel more fatigued than men do (Fauville et al., 2021). Similarly, Zoom fatigue was also experienced in education settings by students who attended virtual classes.

Students feel Zoom fatigue in virtual classes, especially when their cameras are on (Epstein-Shuman & Kushlev, 2022). For example, research by Nadler (2020) has demonstrated that Zoom fatigue occurs after a person starts at the screen for a long time, especially when there is less interaction. Although interaction is important in virtual classes to decrease Zoom fatigue, students can be easily distracted (e.g., doing their own tasks, accessing the internet, and interacting with their cell phones).

Moreover, research by Koo and Jiang (2022) and Koo and Nyunt (2022) revealed that international students learn more about American culture and enhance their English competency in face-to-face classes because of their social interactions. Additionally, Lorenzetti et al. (2023) showed that social interaction is an important element of academic success. These findings demonstrate that international students may have a lower chance of improving English competency in virtual classes because of fewer social interactions. Some studies have shown that Zoom tools increase course engagement in learning, but students continue to face the challenge of Zoom fatigue (Kohnke & Moorhouse, 2022; Peper & Yang, 2021). In addition to these findings, Zoom fatigue could be explained by Nadler's (2020) observation that students' understanding differed between online and face-to-face environments. This difference in locations in virtual classes emphasizes the modes through which Zoom-mediated communication is experienced by professors and students during classes. Therefore, Zoom fatigue hinges on international students' English competency to participate and interact in virtual classes.

English competency

English competency is one of the greatest challenges for international students adjusting to school and social groups (Andrade, 2006; Johnson, 1988; Wan et al., 1992; Yeh & Inose, 2003). English competency is intertwined with their daily lives (e.g., ordering food, getting groceries in a store), their social support (e.g., building social networks, sharing ideas and thoughts), and their academic work (e.g., understanding the courses, doing assignments). Many studies have revealed that low English competency increases international students' mental illness and academic stress to cope with those demands (Mori, 2000; Sandhu & Asrabadi, 1994; Wei et al., 2012). From this perspective, international students' academic achievement is undeniably associated with English competency, which warrants investigation into virtual learning via online video conferencing platforms. Face-to-face classes offer more opportunities to improve English from social interaction with peers and an instructor (Biesenbach-Lucas, 2003). Hence, language competency is an important component that international students consider in virtual learning platforms, which can also influence their academic work at U.S. universities.

Theoretical perspectives

To decrease Zoom fatigue in virtual classes, Zoom-mediated communication should be considered on the basis of international students' English competency for two reasons. First, virtual classes require multitasking, which causes Zoom fatigue. Specifically, Zoom fatigue has been explained by five theoretical nonverbal mechanisms: mirror anxiety, being physically trapped, hyper gaze, producing nonverbal cues, and interpreting nonverbal cues (Fauville et al., 2021; Raake et al., 2022). While international students can grasp information from speakers in face-to-face classes, it is more complex for international students to comprehend the information in virtual settings. As virtual learning platforms display multiple screens, people feel anxious because they are constantly viewing themselves and others, which can lead to depression (Fauville et al., 2021; Fejfar & Hoyle, 2000). Viewing oneself is referred to as mirror anxiety, whereas viewing others is referred to as hyper gaze (Fauville et al., 2021). Moreover, people feel physically trapped because they have to stay centered with the camera. These nonverbal mechanisms catalyze Zoom fatigue because of increased cognitive load (Fauville et al., 2021; Lee, 2020). The cognitive load explains that every individual has a limited-capacity information processing system to encode, store, and retrieve messages in interactions with people and environments (Lang, 2006). Given that, international students with lower English competency are likely to experience greater Zoom fatigue as they process course information throughout a virtual class.

Second, Zoom-mediated communication requires additional cognitive effort because of different and potentially limited communication cues compared with being in the physical classroom. Media richness theory argues that the greater the number of communication cues a medium conveys, the richer the medium is, indicating that communication media convey different cues (Daft & Lengel, 1986; El-Shinnawy & Markus, 1992). For example, face-to-face communication is rich in cues compared with telephone and written documents because face-to-face communication allows rapid mutual feedback and permits multiple communication cues, such as nonverbal, verbal, and contextual cues (El-Shinnawy & Markus, 1992; Suh, 1999). In contrast, Zoom-mediated communication offers limited communication cues that are shown on the screen. For example, international students who are nonnative speakers can use their hand gestures and some body language to deliver their messages, but the Zoom platform shows only part of the body.

Moreover, media richness theory states that an effective communication channel hinges on communication cues (Daft & Lengel, 1986). Specifically, richer communication media holds more communication cues to yield the clearest communication opportunity (e.g., full body posture), whereas low richness holds fewer communication cues, allowing for more ambiguity and distortion in a message (Daft & Lengel, 1986). For example, ironic jokes or sarcasm can sometimes be easily understood face-to-face because there are more communication cues, such as nonverbal and contextual cues (i.e., situation and atmosphere), available to interpret peer reactions; however, virtual learning platforms can be more confusing for international students, who have to capture nuance and meanings from fewer cues, or they may misinterpret the joke. Thus, international students who have low English competency need more communication cues to grasp the full meaning or nuance of the information.

In addition to limited nonverbal cues, online video conferencing platforms provide high-quality visual and audio capabilities, replacing in-person classes with virtual classes facilitated by applications such as Zoom (de Oliveira Dias et al., 2020; Gordon, 2020; Serhan, 2020; Toney et al., 2021). However, these applications cause additional cognitive demands for international students. For example, when one of the students is presenting a presentation through Zoom, other students can simultaneously add information through chats or emojis. Engaging in this practice will demand more cognitive attention for reading and listening simultaneously, prompting Zoom fatigue.

Course engagement

Course engagement can be a pivotal factor for international students to continue their studies in colleges and universities in the U.S. because it motivates them to learn and achieve their academic goals (Appleton et al., 2008; Handelsman et al., 2005). Students' course engagement can be measured in two components: behavioral engagement (e.g., participation, doing homework, taking notes, attendance, etc.) and affective or emotional engagement (e.g., desiring to learn, putting in effort, being confident, etc.) (Handelsman et al., 2005; Newmann et al., 1992; Willms, 2003). To extend this conceptual work, course engagement merits further investigation in virtual classes because the online environment is different from the physical environment. Virtual classes provide various tools (e.g., breakout rooms, captions, and annotation tools) to facilitate class (Kohnke & Moorhouse, 2022; Lee, 2021). Therefore, more studies are needed to investigate how international students' course engagement is related to Zoom fatigue experiences in virtual classes.

International and domestic students show different degrees of course engagement due to cultural differences that are compounded by their English competency. Dangeni (2023) reported that international students engage differently in the classroom depending on their culture, language, and educational background. For example, American students typically prefer assignments that demand critical thinking, whereas Asian students often favor tests that require finding correct answers. Another example is that American students are likely accustomed to asking questions and actively participating in small-group discussions because of their K-12 education experiences. Comparatively, international students might be hesitant to ask questions and participate actively because of differing cultural norms. For example, Asian students (e.g., Taiwanese and Chinese) prefer to be listeners rather than speakers. Furthermore, Asian students feel that it is impolite to interrupt professors in the middle of a lecture (Balas, 2000).

Moreover, Johnson (1988) and Wilson and Komba (2012) reported that low English competency causes poor performance in school. International students might feel shy about their ability to participate in class because their English proficiency can be evaluated instantly in terms of pronunciation and grammar. In addition, international graduate students feel less confident in English because it seems to be associated with their intelligence (Kuo, 2011). Specifically, if international graduate students do not speak fluent English in class, they believe that American students will see them as less intelligent. Furthermore, Kuo (2011) reported that English proficiency affects international students' schoolwork (e.g., writing essays or reports, participating in classroom discussions, and taking notes in the classroom). Therefore, English proficiency is one of the barriers for international students engaging in courses.

Interestingly, the Zoom platform helps international students overcome the English competency barrier and enables students to engage in course material despite being anonymous or being in different spaces with professors. Students show positive reactions to Zoom tools for their learning in Zoom classes (Kohnke & Moorhouse, 2022; Lee 2021; Minhas et al., 2021). Some studies have shown that virtual classes help students learn foreign languages by interacting in small groups (Lee, 2021; Vurdien, 2019) because virtual classes in small groups increase students' motivation and confidence in learning the language (Vurdien,

2019). In addition, the icons available in online learning platforms can be useful tools for engaging in class, such as the chat tool, which is useful for students who are not good at speaking in English (Kohnke & Moorhouse, 2022). Therefore, international students with low English competency will experience less stress and embarrassment in performing their English in virtual classes than in face-to-face classes because there is an indirect way to interact with classmates and professors through various tools (e.g., icons, 1:1 chat).

Additionally, coannotating and screen sharing facilitate student learning in virtual classes (Kohnke & Moorhouse, 2022; Minhas et al., 2021). These tools can assist international students in engaging in classes as they overcome their low English competency by using the available tools (e.g., using a 1:1 chat room, whiteboard, and viewing captions), searching for words, and accessing a translation program. Searching words might help international students follow during Zoom classes. Translation programs are beneficial for improving the speaking and writing of international students. This autonomy ability (e.g., using the internet and Zoom tools) can provide international students with comfort and confidence in their ability to engage in classes. Henceforth, the following hypotheses were proposed:

> H_1: International students' English competency is negatively related to Zoom fatigue in virtual classes for those who study at a U.S. university.
>
> H_2: International students' course engagement is negatively related to Zoom fatigue in virtual classes for those who study at a U.S. university.

METHOD

The study employed a purposive sampling method to recruit participants from the international student population at Minnesota State University, Mankato. A total of 329 participants responded to the Qualtrics survey, but 177 participants were excluded due to incomplete surveys and for nonbinary gender options due to the small proportion of students involved. The study included a final data set of 152 international students. The demographics measured included (1) biological sex (83 females, 55%), (2) age, measured in years (M = 23.30, SD = 4.6), and (3) years in college (M = 3.27 meaning junior, SD = 1.83). The survey included a measure of students' well-being, but it was not analyzed for the purpose of the current study. The survey took approximately 5 minutes to complete.

Control variables

According to previous studies, covariates were measured and included in the analyses to control for the relationships between measures of interest (Epstein-Shuman & Kushlev, 2022; Fauville et al., 2021; Nesher Shoshan & Wehrt, 2022). The participants were asked, "How do you define your gender?" (83 female, 55%), "How many Zoom classes are you taking this semester?" (M = 1.30, meaning one class, *SD* = .60), "How much do you turn on-or-off video during the Zoom classes?" and used a Likert response set ranging from 1 (*Never*) to 5 (*Always*) (*M* = 2.75, *SD* = 1.48) and "How many minutes are you on Zoom in a typical class session?" (*M* = 86.66, meaning almost one hour and a half, *SD* = 39.60).

Independent variables

English competency was measured via the Perceived English Proficiency (PEP) scale adapted from Wei et al. (2012). The PEP includes five items to assess participants' perceptions of their English proficiency in listening, speaking, reading, writing, and overall English ability. The variable consists of five items and uses a Likert response scale ranging from 1 (*very poor*) to 5 (*excellent*). The individual scores of the variables were summed and averaged (*M* = 4.05, *SD* = .78). The five items of the PEP showed high internal consistency (Cronbach's α = .95). Additionally, the average factor loading of convergent validity showed strong intercorrelations among the items ($\lambda = 0.83$).

The Student Course Engagement Questionnaire (SCEQ) was adapted from Handlesman et al. (2005) and was used to measure college students' course engagement. Some of the questions were modified to make them more relevant for students who use Zoom (e.g., "Listening carefully in class or carefully reading online course discussion posts" was changed to "Listening carefully in class or carefully reading Zoom class material"). The variable consists of 23 items representing four subscales (i.e., participation, performance, skills, emotion) and uses a Likert response scale ranging from 1 (*not at all characteristic of me*) to 5 (*very characteristic of me*).

To test the course engagement scale's dimensionality, exploratory factor analysis using promax rotation was conducted via a statistical program to examine construct validity. Initially, some items were loaded on other factors, and those items were removed. In the end, nine items were clustered into three factors: participation, performance, and skills. The model revealed a good fit and retained three factors in the sample: Kaiser–Meyer–Olkin (KMO) = .83, $x^2(34) = 774.39$, $p < .001$ (see Table 1 for factor loadings of each construct and variance). Additionally, all nine items showed high internal consistency (Cronbach's α = .89). To develop a comprehensive measure of "course engagement", the individual scores of the retained variables associated with the three factors were summed and averaged (*M* = 3.44, *SD* = .80).

Table 1: Factor loading and variances of 9 items of course engagement

Course Engagement Items	Factor loading 1	2	3	Percentage of Variance	Cumulative
Factor 1: Participation					
1. Raising my hand or answering questions in the Zoom class.	**.95**	-.00	-.09	53%	53%
3. Asking questions when I don't understand the instructor.	**.83**	.09	-.03		
2. Participating actively in breakout rooms or discussion board.	**.76**	.02	.13		
Factor 2: Skills					
22. Applying course material to my life.	-.01	**.96**	-.01	14.72%	67.72
23. Listening carefully in class or carefully reading Zoom.	.00	**.94**	-.05		
20. Making sure to study on a regular basis.	.20	**.64**	.14		
Factor 3: Performance					
15. Getting a good grade.	-.12	.05	**.92**		
16. Doing well on tests.	.12	.17	**.81**	9.72%	77.45%
4. Doing all the homework problems	.26	-.22	**.78**		

Dependent variable

A 15-item scale to measure Zoom fatigue was developed by Fauville et al. (2021). To increase coherence in college course settings, scale items were modified to represent Zoom course facilitation (e.g., "How mentally drained do you feel after video conferencing?" was changed to "I feel mentally drained after Zoom classes"). The variable used a Likert response scale ranging from 1 (*strongly disagree*) to 5 (*strongly agree*).

To test the dimensionality of the Zoom fatigue scale, exploratory factor analysis using promax rotation was conducted via a statistical program to examine construct validity. In the initial factor analysis, one of the emotional items produced a split factor loading, which resulted in the response "I feel moody after the Zoom class" remaining and the response "I feel emotionally drained after the Zoom class" and "I feel irritable after the Zoom class" being removed.

Table 2: Factors loading and variances of 12 items of Zoom fatigue

Zoom Fatigue Items	Factor loading				Percentage of Variance	Cumulative
	1	2	3	4		
Factor 1: General						
2. I feel exhausted after the Zoom class.	**.95**	-.04	.02	-.01		
3. I feel mentally drained after the Zoom class.	**.94**	.05	-.04	-.03	50.78%	50.78%
1. I feel tired after the Zoom class.	**.89**	-.01	.03	.01		
Factor 2: Visual						
4. I feel my vision gets blurred after the Zoom class.	.03	**.94**	.02	-.13	12.42%	63.21%
5. I feel my eyes get irritated after the Zoom class.	-.07	**.90**	-.03	.11		
6. I feel my eyes hurt after the Zoom class.	.05	**.87**	.01	.03		
Factor 3: Social						
14. I just want to be alone after the Zoom class.	-.05	.06	**.96**	-.02		
13. I avoid social situations after the Zoom class.	-.03	.05	**.89**	.00	11.40%	74.60%
15. I need time by myself after the Zoom class.	.10	-.11	**.84**	.04		
Factor 4: Motivational						
8. I feel like doing nothing after the Zoom class.	-.03	-.06	-.02	**.94**	6.64%	81.24%
9. I feel too tired to do other things after the Zoom class.	-.06	.01	.05	**.92**		
7. I feel dread doing somethings after the Zoom class.	.24	.12	.00	**.57**		

In the end, the twelve items were clustered into four factors: general, visual, motivational, and social. The model revealed a good fit and retained four factors in the sample: KMO = .87, $x^2(64) = 934.13$, $p < .001$ (see Table 2 for factor loadings of each construct and variance). Additionally, the reliability was satisfactory because all 12 items showed high internal consistency (Cronbach's α = .91). To develop a comprehensive measure of "Zoom fatigue," the individual scores of the retained variables associated with the four factors were summed and averaged ($M = 2.67$, $SD = .75$).

RESULT

English competency and Zoom fatigue

Initial analyses involved testing for the significance of correlations between English competency and Zoom fatigue. This analysis revealed a negative relationship between English competency and Zoom fatigue, $r(116) = -.20^*$, $p = .036$. During the survey, some of the data were randomly missing, which influenced the total number of participants shown in the correlations and stepwise regression for the first and second hypothesis tests.

To test the first hypothesis between international students' English competency and Zoom fatigue, a stepwise regression model was used to test the prediction. The first block included control variables (biological sex, number of Zoom classes, Zoom class time, camera-on), and the second block included the independent variable of English competency. The second block of adjusted R^2 was .101, indicating that approximately 10% of the variance in Zoom fatigue in the sample accounted for international students' English competency. Additionally, the linear combination of Zoom fatigue with international students' English competency was significant ($F(5, 105) = 3.46$, $p = .006$). The results indicate that when international students' English competency is greater, international students report lower Zoom fatigue ($b = -.20$, $p = .028$) (see Table 3 for the results of the regression).

Course engagement and Zoom fatigue

To examine the second hypothesis of international student course engagement and Zoom fatigue, correlations between course engagement and Zoom fatigue were examined. This analysis revealed a negative relationship between course engagement and Zoom fatigue, $r(114) = -.24^*$, $p = .01$. The study used a stepwise regression model to test the prediction. The first block included control variables (biological sex, number of Zoom classes, Zoom class time, camera-on), and the second block included the independent variable of course engagement. The second block of adjusted R^2 was .166, which indicated that approximately 17% of the variance in Zoom fatigue accounted for international students' course engagement. Additionally, the linear combination of Zoom fatigue with international students' course engagement was significant ($F(5, 103) = 5.30$, $p <$ .001). The results indicate that when international students report higher course engagement, they experience lower Zoom fatigue ($b = -.35$, $p = <.001$) (see Table 4 for the results of the regression).

Table 3: The effect of English competency on Zoom fatigue

Variables	*B*	β	SE
Block 1:			
Control variables			
Gender (female = 1, male = 0)	.18	.13	.13
Number of Zoom classes	.26	.18	.13
Zoom classes time	.00	.07	.00
Camera-on	.10*	.20*	.05
R^2		.10	
Adjusted R^2		.07	
F value (4, 106)		2.97*	
Block 2:			
Independent variable			
English competency	-.20*	-.20*	.09
R^2		.14	
Adjusted R^2		.10	
F value (5, 105)		3.46**	

Note. * $p < .05$, ** $p < .01$, *** $p < .001$, $N = 111$.

DISCUSSION

The current study investigated how Zoom fatigue is predicted by international students' English competency and course engagement. The study involved an online survey and used a statistical program to run stepwise regression, which confirmed support for the first and second hypotheses.

The first hypothesis predicted English competency to be negatively related to Zoom fatigue among international students attending U.S. universities. This implies that students report lower Zoom fatigue when their English competency is high. This finding aligns with arguments regarding computer-mediated communication and cognitive load. Computer-mediated communication explains that students require extra cognitive effort to interpret, form, or comprehend information because computer-mediated communication involves fewer communication cues than does face-to-face communication according to media richness theory. Nadler (2020) reported how nuances differ between virtual and face-to-face communication because of limited communication cues. Thus, international students might need extra cognitive effort to capture nuance and meanings because of their English proficiency and different cultural backgrounds. In addition, Zoom offers nonverbal cues through various features. These features require extra cognitive demands to international students for multitasking (e.g., listening to lectures and reading chats or emojis). Therefore, virtual classes exacerbate Zoom fatigue among international students.

Table 4: The effect of course engagement on Zoom fatigue

Variables	*B*	β	SE
Block 1: Control variables			
Gender (female = 1, male = 0)	.17	.12	.13
Number of Zoom classes	.25	.18	.13
Zoom classes time	.00	.06	.00
Camera-on	.10	.19	.05
R^2		.09	
Adjusted R^2		.06	
F value (4, 104)		2.70*	
Block 2: Independent variable			
course engagement	-.35***	-.35***	.09
R^2		.21	
Adjusted R^2		.17	
F value (5, 103)		5.30***	

Note. * $p < .05$, ** $p < .01$, *** $p < .001$, $N = 109$.

Furthermore, nonverbal mechanisms associated with the virtual environment, including mirror anxiety, feeling physically trapped, a hyper gaze, and producing and interpreting nonverbal cues, increase the cognitive load. Previous studies have shown that employees feel fatigued during video conferences because of the intensity of experiencing these nonverbal mechanisms (Fauville et al., 2021; Raake et al., 2022). The intense nonverbal cues might be the reason for Zoom fatigue, which intensifies the cognitive load for international students. Therefore, the study shows that international students who have low English competency are likely to experience more Zoom fatigue in virtual classes because of the complexity of managing the richness of cues offered through the media environment while attempting to learn new course material and respond through the different communication channels it offers.

The second hypothesis predicts that course engagement is negatively related to Zoom fatigue among international students attending U.S. universities. This implies that international students report lower levels of Zoom fatigue when they report greater course engagement. This finding aligns with behavioral engagement, as the course engagement factors are participation (i.e., breakout rooms, discussion boards, asking questions, and answering questions), skills (i.e., making sure to study regularly, finding ways to make the course material relevant to one's life, applying a course to one's life), and performance (i.e., obtaining a good grade, doing well on the tests, solving all homework problems). Previous studies have shown that breakout rooms and nonverbal tools (e.g., written chats and icons) are useful tools for students to engage in classes, especially for those who are not fluent in English (Lee 2021; Kohnke & Moorhouse, 2022; Vurdien, 2019), which can decrease Zoom fatigue by enabling students to be involved. Additionally, international students who have low English competency can be more confident in their ability to participate in virtual classes because their faces are not always shown in virtual classes. Moreover, online learning platforms may lessen Zoom fatigue because the virtual classroom allows international students to engage more by using the internet or translation programs to overcome English barriers. Thus, online learning platforms may encourage international students to engage in virtual classes and decrease Zoom fatigue. In other words, international students are less likely to experience Zoom fatigue from engaging in virtual classes. Therefore, this study shows that course engagement is a pivotal element in decreasing Zoom fatigue for international students.

Limitations

Like any other study, this study has potential limitations. Since the data were gathered at one institution, the breadth of applicability and generalizability of the findings are restricted. Therefore, the results of this study should be examined in different institutions with a larger sample size. Additionally, the study did not measure the use of Zoom tools to determine how course engagement is negatively related to Zoom fatigue. Further studies are encouraged to measure the use of Zoom tools (e.g., chat rooms, sharing screens, and breakout room sections) to investigate how Zoom tools affect international students' course engagement.

Despite its limitations, this study is meaningful for investigating how English competency and course engagement are related to Zoom fatigue separately in virtual classes among international students. This study highlights the ambivalence of virtual classes, which can be harmful and beneficial for international students who have low English competency. In summary, international students with low English competency can decrease their Zoom fatigue through course engagement, and it may also offer a means to increase competency levels in a learning environment that is less risky than face-to-face classrooms.

Implications

Further studies should be conducted to decrease international students' Zoom fatigue and increase course engagement. First, future studies can advance the current model by combining the two variables (i.e., English competency and course engagement) to determine how they affect Zoom fatigue. Second, advanced models should explore how English competency could mediate the relationship between course engagement and Zoom fatigues in future studies. Studies of this nature will identify the importance of English competency in the model and encourage future research to investigate how to engage international students in ways to build their language competency in virtual classes. Although some studies show that students engage in virtual classes more when they turn their camera on and when they show their facial and body expressions (e.g., nodding heads, giving thumbs up or down) (Epstein-Shuman & Kushlev, 2022; Peper & Yang, 2021), future work could investigate more thoroughly how it can be applied to international students related to their English competency and examine the ideal length for virtual classes, as Zoom fatigue is associated with the amount of time staring at the screen (Epstein-Shuman & Kushlev, 2022; Nesher Shoshan & Wehrt, 2022). Finally, there should be more studies about interpersonal communication in virtual classrooms with respect to emotional course engagement and Zoom fatigue. On the basis of the factor analysis, emotional factors of course engagement (e.g., having fun in class, desiring to learn the material, and thinking about the course between class meetings) and emotional factors of Zoom fatigue (e.g., feeling emotionally drained, feeling irritable, needing time by themselves after the Zoom classes) were removed. This can highlight the limitations of virtual classes because proximity can restrict the opportunity to build relationships with a professor and classmates (Bejerano, 2008). Therefore, further studies on the relationship between virtual classes and emotional course engagement could be conducted. A potential benefit of this future study would be to provide international students with social and academic support through interaction with other students and professors in virtual classes at U.S. universities.

Acknowledgment

In the preparation of this manuscript, we did not utilize artificial intelligence (AI) tools for content creation. This article does not incorporate content generated by artificial intelligence) tools.

REFERENCES

Andrade, M. S. (2006). International students in English-speaking universities: Adjustment factors. *Journal of Research in International Education*, *5*(2),

131–154. https://doi.org/10.1177/1475240906065589

Appleton, J. J., Christenson, S. L., & Furlong, M. J. (2008). Student engagement with school: Critical conceptual and methodological issues of the construct. *Psychology in the Schools*, *45*(5), 369–386. https://doi.org/10.1002/pits.20303

Bailenson, J. N. (2021). Nonverbal overload: A theoretical argument for the causes of zoom fatigue. *Technology, Mind, and Behavior, 2*(1). https://doi.org/10.1037/tmb0000030

Balas, A. (2000). Using participation to assess students' knowledge. *College Teaching, 48*(4), 122-123. https://doi.org/10.1080/87567550009595827

Bejerano, A. R. (2008). Raising the question #11 the genesis and evolution of online degree programs: Who are they for and what have we lost along the way? *Communication Education, 57*, 408-414. https://doi.org/10.1080/03634520801993697

Biesenbach-Lucas, S. (2003). Asynchronous discussion groups in teacher training classes: Perceptions of native and non-native students. *Journal of Asynchronous Learning Networks,* *7*(3), 24–46. https://olj.onlinelearningconsortium.org/index.php/olj/article/view/1843

Costello, J. (2015). Students' stories of studying abroad: Reflections upon return. *Journal of International Students*, *5*(1), 50–59. https://doi.org/10.32674/jis.v5i1.442

Daft, R. L., & Lengel, R. H. (1986). Organizational information requirements, media richness and structural design. *Management science*, *32*(5), 554-571. https://doi.org/10.1287/mnsc.32.5.554

Dangeni. (2023). Student engagement: A critical conceptualization of the complexity of the international students' experiences. *Journal of International Students* *13*(4), 227-233. https://doi.org/10.32674/jis.v14i3.5702

de Oliveira Dias, M., Lopes, R. D. O. A., & Teles, A. C. (2020). Will virtual replace classroom teaching? Lessons from virtual classes via zoom in the times of COVID-19. *Journal of Advances in Education and Philosophy*, *4*(5), 208-213. https://doi.org/10.36348/jaep.2020.v04i05.004

El-Shinnawy, M. M., & Markus, M. L. (1992). Media richness theory and new electronic communication media: A study of voice mail and electronic mail. *Proceedings of the 13th International Conference on Information Systems,* 91–105. https://aisel.aisnet.org/icis1992/36

Epstein-Shuman, A. & Kushlev, K. (2022). Lights, cameras (on), action! Camera usage during zoom classes facilitates engagement without increasing fatigue. *Technology, Mind, and Behavior,* *3*(3). https://doi.org/10.17605/OSF.IO/M63SG

Fauville, G., Luo, M., Queiroz, A. C. M., Bailenson, J. N., & Hancock, J. (2021). Nonverbal mechanisms predict zoom fatigue and explain why women experience higher levels than men. *SSRN Electronic Journal.* https://doi.org/10.2139/ssrn.3820035

Fejfar, M. C., & Hoyle, R. H. (2000). Effect of private self-awareness on negative affect and self-referent attribution: A quantitative review. *Personality and Social Psychology Review*, *4*(2), 132-142. https://doi.org/10.1207/S15327957PSPR0402_02

Gordon, M. (2020). Synchronous teaching and learning: On-ground versus zoom. *International Journal of Education and Human Developments*, *6*(3), 11-19. https://ijehd.cgrd.org/images/vol6no3/3.pdf

Grayson, J. P. (2008). The experiences and outcomes of domestic and international students at four Canadian universities. *Higher Education Research & Development*, *27*(3), 215-230. https://doi.org/10.1080/07294360802183788

Handelsman, M. M., Briggs, W. L., Sullivan, N., & Towler, A. (2005). A measure of college student course engagement. *The Journal of Educational Research*, *98*(3), 184-192. https://doi.org/10.3200/JOER.98.3.184-192

Johnson, P. (1988). English language proficiency and academic performance of undergraduate international students. *TESOL Quarterly*, *22*(1), 164–168. https://doi.org/10.2307/3587070

Kohnke, L., & Moorhouse, B. L. (2022). Facilitating synchronous online language learning through zoom. *RELC Journal*, *53*(1), 296–301. https://doi.org/10.1177/0033688220937235

Koo, K. K., & Jiang, M. (2022). What does it mean to take online classes as an international student during COVID-19? *Online Learning*, *26*(4), 209-230. https://eric.ed.gov/?id=EJ1374852

Koo, K. & Nyunt, G. (2022). Pandemic in a foreign country: Barriers to international students' well-being during COVID-19. *Journal of Student Affairs Research and Practice*, *60*(1), 123-136. https://doi.org/10.1080/19496591.2022.2056476

Kuo, Y. H. (2011). Language challenges faced by international graduate students in the United States. *Journal of International Students*, *1*(2). https://doi.org/10.32674/jis.v1i2.551

Lang, A. (2006). Using the limited capacity model of motivated mediated message processing to design effective cancer communication messages. *Journal of Communication*, *56*, S57-S80. https://doi.org/10.1111/j.1460-2466.2006.00283.x

Lee, A. R. (2021). Breaking through digital barriers: Exploring EFL students' views of zbreakout room experiences. *Korean Journal of English Language and Linguistics, 21*, 510-524. https://doi.org/10.15738/kjell.21..202106.510

Lee, J. (2020, November 17). *A neuropsychological exploration of zoom fatigue*. Psychiatric Times. https://www.psychiatrictimes.com/view/psychological-exploration-zoom-fatigue

Lorenzetti, D. L., Lorenzetti, L., Nowell, L., Jacobsen, M., Clancy, T., Freeman, G., & Paolucci, E. O. (2023). Exploring international graduate students' experiences, challenges, and peer relationships: Impacts on academic and emotional well-being. *Journal of International Students, 13*(4), 22-41. https://doi.org/10.32674/jis.v14i2.5186

McCabe, J. A., Banasik, C. S., Jackson, M. G., Postlethwait, E. M., Steitz, A., &

Wenzel, A. R. (2023). Exploring perceptions of cognitive load and mental fatigue in pandemic-era zoom classes. *Scholarship of Teaching and Learning in Psychology*. https://doi.org/10.1037/stl0000347

Minhas, S., Hussain, T., Ghani, A., & Sajid, K. (2021). Exploring students online learning: A study of zoom application. *Gazi University Journal of Science, 34*, (2), 171-178. https://doi: 10.35378/gujs.691705

Mori, S. C. (2000). Addressing the mental health concerns of international students. *Journal of Counseling & Development*, *78*(2), 137–144. https://doi.org/10.1002/j.1556-6676.2000.tb02571.x

Nadler, R. (2020). Understanding zoom fatigue: Theorizing spatial dynamics as third skins in computer-mediated communication. *Computers and Composition, 58*, 102613. https://doi.org/10.1016/j.compcom.2020.102613

Nesher S. H., & Wehrt, W. (2022). Understanding zoom fatigue: A mixed-method approach. *Applied Psychology*, *71*(3), 827–852. https://doi.org/10.1111/apps.12360

Newmann, F. M., Wehlage, G. G., & Lamborn, S. D. (1992). The significance and sources of student engagement. *Student engagement and achievement in American secondary schools*, 11-39. https://files.eric.ed.gov/fulltext/ED371047.pdf - page=16

Nietzel, M. T. (2023, November 14). *International college student enrollment roars back in U.S.* Forbes. https://www.forbes.com/sites/michaeltnietzel/2023/11/13/international-college-student-enrollment-roars-back-in-us/?sh=32690a365d35

Peper, E., & Yang, A. (2021). Beyond zoom fatigue: Re-energize yourself and improve learning. *Academia Letters, 257,* 1-7. https://doi.org/10.20935/AL257.

Raake, A., Fiedler, M., Schoenenberg, K., De Moor, K., & Döring, N. (2022). Technological factors influencing videoconferencing and zoom fatigue. *ArXiv Preprint ArXiv*. https://doi.org/10.48550/arXiv.2202.01740

Riedl, R. (2022). On the stress potential of videoconferencing: Definition and root causes of zoom fatigue. *Electronic Markets*, *32*(1), 153–177. https://doi.org/10.1007/s12525-021-00501-3

Sandhu, D. S., & Asrabadi, B. R. (1994). Development of an acculturative stress scale for international students: Preliminary findings. *Psychological Reports*, *75*(1), 435–448. https://doi.org/10.2466/pr0.1994.75.1.435

Serhan, D. (2020). Transitioning from face-to-face to remote learning: Students' attitudes and perceptions of using zoom during COVID-19 pandemic. *International Journal of Technology in Education and Science, 4*(4), 335–342. https://doi.org/10.46328/ijtes.v4i4.148

Suh, K. S. (1999). Impact of communication medium on task performance and satisfaction: An examination of media-richness theory. *Information & Management*, *35*(5), 295–312. https://doi.org/10.1016/S0378-7206(98)00097-4

Toney, S., Light, J., & Urbaczewski, A. (2021). Fighting zoom fatigue: Keeping the zoombies at Bay. *Communications of the Association for Information*

Systems, 48, 40–46. https://doi.org/10.17705/1CAIS.04806
Wan, T., Chapman, D. W., & Biggs, D. A. (1992). Academic stress of international students attending U.S. universities. *Research in Higher Education, 33*(5), 607–623. https://doi.org/10.1007/BF00973761
Wei, M., Tsai, P.-C., Chao, R. C.-L., Du, Y., & Lin, S.-P. (2012). Advisory working alliance, perceived English proficiency, and acculturative stress. *Journal of Counseling Psychology, 59*(3), 437–448. https://doi.org/10.1037/a0028617
Willms, J. (2003). *Student engagement at school: A sense of belonging and participation.* OECD.
Wilson, J., & Komba, S. C. (2012). The link between English language proficiency and academic performance: A pedagogical perspective in Tanzanian secondary schools. *World Journal of English Language, 2*(4). http://dx.doi.org/10.5430/wjel.v2n4p1
Vurdien, R. (2019). Videoconferencing: Developing students' communicative competence. *Journal of Foreign Language Education and Technology 4*(2), 269-298. https://www.ceeol.com/search/article-detail?id=781200
Yao, M. Z., & Ling, R. (2020). What is computer-mediated communication?—An introduction to the special issue. *Journal of Computer-Mediated Communication, 25*(1), 4–8. https://doi.org/10.1093/jcmc/zmz027
Yeh, C. J., & Inose, M. (2003). International students' reported English fluency, social support satisfaction, and social connectedness as predictors of acculturative stress. *Counselling Psychology Quarterly, 16*(1), 15–28. https://doi.org/10.1080/0951507031000114058

Author bios

Esther Son, M.A. (2018, Yonsei University, South Korea; 2024, Minnesota State University, Mankato) is a doctoral student at the University of Maryland, College Park, in the Department of Communication. She studies communication science and explores how individuals engage with emerging media, investigating its profound influence on perceptions, its role in shaping behaviors, and its impact on the dynamics of human interaction. Her work is published in the Bullying Prevention Program, which includes the *Ministry of Education & National Youth Policy Institute*. Email: esther15@umd.edu

Kristen Cvancara, Ph.D. (2004, University of Minnesota, Twin Cities), is a professor at Minnesota State University, Mankato, in the Department of Communication and Media. She studies the use of hurtful communication in close relationships and is a leadership and relationship development consultant. Her research is published in books and journals, including *Personal Relationships, Journal of Family Communication, Communication Quarterly, Social Psychology of Education,* and *Acta Psychologica.* Email: kristen.cvancara@mnsu.edu

Article

Journal of International Students
Volume 14, Issue 5 (2024), pp. 21-40
ISSN: 2162-3104 (Print), 2166-3750 (Online)
jistudents.org

Acculturation of International Graduate Students in U.S. Higher Education Institutions

Bing Gao
Pamela M. Wesely
University of Iowa, USA

ABSTRACT

Every year, the U.S. witnesses an increase in the number of international students pursuing higher education. Researchers, who have focused primarily on international undergraduates, have suggested that international students often encounter various acculturative stressors while adapting to new academic and living environments. Moreover, there is expanding research on coping strategies adopted by most international undergraduates to manage acculturative stressors. Although the number of international graduate students (IGSs) has surpassed that of international undergraduates in the U.S. since 2020, their experiences in higher education contexts have still received relatively less attention than their undergraduate counterparts. This study employed Yakushko's (2010) theoretical model of stress and coping strategies to examine the acculturation experiences of ten IGSs from three U.S. higher education institutions. The findings revealed common acculturative stressors for IGSs, the factors in those stressors, and the coping strategies employed by IGSs and the corresponding consequences.

Keywords: Acculturative stressors, coping strategies, factors impacting IGSs experiences of acculturative stressors, international graduate students, U.S. higher education institutions

In recent years, the U.S. has solidified its position as a destination for higher education, drawing international students from around the globe. International students have been defined as those who have crossed a national border to study outside their country of origin and do not hold permanent residency in the host country (UNESCO Institute for Statistics, 2006). The Institute of International Education (IIE, 2023a) reported that, during the 2022–2023 academic year, approximately one million international students from over 200 countries enrolled in U.S. higher education institutions. Additionally, since the 2020–2021 academic year, the number of IGSs has significantly increased, surpassing the number of international undergraduates (IIE, 2023b). Adjusting to university life might be stressful for all students, but research has shown that unique challenges exist for international students (Nilsson et al., 2008). One significant challenge that international students face is adapting to an environment that differs from their native culture, which often manifests as acculturative stressors (Rai et al., 2021).

Although research has explored the acculturation process among international students, much of it has concentrated on international undergraduates, or some studies have not distinguished between undergraduates and graduates. Thus, there is a need to further investigate the acculturation experiences of IGSs as a distinct group from undergraduate students. The current study was guided by Yakushko's (2010) theoretical model of stress and coping strategies to investigate the acculturation experiences of IGSs in the U.S. Through in-depth interviews with current IGSs, this study examined the types of acculturative stressors that they experienced, the factors in those stressors, and the coping strategies that IGSs used to address those stressors.

LITERATURE REVIEW

Acculturation and Yakushko's (2010) theoretical model

Acculturation is a transformative process involving changes in an individual's cultural practices, behaviors, values, and identities, due to direct, sustained intercultural interactions. Acculturation impacts an individual's psychological well-being and social functioning (Berry, 2003, 2005; Ward & Geeraert, 2016). The acculturation process has been found to bring both personal growth and challenges, as the process might be an exhilarating journey for some while being filled with stressors for others (Ma et al., 2020; Moores & Popadiuk, 2011).

Numerous acculturation models have been developed and debated to illustrate the key factors influencing the acculturation process. The current study employed Yakushko's (2010) theoretical model of stress and coping strategies. This model, initially designed to examine the acculturation of 20 immigrants in Lincoln, Nebraska, involves six domains. The first domain, causal conditions, refers to factors such as reasons for migrating, migration status, and preimmigration expectations. These factors lead to the second domain, the central phenomenon, which pertains to acculturative stressors during the acculturation process. These stressors trigger the third domain, coping patterns, which involve various strategies ranging from constructive to avoidance. The adoption of coping strategies is influenced by two domains: context and intervention conditions. The context includes five levels: individual (e.g., gender, age, social class, and country of origin), family, local ethnic community, local host community, and larger cultural levels. Intervention conditions connect to an individual's resources and values. Finally, coping patterns impact adaptation consequences, which refer to acculturation outcomes achieved through the utilization of coping strategies in areas of society, culture, health, and education.

As a relatively recent theoretical framework, Yakushko's (2010) model has seen limited adoption among researchers. In particular, Ferguson's (2015) study applied this model to examine the stressors faced by Iraqi refugees residing in southern California and the coping strategies they employed. The study identified common stressors, such as self- and family provisions, employment searches, financial needs, education and credential loss, experiences of discrimination, and longing for family in Iraq. The coping strategies revealed in Ferguson's (2015) study included the cultivation of social connections, altruistic behavior, the pursuit of assistance or self-determination, and the utilization of strategies centered around distraction. However, Kuo (2014) emphasized that Yakushko's (2010) model originated from a qualitative study focusing on migrants in a specific geographical area in the U.S. Due to its limited research scope, additional empirical validation is needed to determine the broader applicability of the model in understanding how individuals navigate and culturally adapt to diverse locations.

International students' acculturative stressors

In Yakushko's (2010) model, acculturative stressors have been identified as a central domain of the acculturation process. Many studies have examined the challenges that international students have encountered in foreign countries.

Language struggles

Researchers have shown that language struggles impede the academic adjustment process for international students, particularly international undergraduates (Misra et al., 2003). Specifically, language struggles, observed in spoken and written forms (Chen & Van Ullen, 2011; McLachlan & Justin, 2009), resulted in international students' difficulty comprehending course materials, participating in classroom discussions, and communicating with faculty and peers (Kwon, 2009; Lee, 2013). Moreover, in daily life, language struggles have led to miscommunication, potentially undermining international students' ability to form friendships (Leong, 2015). Thus, the growing body of evidence has highlighted the detrimental impact of language struggles on international students' academic success and everyday communication.

Financial burdens

Financial burdens have been shown to be a primary stressor for most international undergraduates in the U.S. (Perry et al., 2017). At UC Berkeley, 51.6% of international undergraduates cited finances as their top personal concern (UC Berkeley, 2011). According to the F-1 student employment regulations of the U.S. Citizenship and Immigration Services (2023), non-U.S. full-time students on F-1 visas are restricted from off-campus work in their first academic year. Research has shown that these employment regulations discourage international students from seeking job opportunities, leading to their increased dependence on savings or external funding and heightened financial stress (McFadden & Seedorff, 2017).

Other stressors

In addition to the two main acculturative stressors discussed above, research has illuminated additional stressors for international students, including loneliness, homesickness, unfamiliarity with local food, house arrangements, and healthcare systems, lack of social support, and experiences of discrimination (Erturk & Nguyen Luu, 2022; Forbes-Mewett & Sawyer, 2016; Nyland et al., 2013; Poyrazli & Devonish, 2020). While existing studies have identified various stressors for international students, especially a large portion of international undergraduates, research has noted that IGSs studying in the U.S. face unique challenges in adapting to American higher education and broader society, which requires further research (Click, 2018).

Factors influencing acculturative stressors and stress

In Yakushko's (2010) model, the domain of causal conditions explores factors that influence immigrants' experience of acculturative stressors. Some researchers have investigated this domain in the context of international students' acculturation and identified several factors. For example, studies by Bastien et al. (2018) and Luo et al. (2019) demonstrated that factors such as older age, longer residence in the U.S., and greater language competence were predictors of better psychological well-being and lower levels of stress among undergraduate international students in the US. Koo et al. (2021) reported that first-year international college students who were male or from low socioeconomic backgrounds experienced more acculturative stressors than their female counterparts and those from mid- to high-SES backgrounds did.

Additionally, a study conducted by Eustace (2007) revealed that students from collectivistic cultures, who were taught to be silent and passive in classrooms, faced stress when confronted with classrooms that expected active participation, which is common in individualistic cultures. A study by Yu and Moskal (2019) revealed that a lack of institutional diversity and interactional diversity may have led to potential inequalities in cross-cultural learning, hindering personal growth and increasing stress levels among Chinese international students. However, institutional support in areas such as financial assistance, academic learning, and social life has been found to increase the college-life satisfaction of international students and reduce their psychological stress (Cho & Yu, 2015; Glass et al., 2014). Thus, paying attention to factors that influence acculturative stressors and stress is crucial to understanding international students' acculturation experiences.

Coping strategies for acculturative stressors

Yakushko's (2010) model highlights the importance of adopting coping strategies to mitigate acculturative stressors and stress, as these strategies act as mediators between the stressors and the consequences of acculturation. Importantly, scholars have argued that there is no universal solution to mitigate acculturative stressors (Tiwari et al., 2017). Lazarus and Folkman (1984) categorized coping into two dimensions: problem-focused coping and emotion-focused coping. Specifically, problem-focused coping involves taking actions to address external threats and alter the source of stress; emotion-focused coping focuses on managing and expressing emotions in response to stressful situations.

Distinct coping strategies adopted by international students have been explored across different national contexts. For example, studies conducted in the United States, Canada, and Malaysia have indicated that most international undergraduates have adopted both emotion- and problem-focused coping strategies (e.g., seeking support from campus counselors, confiding with siblings, and engaging in constructive activities) to effectively manage acculturative stressors (De Moissac et al., 2020; Ra & Trusty, 2015; Saravanan et al., 2019). However, the well-documented emotion-focused coping strategy of avoidance (e.g. ignoring the problem) has shown more mixed results. While Sumer (2009) reported a positive relationship between avoidance and acculturative stressors for some international undergraduates in the U.S., others have suggested that such a mechanism was negatively associated with stressors for international undergraduates in Thailand (Vergara et al., 2010). Given these mixed findings, it is important to explore the various consequences of employing these coping strategies by IGSs.

The present study poses the following research questions: (1) How do international graduate students describe their acculturative stressors? (2) What factors influence acculturative stressors? (3) What types of coping strategies are available and prove helpful in managing acculturative stressors?

METHOD

The present study employed a multiple case study design (Merriam, 1998). The researchers identified overarching themes among the cases, aiming to gain deeper insights into participants' acculturative stressors and coping strategies based on their distinct experiences and backgrounds.

Context

The present study took place at three U.S. universities in the Northeast and Midwest. From 2022-2023, University A in Northeast hosted approximately 2,837 IGSs, whereas Universities B and C in Northeast and Midwest hosted approximately 1,085 and 1,043 IGSs, respectively. These universities offer support systems for international students, such as international student offices, counseling services, and orientation programs. The choice of these three universities aimed to capture multiple aspects of IGSs acculturation experiences, considering the potential variations in institutional culture, academic climates, and support systems.

Participants

After receiving approval from the Institutional Review Board (IRB) at the University of Iowa, AUTHOR1 used convenience sampling for participant recruitment in order to easily and efficiently access potential participants. The primary selection criterion was that participants had to have been an IGS in the U.S. for at least six months. AUTHOR1 reached out to IGS acquaintances from three universities via email. Out of those contacted, five agreed to participate in the study. Additionally, the international student support office and the College of Education at University C, AUTHOR1's home university, aided in disseminating information about the study campus-wide through emails. Another five participants were recruited. In total, ten participants participated in the study, and details about them can be found in Table 1.

Table 1
Participant Demographics and Academic Backgrounds

Participants	Country	Stay in the U.S.	Institution	Department	Academic Levels
Alex	China	5.5 yrs.	University A	Electrical and Computer Engineering (ECE)	Ph.D. candidate
Ethan	China	2 yrs.	University A	Information Science	Master
Susan	China	6.5 yrs.	University B	Curriculum and Instruction	Ph.D. student
Olivia	Indonesia	3.5 yrs.	University C	Teaching and Learning (T&L)	Ph.D. candidate
Lily	Brazil	1 yr.	University C	T&L	Ph.D. student
Chloe	Turkey	2 yrs.	University C	T&L	Ph.D. student
Emma	South Korea	2 yrs.	University C	Psychological and Quantitative Foundations	Ph.D. student
Ava	South Korea	6.5 yrs.	University C	Educational Policy and Leadership Studies	Ph.D. student
Zoe	China	4.5 yrs.	University C	Counselor Education	Ph.D. student
Leo	Bangladesh	2 yrs.	University C	Human Toxicology	Ph.D. student

This study consisted of semi-structured interviews with ten IGSs in the U.S. These participants were from a diverse range of nations, including China (n=4), South Korea (n=2), Bangladesh (n=1), Indonesia (n=1), Brazil (n=1), and Turkey (n=1). All participants had been residing in the U.S. for at least six months, with durations ranging from one year as the shortest to 6.5 years as the longest and an average duration of 3.55 years. Among the ten participants, nine were pursuing doctoral degrees, whereas one was pursuing a master's degree.

Positionality

In this study, AUTHOR 1 leveraged her six-year experience as an international graduate student in the U.S., providing an insider's perspective. This firsthand insight helped establish rapport with participants, formulate meaningful interview questions, elicit authentic responses, and lead to a deeper understanding of participants' acculturative stressors and coping strategies. AUTHOR 2, a professor in multilingual education and associate dean, provided valuable insights into graduate student experiences in this study. Her job required her to offer support to all graduate students at the collegiate level, and she had served as the advisor of many international students. She contributed a unique viewpoint on the acculturation experiences among IGSs from institutional, professor, and advisor perspectives.

Data collection

Data collection took place in spring 2023. The interview protocol, adapted from the study by Bertram et al. (2014), consisted of ten questions. These questions were designed to probe participants' preconceptions about life and education in the U.S. before their arrival; elicit reflections on their initial experiences and emotions upon setting foot in the U.S.; understand the acculturative stressors that they have experienced in both their daily lives and academic pursuits due to cross-cultural adjustments; gauge their emotional responses to various acculturative stressors; explore the specific coping strategies they utilized to manage or mitigate acculturative stressors; determine the efficacy of these coping strategies; and ascertain their aspirations for additional institutional and professional support. All semi-structured interviews were conducted over Zoom, with each interview lasting approximately one hour. All the interviews were audio-recorded and subsequently transcribed verbatim.

Data analysis

Yakushko's (2010) acculturation model served as the foundation for exploring acculturative stressors and coping strategies among IGSs. The analysis was conducted in two phases and was structured around all the domains of Yakushko's model. In the first phase of data analysis, the researchers utilized a within-case analysis (Merriam & Tisdell, 2016). This involved a thorough analysis of all ten participants' responses, grouping the data on the basis of some domains of Yakushko's (2010) model. In the second phase, a cross-case analysis (Merriam & Tisdell, 2016) was employed to analyze frequent mentions from participants to identify recurrent themes. However, the participants' unique insights, which provided new viewpoints, were also valuable. This phase highlighted both the shared and unique experiences of the participants, illuminating the nuances of their acculturation experiences. Throughout the findings, participants' quotes were labeled with pseudonyms, as outlined in Table 1.

RESULTS

International graduate students' acculturative stressors

Following the central phenomenon of Yakushko's (2010) model, we analyzed participants' experiences with various acculturative stressors and explored their adverse impacts on academic pursuits and daily life.

Struggles with language in academic discourse

Linguistic struggles emerged as the most salient acculturative stressor for participants, manifesting in their use of English for conversations and meeting the rigorous language requirements of graduate students. Specifically, two participants from China, Alex and Ethan, reported difficulties in using English for conversations because of differences from what they had learned in Chinese classrooms. Alex and Ethan encountered difficulties in understanding and articulating ideas clearly, as well as engaging in conversations in English during presentation Q&A sessions, seminars, collaborative research, and conferences. These challenges often led to misunderstandings and embarrassment, and sometimes impeded networking.

Furthermore, the participants reported that the heightened English proficiency expectations in graduate studies increased their language difficulties. Five participants, including Emma, Leo, Lily, Olivia, and Susan, expressed stress in "engaging in in depth, fast-paced discussions and debates" and "reading lengthy, complex academic materials." Additionally, Zoe shared her experience in content-rich graduate seminars: "[American students] spoke superfast... The professor talked a lot about local topics such as movies and jokes. He loves using metaphors. It's hard to understand them without context." Zoe sometimes felt isolated due to the differences between her language and cultural background and those of her professors and fellow students. Moreover, the participants cited here had been in the U.S. for varying lengths of time; it was evident that that language difficulties were prevalent regardless of how long the IGSs had been in the U.S.

Lack of familiarity with new pedagogical approaches

Adapting to distinct U.S. pedagogical approaches was a notable source of stress, as those approaches often differed from participants' previous learning experiences. This challenge was highlighted by doctoral participants who had pursued bachelor's and master's degrees in Asian countries, potentially because they had invested more time in adhering to their home countries' pedagogical approaches. Two participants, Leo and Olivia, shared their U.S. classroom experiences. Specifically, Leo noted the contrast between dynamic classroom discussions in the U.S. and linear lectures in his home country. He expressed:

> In the U.S. ... When a topic is introduced, it is a starting point. It changes as everyone talks about it and shares their different views, allowing the discussion to expand into [sic] various directions. But in my home country, the teacher delivers a 45-minute lecture and then leaves.

Leo characterized U.S. classrooms as "wide discussion classes" and noted the difficulty of predicting exam content due to the dynamic nature of discussions. Therefore, Leo, who was accustomed to a more passive learning experience for an extended period, found the new pedagogical approach overwhelming.

Given the dynamic discussions in U.S. classrooms, Olivia struggled with the emphasis on critical thinking, as it was not emphasized in her home country's educational system. She stated:

> I had to think critically to answer questions [in American classes], but I never did that in my country. Being critical is not an easy thing because I tried to be critical, but I can't be as critical as the other American students.

Olivia's frustration stemmed from both the need for critical thinking and the realization that developing this skill was not an instant achievement. Acculturative stress was thus something that IGSs experienced in their graduate classrooms as well as in other, more personal areas.

Familial burdens and financial burdens

One such personal, non-work-related area for IGSs was their need to manage family expectations and maintain long-distance family relationships. These responsibilities added a layer of pressure to their lives. Chloe shared:

> I came [to the U.S.] with some goals. If I fail, it appears to be leaving my family and country was meaningless. There are pressures to do better. I need to succeed; otherwise, coming to this place has led to a loss of meaning.

Chloe expressed anxiety about failing to meet her goals, such as failing to meet academic standards and not finding a good job after graduation. She believed these failures would diminish the value of her sacrifices for overseas education and family expectations.

Additionally, IGSs felt stress because their commitments to academic responsibilities consumed time and energy, leaving limited energy for maintaining family relationships. Lily described this challenge as follows "Sometimes I get home so exhausted with a mountain of tasks still waiting, but I need to make time to chat with my family and partner... If I failed to balance this commitment, it made my stress even worse." Some IGSs managed family responsibilities as children, spouses, or parents to maintain long-distance relationships. This obligation required them to invest more time and energy than some American graduate students and other international undergraduate students did.

In addition to familial responsibilities, financial burdens were a significant challenge for participants pursuing a Ph.D., regardless of their majors. Specifically, Alex, from STEM, always had a backup plan during his doctoral studies. He took many courses in the first two years in case his advisor faced funding issues. Lily, from humanities and social sciences, also had backup plans owing to the scholarship restrictions. She said, "My main concern is funding. Many funding opportunities are only available for U.S. citizens… If I don't get funding, I'll have to return to my home country, or I'll have to take out a student loan." Financial uncertainty and the implementation of backup plans increased the stress for participants in terms of both emotions and finances.

The factors impacting students' experiences with acculturative stressors

The data analysis, which is based on Yakushko's (2010) causal conditions, has revealed three levels of factors that influenced participants' experiences of acculturative stressors, out of the five in Yakushko's model: the cultural level, the host community/institutional level, and the individual level. The influencing factors differ from acculturative stressors in that the influencing factors are objective facts and therefore described neutrally, whereas acculturative stressors are described negatively owing to their negative impacts on individuals.

Different cultural norms and practices within sociocultural contexts

Cultural norms are the established standards guiding the thoughts and behaviors of individuals within a society, whereas cultural practices refer to prevalent routine behaviors in a culture. Chloe shared her personal struggle in transitioning from her collectivist home country to the U.S. individualistic society. She highlighted the shift from relying on family support to the emphasis on doing things alone. Chloe said, "I can't live without my family, and I can't always find someone who can solve my problems here [in the U.S.]." Playing different roles in collectivist and individualistic societies' contrasting cultural norms has contributed to Chloe's stress.

Alex found it challenging to connect with American students due to the differing communication styles that stemmed from their different cultural practices. He felt that Americans were "straightforward" in expressing their thoughts, but Alex often "remained silent" because he feared that his ideas might not be accepted by others or could lead to unnecessary arguments. Both Olivia and Emma expressed difficulties in quickly adapting to the conversational styles in the U.S. Sometimes, they felt confused about the warm greetings and found it hard to respond immediately, as such greetings were unusual in their home countries.

Diverse power dynamics within institutions and classrooms

Power dynamics within institutions and classrooms emerged as a second-level important factor. Universities have diverse populations of students from different countries and cultural backgrounds, all seeking opportunities and services. However, Leo noted, "We don't have power even though we bring [the university] money." This statement suggested that universities might prioritize the needs of international students, owing to their financial contributions, but this was not the case. Additionally, Lily mentioned that, as an international student, she had a problem with her visa. However, she became upset because "the university did not provide much assistance, they did not know much about my situation." While universities had the authority to allocate opportunities and provide services, participants felt that their needs were not being met, leading to dissatisfaction and anxiety.

As mentioned above, moving from the university level to the classroom setting, the participants experienced stress in adapting from teacher-centered, lecture-based classrooms in their home countries to U.S. classrooms that emphasized active student involvement. As Olivia shared "The education in my home country is heavily reliant on teachers, but here, we need to be independent... We're seeking and expanding knowledge through our own reading and research, and that was hard for me." The U.S. classrooms challenged participants' beliefs regarding teacher authority in classrooms, fostering students' greater independence in knowledge acquisition while leading to increased stress.

Individuals' varied responsibilities assigned in society

Exploring the third level of factor, participants' experiences of some acculturative stressors were influenced by the responsibilities assigned to individuals within the society. First, as international students in the U.S., participants were mandated to meet essential language proficiency requirements to comprehend lectures, engage in class discussions, and engage in conversations. Second, Alex noted that the academic pressure required that graduate students possess an ability to "handle intensity and difficulty of coursework mostly on their own and meet graduation requirements." Third, when dealing with family responsibilities, Alex and Lily experienced financial burdens, possibly due to their perceived obligation to earn money without putting financial pressures on their families. Additionally, Lily stressed not maintaining regular contact with her family members, feeling that it was her duty to maintain those connections. Thus, the responsibilities assigned by society to IGSs constitute a factor influencing participants' experiences of stressors.

Coping strategies for stressors and outcomes

Guided by the four domains in Yakushko's (2010) model, including coping patterns, context, intervention conditions, and consequences, we explored how participants managed acculturative stressors and the corresponding outcomes. Some participants employed problem-focused coping strategies. Among these participants, those from Asian countries tended to rely on self-help and external resources for managing stressors rather than seeking assistance from professors. Specifically, five Asian participants (i.e., Alex, Ethan, Leo, Olivia, Zoe) addressed linguistic challenges in academics by using TED Talks, translation tools, native language textbooks, and lecture recordings. For example, Alex shared that he once watched a TED talk three times until he understood. His commitment led to improvements in listening and comprehension skills. Additionally, Ethan improved his understanding of course material by buying Chinese-translated textbooks that matched his English textbooks. He cross-referenced both languages, benefiting his comprehension and developing his English reading and vocabulary skills. The tendency for some of these IGSs to use external resources rather than consulting professors directly was related to cultural practice. For instance, Ava and Susan mentioned that they hesitated to reach out to professors, and they were uncertain if seeking help for emotional struggles was appropriate. This hesitation stemmed from the hierarchical teacher–student relationship in Asian cultures where approaching professors directly in that way would not be encouraged.

The participants expressed a variety of attitudes about using resources provided by the university to help with coping strategies. Two participants at University A, Alex and Ethan, actively engaged in university and department-provided activities tailored for international students. These activities, such as global community connections, Experience America, and happy hour events, helped them "become familiar with campus life, connect with local students and professors, explore local history and culture, such as American sports, food culture, and festivals." Two participants from Universities B and C, however, expressed dissatisfaction and skepticism about the school's cross-cultural adjustment services. Susan shared, "It is very difficult to contact the international student office to get support." Ava said, "I'm not sure if the services the school offers will be helpful. I tend to rely on my friends, my social circuits will route me up, and they've been helpful." Four participants, including Lily, Leo, Olivia, and Susan, at Universities B and C, primarily adopted an emotion-focused strategy to seek advice and emotional support by sharing their challenges with family and friends from their home countries and fellow international students. Leo, for instance, said that "reaching out to senior Bangladesh students alleviated feelings of isolation... I realized that I was not alone in facing challenges... obtained valuable advice on overcoming challenges." Olivia shared, "When I felt down because of my [course] project, I talked to my family and friends for support. We chatted in our native language, and it made me feel better; then, I was able to focus on my writing again." Thus, the participants had different preferences for managing stressors. Those at Universities B and C placed less emphasis on university-provided resources than did those at University A. This difference might be attributed to two reasons. First, Universities B and C had fewer international students, leading to smaller-scale and less frequent organized activities, and reduced promotion and outreach for tailored resources. Additionally, owing to the limited number of international students at Universities B and C, students might have found it difficult to find companions to attend activities, leading to lower participation rates.

However, several participants used avoidance, an emotion-focused strategy. Specifically, three participants (i.e., Ava, Chloe, and Leo) engaged in recreational activities, such as watching Japanese Anime and American sitcoms and playing video games, to manage linguistic challenges and academic pressures. Despite providing instant relief, Ava emphasized the temporary nature of using the avoidance strategy and stated, "It's instant... I may not be as stressed as I used to be, but the stressors [linguistic challenges] always come back when I moved to a new university in the U.S." Importantly, Ava recognized that relying solely on recreational activities for distraction might not offer a long-term solution to academic adaptation challenges.

Furthermore, regardless of the strategies that students chose to manage stressors, some issues, such as financial burdens, were simply beyond their control. Institutions and faculty could play important roles in this context. As Chloe emphasized, "It would be helpful if advisors and professors gain a better understanding of international students' issues, understand our behaviors, and help us solve problems together." According to Yakushko's (2010) model, IGSs are seen as the primary decision makers in selecting coping strategies, with their choices influenced by the resources provided by institutions (i.e., intervention conditions). However, this study suggests that institutions and faculty could take on roles beyond mere intervention, and they could act as primary agents in collaboration with IGSs to manage stressors together. This idea will be explored in the next section.

DISCUSSION

Guided by Yakushko's (2010) model, we identified common acculturative stressors among ten IGSs, analyzed the factors influencing their experiences of stressors, and explored their coping strategies and corresponding consequences. This study revealed that some participants encountered linguistic challenges and financial burdens. These stressors negatively impact their academic learning and living experiences, corroborating previous research that highlighted the prevalence and adverse effects of these stressors among international student populations (Kuo & Roysircar, 2004; Misra et al., 2003; Perry et al., 2017). Furthermore, this study identified two stressors among participants which have been less emphasized in existing research: a lack of familiarity with new pedagogical approaches and familial burdens. We found that participants from Asian countries who earned bachelor's and master's degrees in their home countries faced challenges in adjusting to new pedagogical approaches in the U.S. This challenge might have stemmed from their prolonged exposure to passive learning approaches, resulting in feelings of being overwhelmed in U.S. classes. Additionally, several participants experienced familial burdens as they managed family expectations regarding their pursuit of academic studies overseas and fulfilled roles as children, spouses, or parents to maintain long-distance family relationships.

Guided by the causal conditions in Yakushko's (2010) model, this study explored the three levels of factors impacting IGSs' experiences of stressors, including variations in cultural norms and practices within sociocultural contexts (cultural level), diverse power dynamics within institutions and classrooms (host community level), and responsibilities assigned to individuals in society (individual level). Some previous studies (Eustace, 2007; Jon, 2012) have focused on the first two levels. For example, Eustace (2007) reported that international students from collectivistic cultures experienced stress while adapting to classrooms, with expectations of active participation common in individualistic cultures. The current study further suggested that the participants' challenge of transitioning from a collectivist to an individualistic society was impacted by distinct cultural norms. Additionally, Jon's (2012) study highlighted power imbalances between domestic and international undergraduates, with the latter often perceiving themselves as having lower status and experiencing discrimination. The current study delved deeper into power dynamics within institutions and classrooms, focusing on the lack of funding for IGSs and the transition from teacher-led to student-centered learning. These power dynamics led to the stress of participants, who found their needs unmet despite their financial contributions to universities and who were accustomed to a teacher-authoritative educational approach. Furthermore, this study revealed the third level of factors as a new discovery. We found that international graduate students in the U.S. navigated various responsibilities, including achieving language proficiency, managing demanding academic workloads, and balancing family obligations. These sets of responsibilities assigned by society collectively constitute a third level of factors influencing participants' stressors.

On the basis of the four domains of Yakushko's (2010) model, including coping patterns, context, intervention conditions, and adaptation consequences, this study examined the coping strategies employed by participants and their corresponding consequences. We found that most participants employed problem-focused and emotion-focused coping strategies to manage their stressors effectively, consistent with previous research on their effectiveness (De Moissac et al., 2020; Ra & Trusty, 2015; Saravanan et al., 2019). Problem-focused coping included using external support, such as TED Talks and translation tools, as well as gaining community and belonging via institution-organized events. Emotion-focused coping focused on emotional support from family and friends. The findings suggested that participants' preferences for managing stressors might have been influenced by differences among institutions in the number of international students, investment in resources, and extent of promotional efforts. Moreover, several participants employed avoidance as a mechanism of emotion-focused coping, such as watching TV shows and playing video games. While these activities provided short-term relief, they were not long-term solutions to stressors. This finding corroborated previous research that linked avoidance with increased acculturative stressors (Sumer, 2009). Overall, the strategies for coping with acculturative stressors varied in effectiveness, with no universal solution (Tiwari et al., 2017).

LIMITATIONS

This study had several limitations. First, the small sample size (n=10) and uneven distribution of participants, with seven from University C and eight from Asian countries, might limit our understanding of acculturation experiences among the diverse demographics of IGSs. However, this study is a qualitative investigation designed to identify themes and trends in a robust way for a small number of people, and the goal is not generalizability to all IGSs. Our findings can serve as a starting point for other researchers to increase the sample size and recruit more participants from different countries and institutions to be more representative of the geographical and cultural diversity of all international students.

Second, for participants who spoke English as a second or foreign language, using English to conduct interviews might have hindered their ability or willingness to express themselves during interviews. We felt this was a minor factor given that all of the students were studying at a high level at English-medium universities, but future researchers might also consider allowing participants to respond or elaborate in their native language, which could facilitate a deeper expression of their thoughts. Finally, this study, like many studies on similar social psychological constructs, relied on self-report data, and so the findings can only be considered as being through the lens of the participants' understandings and experiences.

CONCLUSION

In this study, guided by Yakushko's (2010) model, we examined the common acculturative stressors faced by IGSs in three U.S. higher education institutions, the factors influencing these students' experiences of these stressors, and the coping strategies employed by these students and the corresponding consequences. Some findings of this study corroborate previous research examining the acculturation of international students. For example, we identified that common acculturative stressors, such as linguistic challenges and financial burdens, negatively impacted IGSs' academic learning and living experiences. We also analyzed the primary adoption of problem-focused and emotion-focused coping strategies by IGSs, which led to distinct consequences.

This study also contributes to the understanding of acculturation among IGSs in U.S. institutions. We found that unfamiliar pedagogical approaches and familial burdens stressed these students. The increased stress levels might have stemmed from their prolonged exposure to more passive learning experiences in their home countries and their ability to manage family responsibilities while maintaining long-distance relationships. We also further analyzed the factors that impacted IGSs' experiences of acculturative stressors, including distinct cultural norms and practices within sociocultural contexts, diverse power dynamics within institutions and classrooms, and individuals' varied responsibilities assigned to society.

In considering Yakushko's (2010) model, we suggest connecting the causal conditions to coping strategies more directly. This suggestion stems from the fact that causal factors like the culturally-inscribed experience of the participants in their teacher–student relationships clearly influenced their adoption of coping strategies. That is, the Asian participants' reluctance to seek help from professors might have originated from the predominance of hierarchical teacher–student relationships in Asian cultures, which then led them to find other coping strategies. Additionally, we believe that institutions and faculty could be included in the coping patterns domain to act as primary agents that collaborate directly with IGSs to manage stressors rather than solely intervening during the coping process.

ACKNOWLEDGEMENT

This project was supported by Humane Letters Grant and the University of Iowa College of Education Graduate Student Research Award.

In the preparation of this manuscript, we utilized Artificial Intelligence (AI) tools for content creation in the following capacity:

√ *None*

☐ *Some sections, with minimal or no editing*

☐ *Some sections, with extensive editing*

☐ *Entire work, with minimal or no editing*

☐ *Entire work, with extensive editing*

REFERENCES

Bastien, G., Seifen-Adkins, T., & Johnson, L. R. (2018). Striving for success: Academic adjustment of international students in the US. *Journal of International Students*, *8*(2), 1198-1219. https://doi.org/10.32674/jis.v8i2.143

Berry, J. W. (2003). Conceptual approaches to acculturation. American Psychological Association. In K. M. Chun, P. Balls Organista, & G. Marín (Eds.), *Acculturation: Advances in theory, measurement, and applied research* (pp. 17-37). American Psychological Association. https://doi.org/10.1037/10472-004

Berry, J. W. (2005). Acculturation: Living successfully in two cultures. *International Journal of Intercultural Relations*, *29*(6), 697-712. https://doi.org/10.1016/j.ijintrel.2005.07.013

Bertram, D. M., Poulakis, M., Elsasser, B. S., & Kumar, E. (2014). Social Support and Acculturation in Chinese International Students. *Journal of Multicultural Counseling and Development*, *42*(2), 107-124. https://doi.org/10.1002/j.2161-1912.2014.00048.x

Chen, Y. H., & Van Ullen, M. K. (2011). Helping international students succeed academically through research process and plagiarism workshops. *College & Research Libraries*, *72*(3), 209-235. https://doi.org/10.5860/crl-117rl

Cho, & Yu, H. (2015). Roles of university support for international students in the United States. *Journal of Studies in International Education*, *19*(1), 11-27. https://doi.org/10.1177/1028315314533606

Click. (2018). International graduate students in the United States: Research processes and challenges. *Library & Information Science Research, 40*(2), 153-162. https://doi.org/10.1016/j.lisr.2018.05.004

De Moissac, Graham, J. M., Prada, K., Gueye, N. R., & Rocque, R. (2020). Mental health status and help-seeking strategies of international students in Canada. *Canadian Journal of Higher Education (1975), 50*(4), 52-71. https://doi.org/10.47678/cjhe.vi0.188815

Erturk, S., & Nguyen Luu, L. A. (2022). Adaptation of Turkish international students in Hungary and the United States: A comparative case study. *International Journal of Intercultural Relations, 86*, 1-13. https://doi.org/10.1016/j.ijintrel.2021.10.006

Eustace. (2007). *Factors influencing acculturative stress among international students in the United States.* [Doctoral Dissertation, Kansas State University]. ProQuest Dissertations Publishing. https://www-proquest-com.proxy.lib.uiowa.edu/docview/304834706?pq-origsite=primo&sourcetype=Dissertations%20&%20Theses

Ferguson, C. (2015). *Stress and coping among Iraqi refugee men.* [Master Dissertation, California State University San Marcos].

Forbes-Mewett, & Sawyer, A.-M. (2016). International students and mental health. *Journal of International Students, 6*(3), 661-677. https://doi.org/10.32674/jis.v6i3.348

Glass, Gómez, E., & Urzua, A. (2014). Recreation, intercultural friendship, and international students' adaptation to college by region of origin. *International Journal of Intercultural Relations, 42*, 104-117. https://doi.org/10.1016/j.ijintrel.2014.05.007

Institute of International Education (2023a). *Open Doors 2022 Report: Enrollment Trends.* Retrieved from https://opendoorsdata.org/data/international-students/enrollment-trends/

Institute of International Education (2023b). *Open Doors 2022 Report: Academic Level.* Retrieved from https://opendoorsdata.org/data/international-students/academic-level/

Jon. (2012). Power dynamics with international students. *Higher Education, 64*(4), 441-454. https://doi.org/10.1007/s10734-011-9503-2

Knight. (2004). Internationalization remodeled: Definition, approaches, and rationales. *Journal of Studies in International Education, 8*(1), 5-31. https://doi.org/10.1177/1028315303260832

Koo, K., Baker, I., & Yoon, J. (2021). The first year acculturation: A longitudinal study on acculturative stress and adjustment among the first year international college students. *Journal of International Students, 11*(2), 278-298. https://doi.org/10.32674/jis.v11i2.1726

Kuo, B. C. (2014). Coping, acculturation, and psychological adaptation among migrants: a theoretical and empirical review and synthesis of the literature. *Health Psychology and Behavioral Medicine: An Open Access Journal. 2*(1), 16-33. https://doi.org/10.1080/21642850.2013.843459

Kuo, C.H., & Roysircar, G. (2004). Predictors of acculturation for Chinese adolescents in Canada: Age of arrival, length of stay, social class and English reading ability. *Journal of Multicultural Counseling and Development, 32*(3), 143-154. https://doi.org/10.1002/j.2161-1912.2004.tb00367.x

Kwon, Y. (2009). Factors affecting international students transition to higher education institutions in the United States - From the perspectives of office of international students. *College Student Journal, 43*(4), 1020-1036.

Lazarus, R. S. & Folkman. S. (1984). *Stress, appraisal, and coping.* Springer Publications.

Lee, J. J. (2013). Find on-campus support for international students. An ombudsman is just one type of campus support often underutilized by international students. *US News and World Report.* Retrieved from *https://www.usnews.com/education/blogs/international-student-counsel/2013/07/11/find-on-campus-support-for-international-students*

Leong. (2015). Coming to America: Assessing the patterns of acculturation, friendship formation, and the academic experiences of international students at a U.S. college. *Journal of International Students, 5*(4), 459-474. https://doi.org/10.32674/jis.v5i4.408

Luo, Z., Wu, S., Fang, X., & Brunsting, N. C. (2019). International students' perceived language competence, domestic student support, and psychological well-being at a U.S. university. *Journal of International Students, 9*(4), 954-971. https://doi.org/10.32674/jis.v0i0.605

Ma, K., Pitner, R., Sakamoto, I., & Park, H. Y. (2020). Challenges in acculturation among international students from Asian Collectivist cultures. *Higher Education Studies, 10*(3), 34. https://doi.org/10.5539/hes.v10n3p34

McFadden, A., & Seedorff, L. (2017). International student employment: Navigating immigration regulations, career services, and employer considerations. *New Directions for Student Services, 2017*(158), 37-48. https://doi.org/10.1002/ss.20218

McLachlan, D. A., & Justice, J. (2009). A grounded theory of international student well-being. *Journal of Theory Construction & Testing, 13*(1), 27.

Merriam, S. B. (1998). *Qualitative research and case study applications in education / Sharan B. Merriam.* (2nd edition.). Jossey-Bass.

Merriam, S.B. & Tisdell, E. J. (2016). *Qualitative research: A guide to design and implementation* (4th ed.). Jossey-Bass.

Misra, R., Crist, M., & Burant, C. J. (2003). Relationships among life stress, social support, academic stressors, and reactions to stressors of international students in the United States. *International Journal of Stress Management, 10*(2), 137-157. https://doi.org/10.1037/1072-5245.10.2.137

Moores, & Popadiuk, N. (2011). Positive aspects of international student transitions: A qualitative inquiry. *Journal of College Student Development, 52*(3), 291-306. https://doi.org/10.1353/csd.2011.0040

Nilsson, J. E., Butler, J., Shouse, S., & Joshi, C. (2008). The relationships among perfectionism, acculturation, and stress in Asian international students. *Journal of College Counseling, 11*(2), 147-158. https://doi.org/10.1002/j.2161-1882.2008.tb00031.x

Nyland, C., Forbes-Mewett, H., & Härtel, C. E. J. (2013). Governing the international student experience: Lessons from the Australian international education model. *Academy of Management Learning & Education, 12*, 656-673. https://doi.org/10.5465/amle.2012.0088

Ozer. (2015). Predictors of international students' psychological and sociocultural adjustment to the context of reception while studying at Aarhus University, Denmark. *Scandinavian Journal of Psychology, 56*(6), 717-725. https://doi.org/10.1111/sjop.12258

Perry, C. J., Lausch, D. W., Weatherford, J., Goeken, R., & Almendares, M. (2017). International students' perceptions of university life. *College Student Journal, 51*(2), 279-290.

Poyrazli, & Devonish, O. B. (2020). Cultural value orientation, social networking site use, and homesickness in international students. *International Social Science Review, 96*(3), 1-22.

Ra, Y. A., & Trusty, J. (2015). Coping strategies for managing acculturative stress among Asian international students. *International Journal for the Advancement of Counseling, 37*(4), 319-329. https://doi.org/10.1007/s10447-015-9246-3

Rai, A., Lee, S., Yates, H. T., & Brown, S. L. (2021). Examining relationships between acculturative and life stress of international students in the United States. *College Student Affairs Journal, 39*(2), 165-179.

Saravanan, C., Mohamad, M., & Alias, A. (2019). Coping strategies used by international students who recovered from homesickness and depression in Malaysia. *International Journal of Intercultural Relations, 68*, 77-87. https://doi.org/10.1016/j.ijintrel.2018.11.003

Sumer, S. (2009). *International students' psychological and sociocultural adaptation in the United States*. [Doctoral Dissertation, Georgia State University]. ProQuest. Retrieved from https://www.proquest.com/docview/304891980?pq-origsite=primo

Tiwari, R., Singh, B. G., & Hasan, B. (2017). Acculturative stress and coping strategies of foreign students: A systematic review. *Indian Journal of Health & Wellbeing, 8*, 683-687.

UC Berkeley (2011). *International student needs assessment April 2011.* Retrieved from https://internationaloffice.berkeley.edu/sites/default/files/results_summary.pdf

UNESCO Institute for Statistics. (2006). *Global digest education 2006: Comparing education statistics across the world.* UNESCO. Retrieved from https://uis.unesco.org/sites/default/files/documents/global-education-digest-2006-comparing-education-statistics-across-the-world-en_0.pdf

US Citizenship and Immigration Services (2023). *Students and employment.* Retrieved from https://www.uscis.gov/working-in-the-united-states/students-and-exchange-visitors/students-and-employment

Vergara, M. B., Smith, N., & Keele, B. (2010). Emotional intelligence, coping responses, and length of stay as correlates of acculturative stress among international university students in Thailand. *Procedia, Social and Behavioral Sciences, 5*, 1498-1504. https://doi.org/10.1016/j.sbspro.2010.07.315

Ward, C., & Geeraert, N. (2016). Advancing acculturation theory and research: The acculturation process in its ecological context. *Current Opinion in Psychology*, *8*, 98-104. https://doi.org/10.1016/j.copsyc.2015.09.021

Yakushko. (2010). Stress and coping strategies in the lives of recent immigrants: A grounded theory model. *International Journal for the Advancement of Counseling*, *32*(4), 256-273. https://doi.org/10.1007/s10447-010-9105-1

Yu, Y., & Moskal, M. (2019). Missing intercultural engagements in the university experiences of Chinese international students in the UK. *Compare: A Journal of Comparative and International Education*, *49*(4), 654-671. https://doi.org/10.1080/03057925.2018.1448259

Author bios

Bing Gao, a Ph.D. candidate, is a research assistant in the Teaching and Learning Department at the University of Iowa, USA. Her major research interests lie in the area of cross-cultural and intercultural development of international student populations, Language Policy and Planning, social justice education, and world language education. Email: bing-gao@uiowa.edu

Pamela M. Wesely, Ph.D., is a professor in the Teaching and Learning Department at the University of Iowa, USA. Her major research interests lie in the area of attitudes, motivations, perceptions, and beliefs of stakeholders in K-12 foreign/world language education in the U.S., social justice education, and technology integration in the language classroom.
Email: pamela-wesely@uiowa.edu

Article

Journal of International Students
Volume 14, Issue 5 (2024), pp. 41-66
ISSN: 2162-3104 (Print), 2166-3750 (Online)
jistudents.org

Using Appreciative Inquiry to Empower International Students to Flourish in Research

Lillian Hung
University of British Columbia, Canada

Stephen Cheong Yu Chan
Saint Francis University, Hong Kong, China

Lily Haopu Ren
University of British Columbia, Canada

Hiro Ito
University of British Columbia, Canada

Bubli Chakraborty
University of British Columbia, Canada

ABSTRACT

Despite growing studies on Appreciative Inquiry (AI), rooted in positive psychology, its application in a research laboratory and its associated impact on students' mental health and well-being are underexplored. Thus, this study explores how a positive environment affects students' mental health and well-being. Interpretive descriptions guided the data collection and analysis process. We conducted focus groups and interviews with 23 students recruited through convenience sampling. Reflexive thematic analysis identified three themes: (1) feeling valued by others builds confidence, (2) strength-based guidance fosters growth, and (3) meaningful research work increases resilience. Our study suggests that a positive environment informed by Appreciative Inquiry has the potential to positively affect the mental health and well-being of international students.

Keywords: Appreciative Inquiry, Positivity, International Students, Mental Health, Well-being, Research Lab

INTRODUCTION

The global population, including Canada, is aging (WHO, 2022). According to the government of Canada, the country will face significant population aging in the coming decades, which will profoundly impact society. By 2030, Canada is expected to become a "superaged" country, where one in five people will be over 65 (Statistics Canada, 2022). Concurrently, health worker shortages remain among the greatest challenges in the Canadian healthcare sector (Canadian Nurses Association, 2024).

In Canada, international students are considered "a significant and growing source of permanent immigrants" in response to the demographic shift (Stirrett, 2022, p.1). The expectation is built under the context of "designer immigrants" (Simmons, 1999), in which international students are trained to meet Canadian standards to address the supply and demand of the market after graduation and become temporary foreign workers recruited by Canadian employers (Crossman et al., 2020; Hawthorne, 2012). Compared with foreign-trained professionals, international students who contribute to the future workforce have the advantages of familiarity with local culture and language proficiency (Hawthorne, 2012; Lowe, 2008). Indeed, between 2010 and 2019, the number of international students enrolled in public postsecondary educational institutions in Canada grew rapidly, from 142,200 to 388,800 (Crossman et al., 2021).

However, only approximately three of the ten international students who arrived after 2000 became landed immigrants within ten years of their arrival (Choi et al., 2021). In other words, approximately 70% of international students do not contribute to the Canadian workforce, although their skills are acquired in Canadian educational institutions (Choi et al., 2021). Hence, it is essential to support students' mental health and well-being, including that of international students, to facilitate their successful transition into employment, potentially making high-quality contributions to healthcare, economic and other sectors.
Furthermore, studies have shown that the mental health of most international students has been negatively affected by the pandemic (Firang & Mensah, 2022). Although the literature has indicated the importance of supporting students' mental health and well-being before the pandemic (Clarke, 2023; Evans et al., 2018; Levecque et al., 2017; Wyatt & Oswalt, 2013), the topic has become crucial in its aftermath. Disrupted education systems adversely impact students' mental health, leading to increased reports of depression, anxiety, and other psychological challenges. The shift to online learning has exacerbated feelings of isolation and disconnection among students, affecting their ability to engage with peers and acquire essential professional skills (Azmi et al., 2022).

The challenges brought forth by the pandemic have underscored the importance of peer support, coaching, and mentorship within an academic environment to foster student well-being. In a study by Wu and Liu (2023), students reported experiencing social isolation and a loss of connection with peers due to the shift to online learning. In addition, university students are expected to learn and deliver research output in a fast-paced environment. Oswalt and Riddock (2007) reported that 75% of graduate students feel stressed. In the study by Hyun et al. (2006), 50% of their students reported feeling overwhelmed, and 40% reported being exhausted. The global pandemic has resulted in additional stressors and induced posttraumatic stress disorder (PTSD), depressive symptoms, and other psychological and physical symptoms in the student population (Tang et al., 2020). A study by SenthilKumar et al. (2023) described how the pace of scientific competitive culture and the lack of sufficient support for students from diverse backgrounds influence students' mental well-being, especially for international students.

Traditionally, studies (list some here such as xx xxx and xxx) on student mental health and well-being have investigated the presence or absence of mental health conditions such as depression, anxiety, and burnout. In the literature, well-being has often been reduced to a concept that indicates the absence of mental health symptoms, such as anxiety and depression (Lin et al., 2016). Little attention has been given to positive aspects of mental health, such as happiness, confidence, safety, a sense of belonging, growth, and the motivation to perform. Furthermore, the environmental and cultural drivers of these positive indicators of mental health remain underexplored. For example, there are many unwritten stories about what is valued in research, what makes an international student resilient, and what helps a female immigrant student cope with adversity and maintain positivity to flourish in academic success. Making those unwritten stories visible will help improve the research culture for everyone involved.

There is much complexity in the two concepts of mental health and well-being. While closely related, these concepts are unique and independent (Dodd et al., 2021). There are two broad approaches to well-being in the contemporary psychology literature: hedonic and eudaimonic well-being (Ryan & Deci, 2001). Hedonic approaches often focus on subjective well-being and emphasize constructs such as happiness and affect. Moreover, eudaimonic approaches place greater emphasis on self-actualization and meaning. Those taking a eudaimonic approach also understand that well-being extends beyond subjective appraisals of happiness or life satisfaction (Ryff, 1989)and instead consists of an ongoing process of fostering fulfillment and achieving potential (Deci & Ryan, 2008).
The motivation aspect of self-determination theory (SDT) is also intertwined with the concept of the eudemonic approach; SDT emphasizes personal competence, relatedness, and autonomy. Pursuing intrinsic goals, embracing personal values, maintaining awareness, and behaving autonomously are vital to positively affect psychological, mental, and physical wellness (Ryan et al., 2013). In a study by López-Santacruz and Guízar-Mendoza (2022), students reported a desire to pursue meaningful career paths that enable them to help others and make a positive impact. A sense of purpose was deemed a driver and a source of psychological well-being.

Amidst these unprecedented educational disruptions, the Innovation in DEmentia and Aging (IDEA) Lab was established in 2020 to focus on technology in aging research (IDEA Lab, 2024). This field aims to contribute to society by supporting innovative care for older adults. The research lab provided a platform for students to connect and overcome their sense of isolation, and it aligned with the intrinsic motivation of many students with aspirations to pursue meaningful careers that have a societal impact.

THE IDEA LAB AND APPRECIATIVE INQUIRY

The IDEA Lab was developed by Professor Lillian Hung at the School of Nursing at a Canadian university, to bring students from multiple disciplines together to conduct technology implementation research to improve care for older adults. The lab comprises more than 100 students with diverse backgrounds. In terms of academic training, students ranged from undergraduate to master's and PhD levels. Among these students, more than 80% were visible minorities and females who are traditionally underrepresented in scientific research. The majority of them are international health-related students. This paper refers to international students as those who came from outside Canada to pursue education.

In this lab, students work closely with patient partners (older adults), healthcare organizations, and local community members on projects to innovate care for older adults. The practices in the lab are aligned with practical strategies suggested in the literature to promote an inclusive and supportive training environment (Chaudhary & Berhe, 2020). The IDEA lab has two primary aims:

1) To engage students in multidisciplinary research to increase their knowledge and skills in applied gerontology.
2) To provide a platform for students to research with older adults for social impact.

The students are given options, support, and guidance to take on different roles on the basis of their interests, capacities, and professional goals. For example, students lead projects, collect data, analyze data, present at conferences, write manuscripts and design knowledge translation outputs. Some students were hired as research assistants, whereas others contributed as volunteers. All the students received ongoing support and guidance from the Principal Investigator (PI)/the head of the lab. The projects included implementing virtual reality programs, social robots and other service robots in local hospitals and long-term care homes.

The lab developed its learning culture and environment on the basis of the principles of Appreciative Inquiry (AI) (Cooperrider & Whitney, 2000). Appreciative inquiry has been recognized as an effective approach to organizational development (Bushe, 2013; Cooperrider & Whitney, 2000). However, few studies have reported how AI can be applied in academic research settings. This study examines how a gerontology research lab guided by Appreciative Inquiry influences students' mental health and well-being.

AI was chosen to guide the lab's culture and practice because its core principles—positive collaboration and reflexive practice—align with the lab members' shared desires to foster growth through a strength-based approach. A recent study in the Netherlands demonstrated how AI successfully fostered students' motivation to cocreate with older adults, improving age-friendly services (van den Berg et al., 2019).

AI philosophy takes a positive approach to support human flourishing (Reed, 2006). In a previous geriatric study, AI motivated clinicians to build collective intelligence and team capacity (Hung et al., 2016). AI may empower students to become a positive workforce for the future care of older people. AI focuses on asking generative questions, such as by bringing people together to generate positive energy to address problems (Reed, 2006).

METHOD

Design

Given the complex nature of student experiences, this study employs a qualitative approach to understand how students' experiences in the research laboratory affect their mental health and well-being. Interpretive description (ID) methodology guided the data collection and analysis (Thorne, 2016). ID is suitable for this study because interpretivism values the meaning that participants construct from their subjective experiences. ID is particularly helpful in generating practical knowledge for training the next generation in healthcare to improve senior care. We report the study results following the Consolidated Criteria for Reporting Qualitative Research (COREQ) Checklist (Tong et al., 2007). See Appendix 1 for the COREQ Checklist.

Ethical considerations

We applied several strategies to ensure rigor and address potential bias. First, we have embedded regular team reflection sessions to identify and address ethical issues and biases. All the authors are encouraged to openly discuss their perspectives, concerns, and observations about the research process during these sessions. This collective dialog helps to surface any unconscious biases, ethical dilemmas, or power dynamics that might influence the research. Second, we kept detailed documentation of our research processes, decisions, and challenges encountered to enhance transparency. Third, our research team includes diverse perspectives that help mitigate the risk of bias through robust discussions and a broader understanding of the ethical implications of the research. The University Research Ethics Board approved this study (REB#H22-02402).

Data collection

We developed the interview guide and pilot tested it with a few trainees, who considered the questions understandable, given the participants' educational backgrounds. We then reviewed the interview guide and facilitated two focus groups and six follow-up individual interviews with seven undergraduate and 16 graduate students. All focus groups and interviews were conducted in English. See Table 1 for a timeline of the data collection activities.

Table 1: Data collection activities

Month and Year	Type of Data Collection
August, 2023	Focus Group 1
August, 2023	Focus Group 2
December, 2023	One-to-one interviews

Participants were recruited through convenience sampling from a group email sent to all trainees in the lab, with the goals and reasons for the research project explained. Trainees who expressed interest were invited to participate in the focus group at a mutually convenient time. SC explained the interview questions to all participants who came to the session. With participants' consent, SC conducted and video-recorded all focus groups and interviews over a virtual conferencing platform—zoom meetings. Two focus groups were conducted in August 2023, each lasting an hour. Following the initial data analysis, SC conducted follow-up interviews. All participants in the focus groups were invited to participate in a 30-- to 45-minute follow-up interview. Six participants attended the follow-up interviews in December 2023. SC took field notes for all focus groups and interviews. The BC is a female Asian family partner (a family caregiver of a person living with dementia) of the IDEA Lab. To ensure a safe environment and address power dynamics, the LH, the PI and the founder of the IDEA Lab did not participate in any focus group or interview sessions. Instead, she invited SC, a male psychology professor external to the lab, to collect the data.

The focus group discussions and semistructured interviews included the following topics: experience in the lab, perceptions of the strength-based approach, lab culture, challenges, suggestions for improving the lab, general comments for the supervisor, peer relationships, and experiences working with patient partners. SC, a psychologist and external expert, led the data collection to enhance the study's credibility in two ways. First, he developed specialized skills in qualitative research methodologies, ensuring rigorous research practices. Second, participants felt more comfortable discussing sensitive topics with someone outside their usual academic environment, leading to more open and honest responses. The data were automatically transcribed by Zoom, reorganized by LRs and other trainees from the laboratory, and checked by the SC. Data collection ceased when the team agreed that the data collected were sufficient to address the research question.

Data analysis

Our data analysis aimed to capture individual perceptions and the overall team experience—where commonalities and differences exist. The study focuses on finding answers to the following research question: How does a research lab environment affect students' mental health and well-being? Our analysis was guided by six steps of thematic analysis (Braun & Clarke, 2022) and the six phases introduced by Nowell et al. (2017). In Step 1, all the authors were involved in reading and rereading the transcripts, coding and analyzing them inductively and deductively. LR is a female Asian PhD international student in interdisciplinary studies. HI is a female Asian master's student in public health. LR and HI are trainees supervised by LH. In Step 2, LR sorted the data and performed the initial analysis manually. In Step 3, we discussed the data as a team and developed preliminary themes. The team refined the themes together in Step 4. In Step 5, the team conducted further data analysis and discussion on themes and collectively agreed on the quotations selected together for the paper. Finally, in Step 6, LH wrote the first draft of the manuscript. All the authors edited, reviewed and reached a consensus on the final manuscript.

Ethical considerations

We applied several strategies to ensure rigour and address potential bias. First, regular team reflection sessions were held to identify and address ethical issues and biases. During these sessions, all team members were encouraged to openly discuss their perspectives, concerns, and observations about the research process. This collective dialog helped to surface any unconscious biases, ethical dilemmas, or power dynamics that might influence the research. Second, we kept detailed documentation of our research processes, decisions, and challenges encountered to enhance transparency. Third, our research team included diverse perspectives that helped mitigate the risk of bias and broadened our understanding of the ethical implications of the research.

RESULTS

A total of 23 students participated in the study. The student participants came from diverse professional and cultural backgrounds, reflecting their overall demographics. Almost half of the participants were from health-related fields, including nursing, medicine, and public health. Participants from nonhealth-related professions, such as industry, economics, and international relations, were also included. A total of 91.3% of the participants were female. The participants at all educational levels (undergraduate, graduate and PhD) were represented, with graduate students accounting for the largest portion (43.38%) of the participants.

All participants (100%) were visible minorities, comprising mostly East Asian (69.57%) and South Asian (21.74%) minorities. A total of 4.35% of the students were from African or Persian backgrounds. See Table 2 for their characteristics.

Reflexive thematic analysis identified three themes: (1) Feeling valued by others builds confidence, (2) strength-based guidance fosters growth, and (3) meaningful research work increases resilience. Table 3 shows examples of how the students' quotes were clustered into codes, categories, and final themes.

Table 2: Demographic *characteristics of the participants (n = 23)*

Student Characteristics	N	%
Main Discipline		
Nursing	11	47.83%
Medicine	4	17.39%
Public Health	2	8.70%
Science	1	4.35%
Industry	1	4.35%
International Relations	1	4.35%
Economics	1	4.35%
Kinesiology	1	4.35%
Biology	1	4.35%
Gender		0.00%
Female	21	91.30%
Male	2	8.70%
Levels of Education		
Undergraduate	7	30.43%
Master	10	43.48%
PhD	6	26.09%
Racial background		
East Asian	16	69.57%
South Asian	5	21.74%
African	1	4.35%
Persian	1	4.35%
Total	23	100%

Theme 1: Feeling valued by others builds confidence

In academic institutions, students navigate a highly demanding and competitive environment that often strains their mental health and self-perception. Our findings suggest that the relational dimensions within the lab and a shared commitment to community contribution have a beneficial impact on their well-being. The participants consistently reported that the peer support, positive reinforcement, and acknowledgment they received bolstered their self-confidence and promoted a positive self-image. This was further evidenced by the participants' sense of fulfillment derived from engaging in work they viewed as beneficial to society, imbuing them with a meaningful sense of purpose.

Table 3: Example of Quotes for Theme Development

Theme	Categories	Code	Quotes
Feeling valued by others builds confidence	Social Support	Friendship	*"The social aspect is that I have met so many people through the years, and some have become close friends."*
Strength-based guidance fosters growth	Positivity	Acknowledgment of strengths	*"The professor told the team about my strengths in facilitation, which made me feel included and as if I was a valuable team member."*
Meaningful research work boosts resilience	Re-energized	Reconnect passion	*I was involved in implementing a research project and was privileged to do it at my workplace. At the time, I was feeling burned out and not wanting to go to work. In addition, so just having a research project to implement was refreshing, something new. I got reconnected to the other staff, and my passion was reenergized.*

One student, who described themselves as naturally people-oriented and enthusiastic about research, noted a significant improvement in well-being after working with the lab.

> "I am a people person, passionate about academic research. Before joining the IDEA Lab, I never thought I could facilitate academic meetings or engage with older adults with dementia. It is been especially important to me during the pandemic, as I have been socially isolated. Being back in the community and working with great people has improved my well-being."
> - An international PhD student

Another student expressed how acknowledgment within the lab eased the stress associated with uncertainty about their academic and career choices. This recognition translated into a heightened sense of confidence.

> "My stress level was high in terms of mental health. I often stress where I am headed in life, especially in regard to my studies and career. It is tough to know if I'm making the right choices. However, getting recognition for my work truly helps ease that anxiety. Knowing that others appreciate what I do gives me a boost of confidence."
> -An international master's student

The lab's inclusive, nonhierarchical structure was perceived as a key factor in fostering a sense of belonging among its members. This approach allowed for autonomy in task selection and equitable participation, cultivating personal growth and skill enhancement at the students' pace. Likewise, the supportive environment encouraged mentorship, enhancing leadership and teamwork skills.

> "The nonhierarchical structure allows members to choose tasks on the basis of interest and ensures inclusion and equity among members. Projects and types of tasks are open to everyone, fostering personal development of your will. Members are welcome to contribute in their own way with flexible support. Experienced members mentor new ones, which also strengthens leadership skills." -An international master's student

Students frequently described the lab as a place of discovery, where encouragement to try new things led to self-realization and skill development. Within this nurturing setting, students felt empowered to explore unfamiliar territories, enhancing their capacity to succeed without fear of failure.

> "The support and encouragement made me feel like I belonged. Involvement in writing workshops and manuscript reviews improved my skills and made me feel happy."
> -An international master's student

Another trainee added:

> "I feel encouraged to try. It is a discovery process that helps me realize my potential and develop new skills. In this environment, you are more likely to discover completely new areas and have the courage to take on and see how much you can accomplish instead of being scared of making mistakes."
> -An international master's student

The most salient theme identified was the importance of relationships in supporting student mental health. Positive emotional experiences such as joy, excitement, and satisfaction are linked to enhanced well-being. The social relationships with peers, the PI, patients and family partners provided foundational support for students' psychological health, offering both safety and compassion. For instance, a participant stated,

> "Regarding social aspects, I have met many people through the lab, and some have become close friends. Yeah, it was socialization and a sense of achievement, I think. It helped a lot."
> -An international undergraduate student

Theme 2: Strength-based guidance fosters growth

Teamwork and personal growth were considered pivotal aspects of the academic journey for students at all levels within the lab. The students expressed a profound sense of accomplishment and contentment stemming from the responsibility of project ownership and the reciprocal trust within the team. This feeling of validation and recognition was highlighted as essential to their sense of belonging and value within the group. This is particularly important for international students:

> "As an international student, joining the lab was nerve-wracking initially, but everyone was kind and patient. My confidence grew as I contributed my skills. Working on projects such as filming videos for the Virtual Reality program brought me happiness."
> - An international undergraduate student

> "Joining the lab as a newcomer to Vancouver was comforting. The friendly atmosphere and engagement with innovative projects such as robots made me feel included."
> - An international master's student

> "The collegial feeling of working together was a highlight for me; teamwork made research less intimidating."
> - An international master's student

International students' transition was supported by the welcoming atmosphere and the exciting opportunity to engage with innovative projects, such as robotics. The sense of collegiality was particularly noted for its role in demystifying the research process and integrating new members into the team. Students repeatedly mentioned that participation in research activities, such as knowledge translation, increased confidence. Acknowledging achievements and constructive feedback from team members bolstered team experience and individual well-being. For example, a student expressed the following:

> "My experience with the Telerobot project allowed me to use my strength in creativity and knowledge translation. The lab encouraged me to

> improve as a leader. Writing the Monthly Telerobot Newsletter allowed me to receive feedback and improve as a leader, using appropriate language that resonates with participants and families. I feel empowered by the trust placed in me by the team. Leading tasks such as knowledge translation have reinforced my strengths."
> - An international undergraduate student

The participants also allude to the importance of mentorship and guidance:

> "The professor's awareness of everyone's contributions in the lab and her encouragement have been significant. Her positive approach and support contributed to a supportive and uplifting atmosphere. Her feedback was valuable to me. - An international master's student
> I see the difference between training, coaching, mentoring, and delegating. The lab gave me opportunities to grow. In the lab, my opinion was respected. It makes me think the lab is my home."
> - An international master's student

The professor's recognition of each student's contributions and her consistent encouragement and guidance cultivated a nurturing environment that resonated as a home for some students.

For some students, the lab experience reaffirmed their strengths in project work. It helped them be successfully hired into a job they desired in healthcare, such as the director of long-term care and quality improvement leaders in health authorities.

Empower came from trust, as taking responsibility for a research task reinforced each student's strengths. Positive feedback not only bolstered inclusion but also positively impacted mental health.

> "In a meeting, the professor told the team about my strengths in facilitation, which made me feel included and as if I was a valuable team member. Therefore, it just had a positive overall impact on my mental health as part of this group. She suggested that I get involved in specific ways where my strengths might come into play."
> - An international undergraduate student

Some students found that their work in the lab resonated deeply with their aspirations. A few students spoke about how being in a learning environment that supports their career paths and purpose in life connected them to their personal goals by illuminating their understanding of self.

Additionally, the students expressed a sense of optimism in their ability to achieve their goals due to the confidence built from their work in research. This positive experience was a helpful reminder when challenges and setbacks were encountered.

Theme 3: Meaningful research boosts resilience

The student responses highlighted the necessity of flexibility in adapting to the diverse needs of students. The students discussed the role of autonomy in their work. For example, a student said,

> "They created a sanctuary for many of us, most especially for those international students who are feeling lonely here, feeling that they're able to engage in the opportunity to be in a group that is accepting and welcoming; as mentioned earlier, the value of humility, too, from her end to extend her expertise to us and allow us to exchange our knowledge and skills and can develop our capabilities as individuals toward one goal which is very inspiring and motivating from on my end."
> - An international undergraduate student

Autonomy and personalized recognition within the lab are crucial for increasing students' mental health. One student reflected on how acknowledgment of their geriatric expertise during a meeting significantly boosted their morale, reinforcing the value of shared experiences and expertise.

This environment of flexibility and inclusiveness is essential. The students highlighted that they exceeded expectations when provided with opportunities to work creatively and flexibly, producing quality outcomes. This sense of agency and trust in their abilities is pivotal for motivation and personal growth. For example, one student explained, "One thing I will add is that with flexibility and inclusiveness. I get to be creative and want to do a good job and produce a quality outcome."

The students appreciated the flexibility that allowed them to contribute meaningfully to research and the world from their own spaces. This continued involvement imparted a sense of purpose and connection, significantly mitigating feelings of isolation. For one student, work in the lab meant the following:

> "I had to work remotely, and I appreciate the flexibility. I want to do it again after being asked to make a few videos. In addition, like the feedback I received, I felt valued and seen, and it gave me more motivation to learn and improve."
> - An international undergraduate student

The lab offered a silver lining for those who faced challenges during the pandemic. The recognition and validation of their work within the lab provided a sense of achievement and success when other aspects of life were struggling, thus having a profound impact on their mental health.

> "The lab has done a lot for mental health. I remember that after March 2020, we were all online, and the lab was the only connection I had to school. I was able to contribute to the research by helping with the interviews. I felt like I was able to contribute something to the world. Whenever I was feeling down during the pandemic, a little bit failing at something, I could think about my work at the lab. I know I can do an interview on how to make a conference presentation. My strengths were being used to help others. I thought about my successes in the lab when other places in my life may have been a bit challenging for me."
> - An international undergraduate student

Furthermore, engaging in lab projects offered a refreshing respite from the demands of academic and professional life. One student shared how leading a research project at their workplace reignited their passion and purpose, transforming the mundane into something fulfilling.

> "I can share a little about how it is helped me feel purposeful when implementing. I was involved in implementing a research project and was privileged to do it at my workplace. At the time, I was feeling burned out and not wanting to go to work. In addition, so just having a research project to implement was refreshing, something new. I got reconnected to the other staff, and my passion was reenergized."
> - An international undergraduate student

The outreach in the community, such as interactions with older adults in long-term care homes, enabled students to witness the tangible impact of their work, enhancing their sense of fulfillment and reward.

Moreover, the sense of community within the lab was beneficial during pervasive isolation. The lab fosters connections among students, patient partners, and family partners, creating a unique and supportive community.

> "I felt this way, particularly in grad school, but grad school can be isolating. Many of the things you do are on your own, and I'm sure you know with COVID as well, like I can imagine, whether you're in your undergrad or grad school or working. Like there was a lot of isolation. Therefore, I think a sense of community is fostered with the lab, student members, patient partners, and family partners. The feeling of being a part of a community is something that I think is special about this lab and something I appreciate."
> - An international undergraduate student

Mentorship and guidance from graduate students have been invaluable in alleviating anxieties about the uncertainties of academic life for undergraduate students. The students reported that working together helped them keep each other motivated and inspired, affirming the importance of collective support.

Finally, some discussed the need for financial support, particularly when balancing family obligations and educational expenses. Some students had to work a summer job to pay tuition, causing stress from the competitive demand for time to devote to the research work.

DISCUSSION AND IMPLICATION

This study aimed to understand students' perceptions and experiences regarding their mental health and well-being on the basis of their work and study in an academic lab where operations are informed by AI. Overall, the findings of this study emphasize the role that relationships, teamwork, and flexible support play in the well-being of students, including international students. The students' opportunities for learning and interactions with their team members, peers, and patient partners played a significant role in their mental health and well-being. Our findings corroborate the literature from research-intensive Canadian universities. For example, to improve international students' experiences, Tavares (2024) called for institution-led initiatives to include students through socialization with peers and foster an environment with enhanced equity, diversity, and inclusion, regardless of their identity as international students (Tavares, 2024). Similarly, Lane et al. (2018) reported that teaching practices adopting AI could positively influence students' well-being by increasing their feelings of being connected to their peers and motivated to learn (Lane et al., 2018).

Furthermore, the culture and environment of the research lab, guided by AI principles, supported the students' achievements, growth, and productivity. AI can be a helpful approach to fostering a positive and supportive culture in the lab where students are encouraged to succeed and their international academic, professional, and personal experiences are valued. The findings of our study are congruent with those of a study by Zhang et al. (2022), who reported that the most significant predictors of positive mental health and well-being among graduate students are feelings of satisfaction with their experience in the academic setting, a sense of belonging within them, and satisfaction with their educational supervisor. The study results can inform educators and institutions when designing and implementing well-being support interventions. This knowledge is timely and important.

Notably, the students in the study were from diverse disciplines and levels and various ethnic and racial backgrounds. They each have their own unique needs and strengths. Instead of a one-size-fits-all approach, flexible and tailored strategies are crucial in promoting students' well-being. To foster an inclusive earning environment for international students, future work should investigate student-led programs that cater to underrepresented groups' unique needs. Funding should be invested in student support groups to host events and get-togethers to improve the social connection between international students and students at various levels (SenthilKumar et al., 2023).

Our findings resonate with Ryff's six-factor model of psychological well-being (Ryff, 2014). The use of AI in the research laboratory could foster and facilitate the development of critical components of psychological well-being, including autonomy, environmental mastery, personal growth, positive relationships with others, purpose in life, and self-acceptance. All these values are central to eudaimonic well-being, which goes beyond mere pleasure and emphasizes living with meaning and virtue. The AI approach in the lab allows students to align their actions with their core beliefs and virtues. It enables them to pursue activities that contribute to their personal growth and achievements. This study addresses a critical empirical gap in the literature and informs future strategies for improving student support in academic training.

From the motivational lens, according to self-determination theory (Deci & Ryan, 2012), humans have three basic psychological needs that facilitate their well-being: competence, relatedness, and autonomy. Our findings also suggest that the AI approach taken in the laboratory promotes all these needs. Students claimed that they could master tasks in the flourishing environment, engage in meaningful social interactions with different people in different roles, develop self-directed goals, and make their own decisions. Self-determination can further influence mental health by reinforcing adaptive coping, resilience, and hope. These are valuable resources for students to mitigate symptoms of depression and anxiety (Perlman et al., 2018). For example, Chan and Huang (2022) examined the mediating role of hope in the association between negative emotions and depressive symptoms in university students and reported that hope-related pathways can be a protective factor in terms of university students' psychological outcomes.

University students are expected to play a significant role in supporting the demographic shift of the aging population in Canada. These students could become future taxpayers, formal and informal caregivers, and parents for the next generation. The study results raise awareness of the need to pay more attention to students from a variety of underrepresented backgrounds; more efforts should be made to help them build a sense of belonging and confidence.

Since the COVID-19 pandemic, student training in research has evolved and placed greater reliance on the online environment. Researchers and educators must have a comprehensive understanding of the difficulties and threats that students experience in modern learning environments. This understanding is particularly relevant for junior and undergraduate students, who are more vulnerable and may need more support in the early stages of their training. The need to support junior Chinese students may be particularly relevant for international students, who have been reported to receive mental health-related support relative to their domestic peers despite facing similar levels of stress (Clarke, 2023). Hence, future research should pay attention to the mental health of all university students, particularly international students. Similarly, future research should investigate factors that enable a culture and environment for research, study, and life that nurtures students' personal and professional development within the local context. Future studies are also recommended to explore the implementation of a nurturing environment with an approach of equity, diversity, inclusiveness and accessibility.

STRENGTHS AND LIMITATIONS

Strengths

This study contributes useful insights into the needs of students who identify as international, female, and underrepresented minority populations. One strength of this study is that AI is a promising approach that can bridge the gaps in nurturing the growth of international students and meet the needs of stressful higher education environments. We offer a practical set of strategies—GROW, as shown below—which can be employed heuristically to support others and promote inclusive student support.

Practical tips/strategies

On the basis of our study results and insights from the literature, we created the acronym "GROW" to represent practical tips/strategies for cultivating a positive environment that supports student mental health and well-being in a research lab.

GROW: Practical Tips for Fostering Student Well-Being

G: Give Recognition Promotion

We acknowledge and value each student's contributions, helping to build confidence. Recognition makes students feel appreciated and encourages further engagement and participation in the lab.

R: Relying on strength-based guidance

Guide students by focusing on their strengths, offering mentorship and guidance that helps them grow. Instead of focusing on weaknesses, students should be encouraged to build on their skills and abilities to foster personal and professional development.

O: Offer meaningful work opportunities

Provide students with opportunities to engage in meaningful projects that contribute to real-world impact. Meaningful work increases motivation and resilience, allowing students to persevere even during challenging periods.

W: Well-Being as a Priority

Making well-being a core value of the lab environment. Students should have access to support systems, open communication, and resources to manage their research responsibilities and mental health.

This acronym, **GROW**, serves as a quick and practical reminder of key actions to create a supportive, thriving research lab environment.

Limitations

This study has several limitations. First, the participants were primarily from social science backgrounds, which may not accurately represent the experiences of students from other fields, such as the natural sciences, business, or law. Second, the participants were drawn from a large, urban, and publicly funded university, potentially limiting the transferability of the findings to students at other universities in smaller, remote communities. Finally, none of the participants reported having physical disabilities, which means that the study may not capture the experiences and challenges faced by students with physical disabilities. These factors should be considered when interpreting the results and their applicability to broader student populations.

CONCLUSION

Appreciative inquiry (AI) can enhance the research laboratory environment to support students' mental health and well-being by cultivating a positive atmosphere. The positive research lab environment where each student's contributions are recognized and valued fosters a sense of confidence. The positive approach supports personal and professional growth, as students are guided to build on their talents to expand their research skills. Finally, engaging in research that students find meaningful and impactful reinforces their resilience.

Acknowledgment

In the preparation of this manuscript, we did not utilize artificial intelligence (AI) tools for content creation.

Appendix 1: Consolidated criteria for reporting qualitative studies (COREQ) Checklist by Tong et al. (2007)

No.	Item	Guide questions/description	Answers
Domain 1: Research team and reflexivity			
Personal Characteristics			
1.	Interviewer/facilitator	Which author/s conducted the interview or focus group?	SC, LR and BC
2.	Credentials	What were the researcher's credentials? *E.g. PhD, MD*	PhD and masters
3.	Occupation	What was their occupation at the time of the study?	Professors, PhD student, Master's student and family partner
4.	Gender	Was the researcher male or female?	Four female and one male
5.	Experience and training	What experience or training did the researcher have?	Nursing, psychology, interdisciplinary studies and public health
Relationship with participants			
6.	Relationship established	Was a relationship established prior to study commencement?	Yes
7.	Participant knowledge of the interviewer	What did the participants know about the researcher? e.g. *personal goals, reasons for doing the research*	Goals and reasons for doing the research
8.	Interviewer characteristics	What characteristics were reported about the interviewer/facilitator? e.g. *Bias, assumptions, reasons and interests in the research topic*	Bias, assumptions and power dynamics were reflected and discussed in writing meetings
Domain 2: Study design			
Theoretical framework			
9.	Methodological orientation and Theory	What methodological orientation was stated to	Appreciative Inquiry

		underpin the study? *e.g. grounded theory, discourse analysis, ethnography, phenomenology, content analysis*	
Participant selection			
10.	Sampling	How were participants selected? *e.g. purposive, convenience, consecutive, snowball*	Convenience sampling
11.	Method of approach	How were participants approached? *e.g. face-to-face, telephone, mail, email*	Online meeting
12.	Sample size	How many participants were in the study?	23
13.	Nonparticipation	How many people refused to participate or dropped out? Reasons?	No drop off. Lab members who did not participate were due to other commitments at the time of data collection
Setting			
14.	Setting of data collection	Where was the data collected? *e.g. home, clinic, workplace*	Places at researchers' and participants' convenience
15.	Presence of nonparticipants	Was anyone else present besides the participants and researchers?	No
16.	Description of sample	What are the important characteristics of the sample? *e.g. demographic data, date*	See Table 1 and 2
Data collection			
17.	Interview guide	Were questions, prompts, guides provided by the authors? Was it pilot tested?	No interview questions provided. The interview guide has been pilot tested.
18.	Repeat interviews	Were repeat interviews carried out? If yes, how many?	No repeat interviews were carried out. The six interviews were

			conducted for six different participants.
19.	Audio/visual recording	Did the research use audio or visual recording to collect the data?	Data collection conducted online were recorded.
20.	Field notes	Were field notes made during and/or after the interview or focus group?	SC made field notes for all focus groups and interviews.
21.	Duration	What was the duration of the interviews or focus group?	30 to 45 minutes.
22.	Data saturation	Was data saturation discussed?	Yes.
23.	Transcripts returned	Were transcripts returned to participants for comment and/or correction?	No. We did not return transcript to participants for comment and/or correction due to their heavy school commitments after data collection
Domain 3: analysis and findings			
Data analysis			
24.	Number of data coders	How many data coders coded the data?	One.
25.	Description of the coding tree	Did authors provide a description of the coding tree?	Yes. See Table 3.
26.	Derivation of themes	Were themes identified in advance or derived from the data?	Derived from data.
27.	Software	What software, if applicable, was used to manage the data?	No software was used. Data were analyzed manually.
28.	Participant checking	Did participants provide feedback on the findings?	We did not involve participants to provide feedback on findings due to their heavy school commitments after data collection.

Reporting

29.	Quotations presented	Were participant quotations presented to illustrate the themes/findings? Was each quotation identified? e.g. *participant number*	Yes, we presented quotations to illustrate the themes. Each quotation was identified by adding the participant's education.
30.	Data and findings consistent	Was there consistency between the data presented and the findings?	We made our best effort to ensure consistency between the data presented and the findings
31.	Clarity of major themes	Were major themes clearly presented in the findings?	We made our best effort to clearly present major themes in the findings.
32.	Clarity of minor themes	Is there a description of diverse cases or discussion of minor themes?	We made our best effort to clearly describe diversity in participants' cases

REFERENCES

Azmi, F. M., Khan, H. N., & Azmi, A. M. (2022). The impact of virtual learning on students' educational behavior and pervasiveness of depression among university students due to the COVID-19 pandemic. *Globalization and health*, *18*(1), 1-70. https://doi.org/10.1186/s12992-022-00863-z

Braun, V., & Clarke, V. (2022). Toward good practice in thematic analysis: Avoiding common problems and be(com)ing a knowing researcher. *International Journal of Transgender Health*, 24(1), 1–6. https://doi.org/10.1080/26895269.2022.2129597

Bushe, G. R. (2013). The Appreciative Inquiry Model. In *Encyclopedia of Management Theory*. SAGE. https://doi.org/10.4135/9781452276090

Canadian Nurses Association. (2024). *Health Human Resources*. https://www.cna-aiic.ca/en/policy-advocacy/advocacy-priorities/health-human-resources

Chan, S. C. Y., & Huang, Q. L. (2022). " Better hope, less depressed": The potential mediating role of pathways thinking between negative emotions and depressive symptoms among Chinese university students. . *Hong kong journal of social work*, *56*(1n02). https://doi.org/10.1142/S0219246222000031

Chaudhary, V. B., & Berhe, A. A. (2020). Ten simple rules for building an antiracist. *PLOS computational biology/PLoS computational biology*, *16*(10), e1008210-e1008210. https://doi.org/10.1371/journal.pcbi.1008210

Choi, Y., Crossman, E., & Hou, F. (2021). *International students as a source of our supply: Transition to permanent residency.* Statistics Canada. https://www150.statcan.gc.ca/n1/pub/36-28-0001/2023009/article/00003-eng.htm

Clarke, K. (2023). International graduate students' Mental Health Diagnoses, Challenges, and Support: A Descriptive Comparison to their Non-International Graduate Student Peers. *Journal of international students*, *13*(3), 280-304. https://doi.org/10.32674/jis.v13i3.3148

Cooperrider, D. L., & Whitney, D. (2000). A positive revolution in change: Appreciative inquiry. In *Handbook of organizational behavior, revised and expanded* (pp. 633-652). Routledge.

Crossman, E., Choi, Y., & Hou, F. (2021). International students as a source of our supply: The growing number of international students and their changing sociodemographic characteristics. In: Statistics Canada.

Crossman, E., Hou, F., & Picot, G. (2020). *Two-step immigration selection: A review of benefits and potential challenges*. Statistics Canada.

Deci, E. L., & Ryan, R. M. (2008). Hedonia, eudaimonia, and well-being: an introduction. *Journal of happiness studies*, *9*(1), 1-11. https://doi.org/10.1007/s10902-006-9018-1

Deci, E. L., & Ryan, R. M. (2012). Self-determination theory. *Handbook of theories of social psychology*, *1*(20), 416-436.

Dodd, A. L., Priestley, M., Tyrrell, K., Cygan, S., Newell, C., & Byrom, N. C. (2021). University student well-being in the United Kingdom: a scoping review of its conceptualization and measurement. *Journal of mental health*, *30*(3), 375-387. https://doi.org/10.1080/09638237.2021.1875419

Evans, T. M., Bira, L., Gastelum, J. B., Weiss, L. T., & Vanderford, N. L. (2018). Evidence for a mental health crisis in graduate education. *Nature biotechnology*, *36*(3), 282-284. https://doi.org/10.1038/nbt.4089

Firang, D., & Mensah, J. (2022). Exploring the Effects of the COVID-19 Pandemic on International Students and Universities in Canada. *Journal of international students*, *12*(1), 1. https://doi.org/10.32674/jis.v12i1.2881

Hawthorne, L. (2012). Designer immigrants? International students and two-step migration. In. https://doi.org/10.4135/9781452218397.n23

Hung, L., Lee, P. A., Au-Yeung, A. T., Kucherova, I., & Harrigan, M. (2016). Adopting a Clinical Assessment Framework in Older Adult Mental Health. *Journal of psychosocial nursing and mental health services*, *54*(7), 26-31. https://doi.org/10.3928/02793695-20160616-05

Hyun, J. K., Quinn, B. C., Madon, T., & Lustig, S. (2006). Graduate Student Mental Health: Needs Assessment and Utilization of Counseling Services. *Journal of college student development*, *47*(3), 247-266. https://doi.org/10.1353/csd.2006.0030

Innovation in DEmentia and Aging (IDEA) Lab. (2024, September 24). *IDEA Lab*. https://idea.nursing.ubc.ca/about/

Lane, K., Teng, M. Y., Barnes, S. J., Moore, K., Smith, K., & Lee, M. (2018). Using Appreciative Inquiry to Understand the Role of Teaching Practices in Student Well-being at a Research-Intensive University. *The Canadian journal for the scholarship of teaching and learning*, *9*(2). https://doi.org/10.5206/cjsotl-rcacea.2018.2.10

Lerchenfeldt, S., Attardi, S. M., Pratt, R. L., Sawarynski, K. E., & Taylor, T. A. H. (2021). Twelve tips for interfacing with the new generation of medical students: iGen. *Medical teacher*, *43*(11), 1249-1254. https://doi.org/10.1080/0142159X.2020.1845305

Levecque, K., Anseel, F., De Beuckelaer, A., Van der Heyden, J., & Gisle, L. (2017). Work organization and mental health problems in PhD students. *Research policy*, *46*(4), 868-879. https://doi.org/10.1016/j.respol.2017.02.008

Lin, D. T., Liebert, C. A., Tran, J., Lau, J. N., & Salles, A. (2016). Emotional intelligence as a predictor of resident well-being. *Journal of the American College of Surgeons*, *223*(2), 352-358.

López-Santacruz, H. D., & Guízar-Mendoza, J. M. (2022). A New Challenge for Dental Education: Generation Z. *Odovtos*, *24*(3), 36-40. https://doi.org/10.15517/ijds.2022.50804

Lowe, S. J. (2008). *Designer Immigrants': Eliminating Barriers*. Toronto Region Immigrant Employment Council. Retrieved August 31 from https://triec.ca/designer-immigrants-elimi/

Nowell, L. S., Norris, J. M., White, D. E., & Moules, N. J. (2017). Thematic Analysis: Striving to Meet the Trustworthiness Criteria. *International journal of qualitative methods*, *16*(1), 1-13. https://doi.org/10.1177/1609406917733847

Oswalt, S. B., & Riddock, C. C. (2007). What to Do About Being Overwhelmed: Graduate Students, Stress and University Services. *The College student affairs journal*, *27*(1), 24. https://go.exlibris.link/n9tyqKfx

Perlman, D., Taylor, E., Molloy, L., Brighton, R., Patterson, C., & Moxham, L. (2018). A Path Analysis of Self-determination and Resiliency for Consumers Living with Mental Illness. *Community mental health journal*, *54*(8), 1239-1244. https://doi.org/10.1007/s10597-018-0321-1

Reed, J. (2006). *Appreciative inquiry: research for change* (1 ed.). Sage Publications. https://go.exlibris.link/cDFcKjHt

Ryan, R. M., & Deci, E. L. (2001). On happiness and human potentials: A review of research on hedonic and Eudaimonic well-being. *Annual review of psychology*, *52*(1), 141-166. https://doi.org/10.1146/annurev.psych.52.1.141

Ryan, R. M., Huta, V., & Deci, E. L. (2008). Living well: A self-determination theory perspective on eudaimonia. *Journal of Happiness Studies*, *9*, 139-https://doi.org/170.10.1007/s10902-006-9023-4

Ryff, C. D. (1989). Happiness Is Everything, or Is It? Explorations on the Meaning of Psychological Well-Being. *Journal of personality and social psychology*, *57*(6), 1069-1081. https://doi.org/10.1037/0022-3514.57.6.1069

Ryff, C. D. (2014). Psychological well-being revisited: advances in the science and practice of eudaimonia. *Psychotherapy and psychosomatics*, *83*(1), 10. https://doi.org/10.1159/000353263

SenthilKumar, G., Mathieu, N. M., Freed, J. K., Sigmund, C. D., & Gutterman, D. D. (2023). Addressing the decline in graduate students' mental well-being. *American journal of physiology. Heart and circulatory physiology*, *325*(4), H882-H887. https://doi.org/10.1152/ajpheart.00466.2023

Simmons, A. B. (1999). Economic integration and designer immigrants: Canadian policy in the 1990s. *Free markets, open societies, closed borders*, 53-69.

Statistics Canada. (2022). Census of Population. In.

Stirrett, S. (2022). International students deserve to be treated as more than just a revenue stream. *Globe and mail*. https://go.exlibris.link/zTclHYNl

Tang, W., Hu, T., Hu, B., Jin, C., Wang, G., Xie, C., Chen, S., & Xu, J. (2020). Prevalence and correlates of PTSD and depressive symptoms one month after the outbreak of the COVID-19 epidemic in a sample of home-quarantined Chinese university students. *Journal of affective disorders*, *274*, 1-7. https://doi.org/10.1016/j.jad.2020.05.009

Tavares, V. (2024). Feeling excluded: international students experience equity, diversity and inclusion. *International journal of inclusive education*, *28*(8), 1551-1568. https://doi.org/10.1080/13603116.2021.2008536

Thorne, S. (2016). *Interpretive description: Qualitative research for applied practice*. Routledge.

Tong, A., Sainsbury, P., & Craig, J. (2007). Consolidated criteria for reporting qualitative research (COREQ): a 32-item checklist for interviews and focus groups. *International journal for quality in health care*, *19*(6), 349-357. https://doi.org/10.1093/intqhc/mzm042

van den Berg, A., Dewar, B., Smits, C., Jukema, J. S., University of the West of Scotland, P. S., Saxion University of Applied Sciences, D. T. N., & Windesheim University of Applied Sciences, Z. T. N. (2019). Experiences of older adults and undergraduate students in cocreating age-friendly services in an educational living . *International practice development journal*, *9*(2), 1-14. https://doi.org/10.19043/ipdj.92.002

WHO, W. H. O. (2022, October 1). *Aging and health*. Retrieved August 31 from https://www.who.int/news-room/fact-sheets/detail/ageing-and-health

Wu, J., & Liu, Q. (2023). A longitudinal study on college students' depressive symptoms during the COVID-19 pandemic: The trajectories, antecedents, and outcomes. *Psychiatry research*, *321*, 115058-115058. https://doi.org/10.1016/j.psychres.2023.115058

Wyatt, T., & Oswalt, S. B. (2013). Comparing Mental Health Issues Among Undergraduate and Graduate Students. *American journal of health education*, *44*(2), 96-107. https://doi.org/10.1080/19325037.2013.764248

Zhang, F., Litson, K., & Feldon, D. F. (2022). Social predictors of doctoral student mental health and well-being. *PloS one*, *17*(9), e0274273-e0274273. https://doi.org/10.1371/journal.pone.0274273

Author bios

LILLIAN HUNG, PhD, RN, is an Associate Professor at the School of Nursing, University of British Columbia (UBC), Canada Research Chair in Senior Care, and the founder and head of Innovation in DEmentia and Aging (IDEA) Lab. Her research is at the forefront of exploring how emerging technologies, including robotics and assistive devices, can support and impact dementia care for older adults. Dr. Hung's research findings were used to inform policy, education, and practice in aging research and practice improvement in hospitals and long-term care settings. Email: Lillian.hung@ubc.ca

STEPHEN CHEONG YU CHAN, PhD, is an Assistant Professor in the Felizberta Lo Padilla Tong School of Social Sciences at Saint Francis University, Hong Kong. His expertise includes psychology and research subjects including Positive Psychology, the Psychology of Aging and Research Methods in Psychology. Dr. Chan's research interests fall into aging and positive psychology while his current research is mainly related to carer studies, positive psychological interventions and positive psychology in older adults. Email: cy4chan@sfu.edu.hk

LILY HAOPU REN, MHLP, is a PhD student in interdisciplinary studies at UBC. Lily is a Research Project Manager at UBC's Innovation in Dementia and Aging (IDEA) Lab. She graduated with Master of Health Leadership and Policy in Seniors Care from UBC. Ms. Ren is interested in ethical considerations in technology implementation for dementia care delivery in hospital settings. Email: lily.ren@ubc.ca

HIRO ITO, BA, is a second-year Master of Science student at the School of Population and Public Health, UBC, and a Research Project Manager at UBC's Innovation in Dementia and Aging (IDEA) Lab. She graduated with a Bachelor of Arts in Psychology at UBC. Ms. Ito's research interests include the psychosocial and cultural aspects of health, aging and dementia, and accessibility. Email: hiro.ito@ubc.ca

BUBLI CHAKRABORTY is a family partner at the IDEA Lab. She is the caregiver of her family member living with dementia. She graduated with a Master of Environmental Studies degree at York University. Ms. Chakraborty is interested in supporting researchers in codesigning research projects and coproducing knowledge translation outputs to improve the care of people living with dementia. Email: nibedita.chakraborty@ubc.ca

Article

Journal of International Students
Volume 14, Issue 5 (2024), pp. 67-84
ISSN: 2162-3104 (Print), 2166-3750 (Online)
jistudents.org

Calling for Equitable Access to the Canadian Labor Market: Exploring the Challenges of International Graduate Students in Canada

Trung Tu Nguyen
Thompson Rivers University, Canada

Manu Sharma
Thompson Rivers University, Canada

ABSTRACT

In this paper, we identify the main challenges faced by international graduate students seeking employment in the Canadian labor market after completing Canadian Master of Education programs. We approach this issue from our combined perspectives: a professor of higher education and a recent international graduate with a Master of Education program. Drawing on the theoretical framework Responsibility of the University in Employability (RUE) (López-Miguens et al.*, 2021), we argue that universities play a significant role in preparing international students for successful integration into the Canadian workforce. After conducting a thematic analysis of the relevant literature, we identify the five most common key challenges faced by international students: racialized complexities of a credential regime, problems of deskilling and devaluation of immigrants, the triple glass effect, foreign accent bias, and a lack of soft skills according to the Canadian norm. In response to these thematic findings, we offer two key recommendations for Canadian universities: helping international students build networks and employment contacts and helping international students take part in work-integrated learning and vocational programs that ease their transition into employment after graduating from a Canadian Master of Education program.*

Keywords: Canada, employability, international students, Master of Education, postsecondary

INTRODUCTION

Employability is the ability to get and keep a paid job. Employability is a major concern for international students who come to study in Western countries (Zhao et al., 2024; Li et al., 2024). According to Guo (2015), in 2005, the Canadian government introduced the express entry program to speed up the process of skilled immigrants' applications in less than six months so that they could begin to contribute to Canada's economy and job market after a shorter period of time. The Canadian Experience Class (CEC) stream was introduced in 2008 to account for the proportion of economic immigrants admitted to Canada (Nunes & Arthur, 2013). The CEC has allowed skilled foreign workers and international graduates of Canadian postsecondary institutions with work experience in Canada to apply for permanent residency without the need to leave Canada to complete the application process. Before 2008, international graduates were required to return to their home country to apply for permanent residency (Tamburri, 2019). In 2013, the government further eased CEC requirements by reducing the work requirement period from fourteen months to twelve months in three years, instead of two years, after graduation (Tamburri, 2019). After spending at least three of the last five years working and residing in Canada, permanent residents may apply for Canadian citizenship (Government of Canada, 2024).

Conducting research on international students' integration into the Canadian workforce, Nunes and Arthur (2013) stated that international students were positioned as potential skilled immigrants, owing to their past work experience, by the Canadian government, which has enacted policies to ease the immigration process for international students. To properly recognize the importance of international students to Canada in the Immigration and Refugee Protection Act and help Canada become more competitive in significant competition with other developed countries, the AUCC suggested that the Canadian government should enhance and simplify the policy related to international students and facilitate the recruitment of international students (in terms of the complexity involved and the related public debate; see also Omidvar, 2024). In particular, the Immigration and Refugee Protection Act should focus on facilitating international student recruitment as an important objective for Citizenship and Immigration Canada. Finally, the federal government should take a government-wide approach to international student recruitment and prioritize increasing resources for CIC's processing of student visa applications (AUCC, Ottawa (Ontario), 2001).

However, according to Reitz et al. (2014), in Canada, highly skilled foreign workers (including international students) often have trouble finding jobs commensurate with their qualifications. Two possible reasons for those difficulties are as follows: first, employers do not recognize foreign credentials and work experience; second, their language skills are still developing according to employers. Drawing on the lived experiences of the authors, the paper argues that despite the richness that international students bring to Canada's society and economy, they encounter significant difficulties in obtaining employment opportunities after completing their studies in Canada. The edited volume of Raby, Singh, and Bista (2022) presents many cases that illustrate the challenges that many international graduates and highly skilled immigrant professionals in Canada encounter when attempting to integrate into the Canadian labor market.

Importantly, there is no policy available at the university level that addresses the university's responsibility of providing employment opportunities during or after graduate students complete their Master of Education program. In this paper, the driving reflections from the authors are from one particular university's Master of Education program, but these are comparable to other Canadian university programs that have created a Master of Education program with a financial motivation to assist the university. Notably, no guarantees of work or employability are offered to international students upon the completion of the Master of Education program; rather, it is seen only as a potentially viable pathway to gain permanent residency in Canada, which is currently at risk, as evidenced by international student protests across Canada (Pandher & Dhami, 2024).

POSITIONALITIES

As this paper originated from the authors' experience with the topic, it is important to provide this experience as well as their positionalities.

The first author, who self-identifies as a Vietnamese male, was a graduate of the Master of Education program at a mid-sized university in British Columbia. After graduation, he stayed in Canada to look for jobs and struggled in the process. He has experienced and witnessed the challenges that international racialized people faced in their integration into Canadian society and the labor market after various unsuccessful attempts at professional long-term full-time employment positions.

The second author identifies as a South Asian Canadian as she was born and raised in Toronto as a second-generation immigrant. Over the past five years, she has worked with several international students at a mid-sized university in British Columbia and thus has secondhand knowledge of the trends and challenges that many of her students face in finding stable and meaningful employment. She has supported Author 1 as a graduate student and now as a colleague in the field of postsecondary education.

Following Author 1's (and many other international students') experience of challenges going into the employment sector after graduation, it is important to turn our attention to the following questions: Why does Canada want international students? What does the literature say about the matter? How, if any, can the challenges faced by international students be mitigated by higher education institutions? It is with this line of questioning that we have decided to embark upon this paper. When reflecting upon the lack of accountability toward international students by graduate programs that are often in existence due to international students' financial contributions and comparing this back to the challenges faced by international students in the Canadian employment market, we wonder if this reflects a deficit in attitudes toward the capabilities and assets that international students bring to Canada. We hope to provide insights from our own narratives both as a mentor to international students (Author 2) and as an international student with lived experience (Author 1). We would like to further explore the ethical responsibility of universities and Canadian employers toward international students who graduate from Canadian universities and seek equitable working opportunities at fair wages for their international experience and education.

THEORETICAL FRAMEWORK

This paper uses the theoretical framework of López-Miguens et al. (2021), who measured the responsibility of the University in Employability (RUE) as the ability of a university to impart general and specific values, skills, and mindsets to its students and to carry out matching activities with employers as much as it enhances the employability of future graduates. The research was grounded in positional conflict theory (Brown et al., 2003, as cited in López-Miguens et al., 2021) and the resource-based view (Barney, 1991, as cited in López-Miguens et al., 2021). It also considers broader employability studies, such as career studies, management, and psychology.

According to international students, the main motivation for pursuing studies abroad is to find work in the country in which they are studying (Fakunle & Pirrie 2020; Gribble et al., 2015; Soares & Mosquera, 2020); thus, employability matters. The term employability has a wide range of definitions in this paper; we draw upon Römgens et al.'s (2020) work, which states that all employability definitions focus on a competence-based approach that is centered on an individual's skills and ability to obtain and maintain employment throughout their career. Thus, this definition of employability and the theoretical framework of RUE need to be a cornerstone in programs such as a Master of Education to ensure that the long-term benefits of the program are given to both the university and international students.

However, López-Miguens et al. reported that the quality of teaching staff and the mismatching activities between universities and employers played more important roles than university reputation in terms of graduate employability. In other words, if the teaching staff and the opportunities to match international students with potential employers are not aligned, then the RUE cannot be fulfilled. According to López-Miguens et al. (2021), universities bear some of the responsibility for the results that their students achieve in their social, local, and international communities. They have the ability and potential to equip students with necessary skills so that they can become responsible citizens in society and improve their employability for future employment. Therefore, López-Miguens et al. (2021) maintained that the main objective of universities is prioritizing employability.

According to López-Miguens et al. (2021), multiple parties are interested in RUE. For sustainable human development, society wants universities to provide competent students. On the other hand, government organisations want to achieve fruitful results in their investments in universities through the integration of graduates in the workforce and the prevention of unemployment. Additionally, employers need graduates with not only domain-relevant knowledge but also attributes such as empathy with their surroundings, flexibility, adaptability, and teamwork. In summary, RUE is one of the primary objectives of the Bologna Process for universities within the framework of the European Higher Education Area, despite the interest of multiple parties (Paris Communiqué, 2018). As a result, López-Miguens et al. claimed that universities are becoming increasingly socially responsible, and we use this theoretical lens to inform our paper.

METHOD

We used literature review to identify, analyze, and synthesize existing research on the employment challenges faced by international graduate students in Canada. To find relevant literature for this paper, the following keywords were used: immigrants, employability, barriers, challenges, postsecondary, Canada. The search engines used were Google Scholar, PubMed, and the local university's library database, which draws upon JStor and Scopus and relevant government and institutional reports. For the years of the search, we aimed for the past ten years (2014--2024) but ended up having to review the most relevant articles that went back to 2006 and included studies beyond the Canadian context. The relevant studies we included (a) focused on international graduate students in Canada, (b) addressed employment challenges, (c) were published between 2006 and 2024, and (d) were written in English. Studies focusing on undergraduate students or those published before 2006 were excluded. After the review and analysis of the relevant literature, the following five themes emerged as the five key challenges: credential recognition, deskilling and devaluation, the triple glass effect, foreign accent bias, and a lack of soft skills.

FINDINGS

We provide the following literature review on the five most common challenges that immigrants face when trying to integrate into the Canadian workforce.

1. Racialized complexities of a credential regime

Guo (2015) contested that there was a racialized skills regime in Canada through the lens of critical race theory and argued that the knowledge and skills of recent immigrants in Canada were racialized and materialized on the basis of ethnicity and nationality. According to Guo, a racialized regime of skill has produced normative, white, docile corporate subjects who adhere to Canadian norms and organizational cultures.

Liu and Guo (2021) reported that

> Recognition of international qualifications in Canada involves 13 jurisdictions, 55 ministries, more than 50 regulated occupations, more than

400 regulatory bodies, 5 assessment agencies, more than 240 postsecondary institutions and a large community of immigrant service agencies, not to mention numerous employers (p. 740).

Multilayers of authorities and myriad policies created an institutional complexity that governed the local settings in which immigrants must wait a long time to conform to the qualification assessment process or look for other lines of employment whose skills are unappreciated. Institutional complexity diminishes immigrants' prior social investments in education and work experience. During the prolonged recognition process of their international qualifications, many of them had to work in 'survival jobs' not commensurate with their prior professional experiences or related to their skills, enduring low pay and precarious working and living conditions.

Raza et al. (2013) confirmed that the devaluation of foreign qualifications was one element that impacted the labor market outcomes of visible minority immigrants in Canada. According to Raza et al., visible minority immigrants are more likely to be stuck in low-income jobs than other immigrants are. One of the reasons for their earnings disadvantage was discrimination against visible minority immigrants (Pendakur & Pendakur, 1997, as cited in Raza et al., 2013).

According to Guo, immigrants' international qualifications, job skills and work experience tend to be devalued and denigrated based on their skin color (Guo 2015). Liu and Guo (2021) claimed that the color of the skill associated with immigrants' skin color caused deskilling and devaluation, which will be discussed in the next section. In summary, the knowledge and skills of recent immigrants in Canada have been racialized and led to white privilege and dominance.

2. Deskilling and devaluation of immigrants in Canada

In contemporary workplaces, skill has been denoted as a strategy to achieve high employability, productivity, and economic competitiveness. However, the definition of skill was problematic and contested by Guo (2015) in the circumstances of immigrants looking for employment in Canada. Guo argued that skill is nothing but an ideology, 'skill is not neutral; it is socially constructed'. It was necessary to consider skill as a relational concept that was entailed in social, cultural, and economic organizations. In fact, Guo tried to answer the following questions: "Why are immigrants' knowledge and skills devalued? What counts as legitimate knowledge and skill? Whose knowledge and skills are considered valuable? Whose knowledge and skills are silenced? Are knowledge and skill racialized…" (p. 237) on the basis of immigrants' races or ethnicities?

Liu and Guo (2021) and Guo (2009) reported that while trying to have their international qualifications and professional experiences recognized, immigrants in Canada faced denigration, devaluation, and deskilling. Despite Canada's need for highly skilled immigrants, many of them encountered deskilling and downward social and occupational mobility after arriving in Canada (Guo, 2015). According to Guo, even when knowledge and skills are considered legitimate, the skills and work experience of internationally trained professionals are often doubted or considered inferior. Some immigrants had to shift to low-skilled jobs in sales, services, and manufacturing, even though they had previously worked in science, engineering, business, and management positions. This situation posed challenges to their integration and eliminated the benefit of their skills.

In another research study, Reitz et al. (2014) investigated the situations of immigrants who arrived five years before 1996, 2001, and 2006. The proportion of immigrants with university degrees was always greater than that of the Canadian-born population, from nearly two times in 1996 to at least two-and-a-half times in 2006. Despite this, immigrants have difficulty accessing high-skilled occupations such as managerial or professional occupations. Reitz et al. reported that for immigrant men with university degrees, the percentage in high-skilled jobs was 50.4% in 1996, increasing to 54.2% in 2001 but then decreasing to 43.5% in 2006. For immigrant women, the percentage of highly skilled employees was 34.6% in 1996, increasing to 42.3% in 2001 but decreasing to 34.4% in 2006. Reitz et al. also discovered that the proportion of highly skilled immigrants in the lowest-skilled jobs, such as cashiers, kitchen helpers, and cleaners, increased steadily, from 1.5 times the proportion for the Canadian-born population to 2.3 and 2.4 times over the same period. While skilled immigrants constitute an expanding segment of the Canadian workforce, they find it harder to obtain professional and managerial jobs over time (Reitz et al., 2014). Reitz et al. demonstrated that the devaluation of immigrant skills resulted in lower salaries than did their equally qualified Canadian-born counterparts in jobs at the same skill level. They reported that racial and cultural differences, in addition to country of origin, gender, age and other qualities, play a vital role in devaluing the qualifications and skills of immigrants (Li, 2008).

Reitz et al. (2014) estimated the total incomes that immigrants failed to obtain due to unused or underutilized skills as $4.8 billion in 1996, $6.02 billion in 2001, and $11.37 billion in 2006 in Canada. This demonstrated that immigrant skill underutilization not only exists in Canada but also has deepened. The inferior value of immigrant skills caused immigrants to receive lower salaries than equivalently qualified Canadian-born professionals even when they work at the same skill level. Reitz et al. concluded that racial discrimination was the cause of the devaluation and denigration of immigrants. Similarly, Maitra (2015) noted that the requirement of the Canadian experience or credentials is euphemisms for hiding the references for race or gender.

3. Triple glass effect

Guo (2015) claimed that immigrant workers encountered a 'glass gate' that prevented them from entering guarded professional communities. Professional associations and prior qualification assessment agencies were among the institutions and players who guarded the professional communities by devaluing immigrants' foreign qualifications and work experience. They acted as gatekeepers and deemed immigrants' skills and experience deficient.

Even after immigrants' skills and experience were successfully recognized by the mentioned gatekeepers, immigrants hit the second layer, called the 'glass door', which blocked their job opportunities at high-paying companies, which are key players in the labor market. The employers rejected immigrants because they lacked Canadian work experience, or their past work experience was considered inferior to the Canadian experience. Furthermore, immigrants faced difficulties in securing high-paying employment because of their skin color or nonnative English accents. Oreopoulos (2009, 2011) stated that a foreign-sounding name such as Chinese, Indian, or Pakistani might cause the number of job interviews to be 40% lower.

Guo (2015) called the third layer, which blocks immigrants from moving into management jobs due to their different ethnicities and cultures, the 'glass ceiling'. Guo stated that some immigrants worked at the same positions as their white colleagues but were unable to be promoted and paid less. Guo referred to those situations as racialized disparities in earnings.

The triple glass effect is a metaphor that symbolizes multiple structural barriers that cause immigrants to be unemployed or underemployed (Guo, 2015). As such, immigrants encounter unemployment, underemployment, low incomes, and downward social mobility from their social levels in their home countries.

4. Foreign accent bias

Framing immigrants' foreign accents as a lack of communication skills also played a vital role in the racialization of skills. This strategy, according to Creese and Kambere (2003), acts as a justification for disclaiming any employment offer or social inclusion for immigrants without touching the subtlety of equality in the liberal context. Research by Creese and Kambere with African immigrant women revealed that an African accent was usually a rationale for them being rejected in the labor market, although most of them had advanced postsecondary degrees from English language universities or colleges. According to a participant, her foreign accent was a large barrier when it came to jobs such as receptionist, teacher of English, and customer service. Owing to their accents and skin colors, they were marked as 'other'. Creese and Kambere showed that language skills were used as a systematic barrier that prevented immigrants from crossing to become Canadian, even though formal citizenship processes were in place. They claimed that accents were just a euphemism to exclude, marginalize, and discriminate against African immigrant women.

Li (2008) studied the effect of foreign skills, including language fluency, on the incomes of immigrants in Canada and reported that not all foreign skills are devalued in Canada. In particular, foreign skills held by British, North and West European immigrants brought about advantages in their incomes, whereas foreign skills held by black, Chinese, or South Asian immigrants produced disadvantages. On the basis of Li's findings, we can assume that such racialization of foreign skills was also reflected in the judgment of immigrants' foreign accents. It could be said that not all foreign accents bring disadvantages, but the identity associated with the accent is the problem.

As foreign accents of immigrants from certain origins were not acceptable, some career bridging programs were provided by service agencies to help immigrants reduce their accents (Guo, 2009). These types of programs admit that there was racism against foreign accents in the job market. Instead of going against racism, the service agencies influenced immigrants to take part in their programs and find ways to assimilate into the workforce. The intention of those programs of accent reduction was to improve immigrants' presentability and employability through achieving accentless English proficiency. One of the program administrators said that the voice tone of an immigrant made her sound defensive and confrontational, and they guided her to reduce her accent and make her properly understood by the native. According to the program administrators, nonnative accents were not only different but also signal that the speakers were incompetent and deficient in the workplace. Therefore, they needed to be corrected and normalized to sound as native as possible. This practice of accent reduction highlights a colonial mentality in which native accents are perceived to be superior to nonnative accents.

5. Lack of soft skills according to the Canadian norm

Even though immigrants might have competent qualifications and skills, they were viewed from a deficit view as lacking soft skills such as communication and decision-making skills and hence could hardly be promoted to management positions (Reitz et al., 2014). Many soft skills training programs in Canada have adopted a list of nine important skills comprising interpersonal, communication, behavioral and organisational skills (Noorani, 2011). In Canadian ways of thinking, immigrants need to acquire those skills to integrate into the Canadian workplace. For example, it was the Canadian norm to 'make direct eye contact', 'shake hand firmly', and 'have water cooler chit chat' at the workplace. It was important to avoid 'religion, politics, sex, money' or 'getting too personal in the workplace'. Other soft skills that immigrants need to acquire belong to their presentation: suitable dress, hygiene, facial expressions, and body language.

Soft skills are often discreetly defined by employers, so they tend to vary from company to company and from context to context. Employers determined soft skills as a strategy for boosting employees' performance. Guo (2015) asserted that soft skills or personal qualities and attributes, in recent years, may be emphasized to promote discrimination, legitimizing gender inequalities and racism. According to Guo, the racialization of skills was also seen in soft skills training for immigrants. This reflected that high-skilled immigrants' rich soft skills were devalued and deskilled; then, they were assumed to lack soft skills, which are usually locally defined by employers and vary according to specific contexts. In other words, immigrants are thought to lack behavioral competencies in the workplace (Grugulis & Vincent, 2009).

In fact, a campaign was launched nationally by numerous service and training agencies to advertise soft skills training. The banners of these soft skills training campaigns read as 'Nine soft skills no immigrant should be without!', 'Learning to fit in the workplace: Soft skills training', 'Enhance skilled immigrants' essential soft skills to boost success', and 'Soft skills are the keys to success at work'.

These soft skills training programs shifted the blame for being unemployed to immigrants by implying that they lacked skills. The hidden objectives of the programs were to 'whiten' immigrants and to inject Canadian ways of thinking, acting, and behaving into their minds. The result of this whitening process was the formation of white, docile workers who would leave out their past skills and adopt Canadian culture at workplaces to become real Canadians.

DISCUSSION AND IMPLICATIONS

According to UNESCO (2019) and the Organization for Economic Cooperation and Development (2020), the number of international students increased from two million in 2000 to over 5.6 million in 2019. The three key host countries with 39% of all international students in higher education are the United States, the United Kingdom, and Canada (OECD, 2020). The financial contribution of international students is vital for host countries' universities and, later, the workforce. In 2021, due to the COVID-19 pandemic, the number of international students enrolled in Canada decreased by approximately 17% (Statista, 2021a). Nevertheless, international students still accounted for more than 25% of total postsecondary enrollments (530,540 out of 2.15 million; Statista, 2021b).

The Association of Universities and Colleges of Canada (AUCC) (2001) wanted to discuss the topic of international students in response to the deliberations of the Standing Committee on Citizenship and Immigration Canada on Bill C-11, the Immigration and Refugee Protection Act, and three main reasons for recognizing the importance of international students to Canada in this Act. First, international students help bring an international perspective and diversity to classrooms and internationalize the campuses of Canadian colleges and universities. Second, there would be significant economic benefits from foreign students for both higher education institutions and the communities they serve (AUCC, 2001). Universities and colleges would gain additional revenue to support their academic endeavors. Local communities gain economic benefits from international students' expenses for house/room rentals, food, books, and other costs of living expenses (AUCC, 2001). In another study on the benefits from international students, Nunes and Arthur (2013) estimated that international students contributed more than $6.5 billion to the Canadian economy each year in the recent period. In 2018, it was estimated that international students contributed $22.3 billion to the Canadian economy and $4.7 billion to British Columbia's province's economy (Global Affairs Canada – Canmac Economics Limited, 2020). Third, Canada lagged behind its counterparts, such as Australia, the United Kingdom, and the United States, because of a lack of coherent international recruitment strategies, promotions and advertisements, and a reasonable approach to immigration policies and practices. There was a need for Canada to catch up with other countries.

Many countries have become ethno-culturally diverse due to an increasing number of immigrants in their population (which also raises the problem of cross-cultural challenges; see Astley, 2024). In 2013, the United Nations estimated that

232 million people lived outside their countries of birth. Fifty-nine percent of them lived in developed nations, and 41% lived in developing countries (United Nation, 2013). On another note, the foreign-born population in the Organization for Economic Cooperation and Development (OECD) countries accounted for 10% of the total population in 2014 (OECD, 2014). That of Canada reached 20.6%, which was double the OECD average. Canada is safe in that it is twice as culturally diverse as other OECD countries.

On the other hand, according to the Canadian Association for Graduate Studies (2005), people with graduate degrees are referred to as 'highly qualified personnel'. Based on Author 1's experience, at the graduate level, international students deepen their knowledge, acquire the ability to conduct research, and develop professional skills considered valuable assets in today's knowledge economy. The professional skills that complement disciplinary knowledge and technical skills remain the most important aspects of any graduate training. According to the Canadian Association for Graduate Studies (CAGS), two important skills in which graduate students are trained are communication and management skills. These skills allow graduates to work efficiently in a wide range of situations involving projects with different objectives, timelines, and stakeholders. A highly skilled workforce was necessary to fuel Canada's ambition for, and achievement of, healthy economic growth, enhanced quality of life and quality of democracy (CAGS, 1999).

To resolve its shortages of labor and the effects of an aging population, Canada has competed to attract the most talented, skilful, and resourceful international workers. International workers benefitted Canadian workplaces in terms of global knowledge, enhanced diversity, and multiculturalism. However, their knowledge, skills, and work experience have not been fully respected and utilized in Canada.

In light of the above further context, we believe it is important to ask the following question: What is the institution's responsibility toward international students in regard to finding work after the completion of their degree/program? (see also McCowan, 2015; López-Miguens, et al., 2021; Sin et al., 2016).

Research has shown that universities have rolled out programs to improve the employability of their graduates, but international students still receive little support from their institutions in finding jobs after graduation (Han et al., 2022). In the most recent article about international student recruitment, Crawley and Ouellet (2024) stated that Canadian institutions have prioritized filling seats in business programs over meeting the need for workers in the skilled crafts and health care industry when recruiting international students. According to Crawley and Ouellet, experts have shown that the federal government, provincial governments, Canadian colleges, and universities themselves have not directed their efforts toward recruiting international students in a way that would primarily address employment shortages in the nation. According to Rupa Banerjee, an associate professor at Toronto Metropolitan University, graduates of programs that are not desirable in the labor market are not able to find relevant jobs and face difficulties in transitioning to and becoming lawfully permanent citizens of Canada (Crawley & Ouellet, 2024).

Perić and Delić (2016) suggested that universities concentrate their social responsibility efforts on improving their graduate employability. In this context, the question is whether universities are implementing strategies that are accountable to their internal (students) and external stakeholders (employers, society, government), considering that they play a critical role in developing their internal stakeholders, building human capital such as high-order thinking, self-management, and career-building skills, and social capital such as networking skills and professional networks before students transition to the workforce (Clarke, 2018). As organizations with social responsibility, universities hold greater responsibility for their internal and external stakeholders than many other organizations do (Claver-Cortés et al., 2020; See also Petruzziello et al., 2023). This social responsibility manifests in multiple key areas: first, sustainable human development by providing competent graduates for society; second, return on investment for governments by helping graduates successfully integrate into the labor market and reducing unemployment; and third, meeting employer needs by providing well-rounded graduates who are competent at not only domain-relevant knowledge but also essential qualities such as flexibility, adaptability, teamwork, and empathy. Universities not only provide educational services but also create a platform for active involvement in economic and social development (Peric, 2012; Quezada, 2011; Sánchez-Hernández & Mainardes, 2016, as cited in López-Miguens et al., 2021). Therefore, the important question is to what degree universities carry out this obligation and produce graduates who are employable.

Sin and Amaral (2017) and López-Miguens et al. (2021) determined that universities play a primary role in the development of student employability, but only humble levels of activities are carried out to improve student employability. Sin and Amaral (2017) reported that there is a low level of collaboration between universities and employers. Therefore, universities must change strategies and incorporate a responsible approach into both their operations and curricula. In this context, López-Miguens et al. suggested a way to quantify RUE by considering three formative factors that fall under the accountability of university managers: university reputation, teaching staff and matching activities with employers.

RECOMMENDATIONS FOR CANADIAN INSTITUTIONS

The authors would like to revisit the following question: how can educational institutions help mitigate the challenges faced by their international graduate students during workforce integration? In response, we offer two recommendations: (1) Helping international students build networks and employment contacts and (2) helping international students take part in work-integrated learning and vocational programs.

1. Helping international students build networks and employment contacts

The participants in Nunes and Arthur's (2013) research advised that career services personnel assist international students in building networks, especially with local people, professional contacts by part-time jobs or internships, and meeting prospective employers before they graduate. Personnel should know how to help international students achieve their goals in terms of career development and permanent residency. They could organize career fairs and invite large companies to attend fairs and interact with international students, who often do not have networking activities such as local students. Part-time jobs and internships helped international students gain Canadian work experience and become accustomed to the Canadian workplace. Furthermore, career service personnel must act as a link between enterprises and CICs and advise them on how to hire international students. It would also be beneficial if universities and colleges could ask for funds from the Canadian government to increase headcounts and improve services and activities for international students.

Career counsellors could set up workshops to help students develop networking skills, understand professional networks, and assist them in building their networks through attending career fairs and volunteering. These activities could target international students in their first or second years. Counsellors might inform international students about on- and off-campus resources and stimulate them to develop their skills and confidence in networking in Canadian culture and the workplace. Nunes and Arthur (2013) also recommended that current international students act as peer mentors for new international students. Career services personnel should consider rolling out various types of mentoring programs for international students. The mentoring programs could focus on social networking, career development and strategies for accessing the Canadian labor market.

Nunes and Arthur (2013) noted that graduate students lacked information about employment opportunities and received less support from career service personnel than undergraduate students did. Therefore, career services are advised to pay more attention to the needs of graduate students and help them more. They might consider developing additional resources for international graduate students. The resources might consist of information about companies that are interested in recruiting persons with graduate degrees. In addition, they could organize workshops that teach graduate students to market their skills and train their networking skills.

2. Helping international students take part in work-integrated learning and vocational programs

Han et al. (2022) mention that postsecondary institutions also play an important role in international graduates' integration into the labor market by equipping them with transferable and marketable skills through work-integrated learning and vocational programs. Nourpanah (2019) conducted a study of international graduates who took part in vocational nursing programs and then went to work and became permanent residents. Nourpanah reported that vocational programs provided relevant work-related skills and put international graduates at an advantage in looking for employment after graduation (see also Goodwin & Mbah, 2019; Pham et al., 2018; Popadiuk & Arthur, 2014; Tran & Soejatminah, 2016).

In light of these recommendations, the authors hope to shed light on the situation that many international students encounter as they attempt to enter the Canadian labor market and thus call upon universities and the Canadian government for an ethical response that helps provide an employment opportunity that contributes in a meaningful way to Canadian society and, at the same time, upholds and respects the talents and skills that international graduate students bring with them.

REFERENCES

Association of Universities and Colleges of Canada. (2001). Recognizing the Importance of International Students to Canada in the Immigration and Refugee Protection Act. https://files.eric.ed.gov/fulltext/ED455736.pdf

Astley, M. (2024). Cross-cultural challenges faced by international students: A case study of Indian postgraduate students at a London-based business school. *Journal of International Students, 14*(4), 971-988.

Canadian Association for Graduate Studies (CAGS). (2005). *Your Future: A Guide for Potential Graduate Students*. Retrieved from https://www.cags.ca/documents/publications/CAGSHandbook05.pdf

Clarke, M. (2018). Rethinking graduate employability: the role of capital, individual attributes and context. *Studies in Higher Education, 43*(11), 1923-1937. https://doi.org/10.1080/03075079.2017.1294152

Crawley, M., & Ouellet, V. (2024, May 9). Canada's foreign student push "mismatched" job market, data shows. *CBC*. https://www.cbc.ca/news/canada/toronto/international-students-college-university-fields-study-data-1.7195530

Creese, G., & Kambere, E. N. (2003). "What Color Is Your English?". *Canadian Review of Sociology and Anthropology, 40*(5): 565–573.

Fakunle, O., & Pirrie, A. (2020). International students' reflections on employability development opportunities during a one-year masters-level program in the UK. *Journal of International Students, 10*(S2), 86-100.

Global Affairs Canada – Canmac Economics Limited. (2020, August). *Economic Impact of International Education in Canada 2017 – 2018 Final Report*. Retrieved November 17, 2022, from https://bccie.bc.ca/wp-content/uploads/2020/12/economic_impact_international_education_canada_2017_2018.pdf

Goodwin, K., & Mbah, M. (2019). Enhancing the work placement experience of international students: toward a support framework. *Journal of further and higher education, 43*(4), 521-532.

Government of Canada. (2024, January 11). *Apply for citizenship: Who can apply*. Retrieved April 14, 2024, from https://www.canada.ca/en/immigration-refugees-citizenship/services/canadian-citizenship/become-canadian-citizen/eligibility.html

Gribble, C., Blackmore, J., & Rahimi, M. (2015). Challenges to providing work integrated learning to international business students at Australian universities. Higher Education, Skills and Work-Based Learning, 5(4), 401–416.https://doi.org/10.1108/HESWB L-04-2015-0015

Grugulis, I., & Vincent, S. (2009). "Whose Skill Is It Anyway? 'Soft' Skills and Polarization". *Work, Employment and Society, 23*(4), 597–615.

Guo, S. (2009). "Difference, Deficiency, and Devaluation: Tracing the Roots of Non/recognition of Foreign Credentials for Immigrant Professionals in Canada." *Canadian Journal for the Study of Adult Education, 22*(1), 37–52.

Guo, S. (2015). The color of skill: Contesting a racialised regime of skill from the experience of recent immigrants in Canada. *Studies in Continuing Education, 37*(3), 236–250. https://doi-org.ezproxy.tru.ca/10.1080/0158037X.2015.1067766

Han, Y., Gulanowski, D., & Sears, G. J. (2022). International student graduates' workforce integration: A systematic review. *International Journal of Intercultural Relations, 86*, 163-189.

Kim, S. (2024). Subjective well-being of international students: Interplay of perceived discrimination, health status, and community satisfaction. *Journal of International Students*, *14*(4), 570–590. https://doi.org/10.32674/jis.v14i4.6480

Lee, E. S., Szkudlarek, B., Nguyen, D. C., & Nardon, L. (2020). Unveiling the Canvas Ceiling: a multidisciplinary literature review of refugee employment and workforce integration. *International Journal of Management Reviews, 22*(2), 193–216.

Li, J., Liu, X., & Mullins, P. (2024). Exploring the career development challenges and expectations of international students during the COVID-19 pandemic. *Journal of International Students*, *14*(4), 591-605.

Li, P. S. (2008). "The Role of Foreign Credentials and Ethnic Ties in Immigrants' Economic Performance." *Canadian Journal of Sociology, 33*(2), 291–310.

Li, X., DiPetta, T., & deVires, P. (2016). Canadian Higher Education Internationalization: Experiences of Chinese Students. *The Journal of Educational Thought (JET)/Revue de la Pensée Éducative*, *49*(3), 265–283.

Li, X., DiPetta, T., & Woloshyn, V. (2012). Why do Chinese study for a Master of Education degree in Canada? What are their experiences?. *Canadian Journal of Education/Revue Canadienne De l'éducation*, *35*(3), 149–163. Retrieved from https://journals.sfu.ca/cje/index.php/cje-rce/article/view/1076

Liu, J., & Guo, S. (2021). *Navigating transition to work: Recent immigrants' experiences of lifelong learning in Canada.* International Review of Education

López-Miguens, M. J., Caballero, G., & Álvarez-González, P. (2021). Responsibility of the University in Employability: Development and validation of a measurement scale across five studies. *Business Ethics, the Environment & Responsibility, 30*(1), 143-156.

Maitra, S. (2015). "The Making of the 'Precarious': Examining Indian Immigrant IT Workers in Canada and Their Transnational Networks with Body Shops in India". *Globalization, Societies and Education, 13*(2), 194–209.

Noorani, N. (2011). "Nine Soft Skills No Immigrant Should Be Without!" http://www.prepareforcanada.com/wp-content/uploads/9SoftSkills_PrepareforCanada.pdf

Nourpanah, S. (2019). Drive-by education: the role of vocational courses in the migration projects of foreign nurses in Canada. *Journal of International Migration and Integration, 20*(4), 995–1011.

Nunes, S., & Arthur, N. (2013). International students' experiences of integrating into the workforce. *Journal of Employment Counseling, 50*(1), 34-45. https://doi.org/10.1002/j.2161-1920.2013.00023.x

Omidvar, R. (2024). Be wary of simple fixes on immigration; With foreign students, Canada has gotten tangled up in a sticky problem of our own making. *Globe & Mail (Toronto, Canada)*, A11-A11.

Oreopoulos, P. (2009). *Why Do Skilled Immigrants Struggle in the Labor Market? A Field Experiment with Six Thousand Resumes.* NBER Working Paper No. 15036. Cambridge, MA: National Bureau of Economic Research.

Oreopoulos, P. (2011). "Why Do Skilled Immigrants Struggle in the Labor Market? A Field Experiment with Thirteen Thousand Resumes". *American Economic Journal: Economic Policy, 3*(4), 148–171.

Organization for Economic Co-operation and Development (OECD) (2020). *Education at a Glance 2020: OECD Indicators.* Paris: OECD Publishing. https://doi.org/10.1787/69096873-en

Organization for Economic Co-operation and Development (OECD). (2014). *International Migration Outlook.* Paris: Organization for Economic Co-Operation and Development.

Pandher, J., & Dhami, S. (2024, Aug. 27). Thousands of international students in Canada face deportation, sparking protests nationwide. Citynews. https://toronto.citynews.ca/2024/08/26/canada-international-students-deportation-protests/

Paris Communiqué. (2018). *EHEA Ministerial Conference Paris*. Retrieved from http://www.ehea2018.paris/Data/ElFinder/s2/Communique/EHEAParis2018-Communique-final.pdf

Perić, J., & Delić, A. (2016). Developing social responsibility in Croatian Universities: a benchmarking approach and an overview of current situation. *International Review on Public and Nonprofit Marketing, 13*(1), 69–80. https://doi.org/10.1007/s12208-015-0144-5

Petruzziello, G., Mariani, M. G., Guglielmi, D., van der Heijden, B. I., de Jong, J. P., & Chiesa, R. (2023). The role of teaching staff in fostering perceived employability of university students. *Studies in Higher Education*, *48*(1), 20-36.

Pham, T., Saito, E., Bao, D., & Chowdhury, R. (2018). Employability of international students: Strategies to enhance their experience on work-integrated learning (WIL) programs. *Journal of Teaching and Learning for Graduate Employability*, *9*(1), 62-83.

Popadiuk, N. E., & Arthur, N. M. (2014). Key relationships for international student university-to-work transitions. *Journal of career development*, *41*(2), 122-140.

Raby, R. L., Singh , J. K. N., & Bista, K. (2022). Dimensions of International Student Critical Employability. *Book Series.* Retrieved from https://www.ojed.org/index.php/gsm/article/view/5154

Ramjattan, V. A. (2023). International students and their raciolinguistic sensemaking of aural employability in Canadian universities. *International journal of the sociology of language*, *2023*(282), 159-180.

Raza, M., Beaujot, R. & Woldemicael, G. (2013). Social Capital and Economic Integration of Visible Minority Immigrants in Canada. *Int. Migration & Integration, 14*, 263–285. https://doi.org/10.1007/s12134-012-0239-3

Reitz, J. G., Curtis, J. & Elrick, J. (2014). "Immigrant Skill Utilization: Trends and Policy Issues." *Journal of International Migration and Integration, 15*(1), 1–26.

Römgens, I., Scoupe, R., & Beausaert, S. (2020). Unraveling the concept of employability, bringing together research on employability in higher education and the workplace. *Studies in Higher Education* (Dorchester-on-Thames),45(12), 2588–2603.

Sin, C., & Amaral, A. (2017). Academics' and employers' perceptions about responsibilities for employability and their initiatives toward its development. *Higher Education, 73*(1), 97–111. https://doi.org/10.1007/s10734-016-0007-y

Sin, C., Tavares, O., & Amaral, A. (2016). Who is responsible for employability? Student perceptions and practices. *Tertiary Education and Management*, *22*(1), 65-81.

Soares, M., & Mosquera, P. (2020). Linking development of skills and perceptions of employability: The case of Erasmus students. *Ekonomska Istraživanja, 33(1), 2769–2786.* https://doi.org/10.1080/1331677X.2019.1697330

Statista. (2021a). *Number of study permit holders with a valid permit in Canada from 2000 to 2020.* Retrieved from https://www.statista.com/statistics/555117/number-of-international-students-at-years-end-canada-2000–2014/

Statista. (2021b). *Education in Canada - Statistics & Facts*. Retrieved from https://www.statista.com/topics/2863/education-in-canada/

Tamburri, R. (2019, May 1). *Changes to immigration rules are a boon to international student recruitment.* University Affairs. https://universityaffairs.ca/news/news-article/changes-to-immigration-rules-are-a-boon-to-international-student_recruitment/

Tharenou, P., & Kulik, C. T. (2020). Skilled Migrants Employed in Developed, Mature Economies: From Newcomers to Organizational Insiders. *Journal of Management, 46*(6), 1156–1181.

Tran, L. T., & Soejatminah, S. (2016). 'Get foot in the door': International students' perceptions of work integrated learning. *British Journal of Educational Studies*, *64*(3), 337-355.

UNESCO. (2019). Outbound internationally mobile students by host region. Retrieved from http://data.uis.unesco.org/Index.aspx?queryid=172

United Nations. (2013). *International Migration Report 2013*. New York: United Nations, Department of Economic and Social Affairs, Population Division.

Yin, Z., Ong, L. Z., & Qiao, M. (2024). Psychological factors associated with Chinese international students' well-being in the United States: A systematic review. *Journal of International Students, 14*(4), 529–551. https://doi.org/10.32674/jis.v14i4.6428

Zhao, X., Kung, M., & Bista, K. (2024). How UK PhD programs have prepared international students for work: perspectives of Chinese doctoral students in the social sciences. *Journal of International Students, 14*(1), 171-188.

Author bios

TRUNG TU NGUYEN, MEd, is a graduate of the Faculty of Education and Social Work at Thompson Rivers University in Canada and an Academic Advisor of the Schulich School of Engineering at the University of Calgary in Canada. His major research interests lie in the area of international students' integration into the Canadian labor market. Email: tuwalker82@gmail.com

MANU SHARMA, PhD, is an Associate Professor in the Faculty of Education and Social Work at Thompson Rivers University in Canada. Her major research interests lie in the areas of critical social justice theory and equitable public education for all: social justice initiatives in higher education/teacher education/community, international comparative studies, legal issues in education, and critical race theory. Email: masharma@tru.ca

Article

Journal of International Students
Volume 14, Issue 5 (2024), pp. 85-107
ISSN: 2162-3104 (Print), 2166-3750 (Online)
jistudents.org

Latin American University Exchange Students' Experiences with Intercultural Sensitivity Development: The Role of Emotions

Sarah Carrica-Ochoa
University of Navarra, Spain

Eleanor Joanne Brownb
University of York, UK

ABSTRACT

We studied the affective component of intercultural competence: intercultural sensitivity. Specifically, this mixed methods study will be used to understand how Latin American students experienced their experience studying abroad in the UK, including what and how they learned and changed. The study explores the relationships between intercultural sensitivity and experiences of intercultural contact to predict the variables that impact its development. This study contributes to our understanding of the phenomenon of learning abroad, particularly in the context of UK higher education. Results suggest that emotions are key to the experience of studying abroad, both positive and negative, and these impact the ways that one learns about oneself and about others and one's ability to reflect on one's own culture as well as being open to a new culture.

Keywords: Global citizens, Higher education, Intercultural competence, Intercultural sensitivity, Study abroad.

This paper presents a study examining the experiences of Latin American students in the UK and the factors they identify as shaping the development of their intercultural sensitivity (IS). The Latin American population in the UK, now approximately a quarter of a million (Blair, 2019), has grown fourfold since 2001, making them the second fastest-growing non-EU migrant group in the country (McIlwaine, Cock, & Linneker, 2011, 2026). With the UK's departure from the European Union and the resulting changes in the freedom of movement, it is increasingly critical to understand the experiences of international students from other regions. This understanding not only informs institutions about the motivations and decisions of these students in selecting the UK as their study destination but also offers opportunities to foster environments that better support the development of IS. This research aims to explore IS development from the perspective of Latin American students, with a focus on changes in their identities and emotional responses to cultural diversity. The findings highlight potential relationships between acculturation strategies, identity development, and IS, providing valuable insights for host universities to create inclusive and supportive environments for international students.

LITERATURE REVIEW

Globalization has significantly increased international student mobility, presenting unique challenges as students adapt to new cultural and educational environments. Intercultural sensitivity and emotional management are crucial for their adaptation and success. This literature review highlights key studies and theoretical perspectives related to intercultural sensitivity and emotion among international students.

Intercultural sensitivity is the ability to recognize, respect, and adapt to cultural differences and is essential for effective interaction in multicultural settings. Milton J. Bennett's developmental model of intercultural sensitivity (DMIS) describes a continuum of stages (denial, defense, and minimization) to ethnorelative stages (acceptance, adaptation, and integration) through which individuals can progress as they develop greater intercultural sensitivity and competence. His work focused on how individuals perceive and respond to cultural differences, and his model has become a fundamental tool in the field of intercultural education. The DMIS was one of the first theoretical frameworks to directly link the concept of intercultural sensitivity with personal development and intercultural competence.

Hammer, Bennett, and Wiseman (2003) revised this model to emphasize the integration phase, where individuals adapt not only their behaviors but also their cultural identities through continuous interactions with diverse cultures. Bennett (2013) argues that in the contemporary era, the model requires consideration of not only individual adaptation but also the impact of globalization on collective cultural identity. This revision has influenced how educational institutions approach the teaching of intercultural competence.

Chen and Starosta's (1996) model offers a comprehensive view of intercultural competence by integrating affective, cognitive, and behavioral components, stressing the importance of attitudes and emotions alongside knowledge and skills. This study focuses on the gap between knowing and acting in intercultural sensitivity, which involves empathy and the rejection of ethnocentrism (Downing & Husband, 2002).

We adopt the Chen & Starosta model as the theoretical framework for this study because of the importance it places on the emotional component. The management of emotions is critical for international students, who often experience stress, anxiety, and loneliness while adapting to new cultural and academic environments. Lazarus and Folkman's theory of stress and coping (1984) describes how individuals evaluate and cope with stressful situations. The context of international students has been used to explore how they manage the stress associated with cultural adaptation. Gross's emotion regulation theory in intercultural contexts (2015) explores how individuals manage their emotions when faced with significant cultural differences.

Kim's theory of cross-cultural adaptation (2001) posits that intercultural adaptation is a dynamic process involving personal growth and adjustment to a new environment. It includes factors such as cultural openness and the ability to manage stress. In this vein, Ward, Bochner, & Furnham (2001) integrated Kim's theory with Berry's acculturation model (1997), emphasizing the importance of both psychological and sociocultural adaptation. Their combined model provides a comprehensive understanding of the adaptation process of international students.

The literature underscores the interdependence of intercultural sensitivity and emotional regulation in the adaptation of international students. Integrating theoretical models such as Bennett's revised DMIS, Deardorff's framework, Chen & Starosta's approach, Gross's emotion regulation theory, and the adjustment models of Gudykunst and Tabor & Milfont provides a comprehensive understanding of these processes.

METHOD

This study employs a phenomenological research design (Weber, 1949), integrating both quantitative and qualitative data collection methods to provide a comprehensive understanding of the subject. By investigating the lived experiences of participants (Converse, 2012), the research seeks to deepen insight into the development of intercultural sensitivity (IS) and the acculturation processes among international students.

Research Objectives

1. To examine the degree of intercultural sensitivity (IS) exhibited by international students in contexts characterized by cultural diversity and coexistence.
2. To analyze the meanings and interpretations that students attribute to their experiences within a culturally different environment, with a specific focus on their identity formation.

Participants

This study employed a purposive sampling strategy (Creswell, 2005) to recruit eight participants aged 20--29 years who were enrolled in the UK. Their prior international travel experiences varied; most had taken short tourist trips, primarily within Latin America, whereas some had visited Europe and the USA multiple times. Only one participant had previously been to the UK, two had studied or interned in Europe, and one had lived abroad in Europe and North America during childhood.

Table 1. Participants characteristics (n = 8)

Come from		**Studying Abroad Before**		**Arrival study level**	
Mexico	4	Yes	2	High School	2
Salvador	1	No	6	Undergraduate	5
Ecuador	1			Master	1
Chile	2				
National identity		**Living Abroad Before**		**Occupation**	
Latino American	5	Between half-1 year	4	Studying	7
Latino American + Spanish	2	Between 1-2 years	1	Working	0
Latino American + French	1	Between 2-3 years	2	Both	1
		Between 4-5 years	1		
Language level		**Working Abroad Before**		**Actual Studying**	
Proficiency English	8	Yes	2	Undergraduate	2
Proficiency English+French	4	No	6	Master	4
				PhD	2
International School		**UK Residence**			
Yes	3	Durham	1		
No	5	Manchester	2		
		York	5		

Data collection

We utilized interviews and questionnaires for data collection. The questionnaires provided detailed information about the adopted strategies, whereas the interviews assessed the participants' meanings behind these strategies.

The questionnaire included four sections: a) Sociodemographic information; b) Sociocultural aspects (academic level and occupation); c) International experiences (education, travel, friendships, living abroad); and d) Intercultural sensitivity factors measured by the Intercultural Sensitivity Scale (ISS) (24 items; Cronbach's alpha: 0.86) (Chen & Starosta, 2000; Spanish validation: Vilá, 2006). This scale, validated for adult college students, was appropriate for our study.

The semistructured interviews (Kvale, 2015) focused on key variables of intercultural inclusion (Passiatore et al., 2019) within a migration context (Eguiluz, 2017) and comprised three sections: sociodemographic aspects, immigration experiences, and intercultural sensitivity.

Figure 1: Procedure and instruments

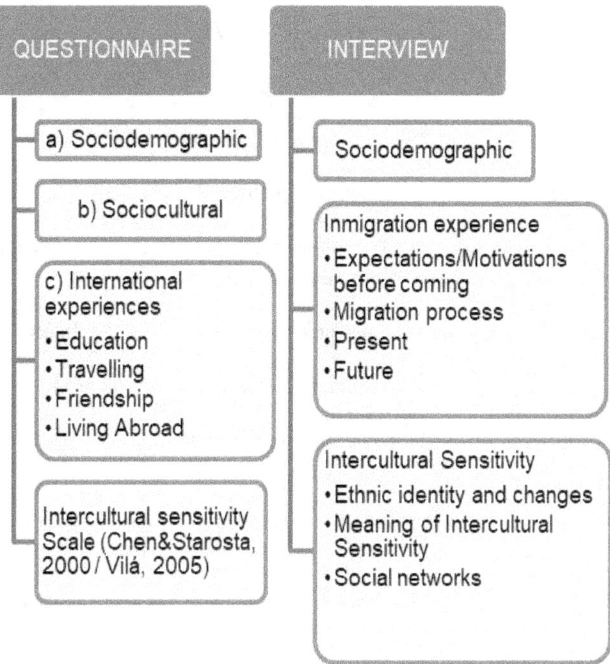

Analysis

The questionnaires and interviews were conducted and analyzed in Spanish to ensure that the participants could express themselves freely and that their voices were accurately represented.

The study's research methods were approved by both universities' ethics boards.

Quantitative analysis was performed via SPSS25, with a focus on descriptive statistics, frequencies, and percentages. Qualitative analysis utilized NVivo12 for thematic narrative analysis (Riessman, 2008; Lester, 2020). Information categorization was based on Chen's six characteristics of intercultural sensitivity and themes emerging from participants' narratives (Gibbs, 2012). The analysis followed the four steps of phenomenological analysis outlined by Giorgi and Giorgi (2003).

Figure 2. Method design

	QUALITATIVE	QUANTITATIVE
DATA COLLECTION	Questionnaires + In-depth Interviews	Questionnaires
DATA ANALYSIS	Data systematization	Sata systematization
	Categories (previous + emergings)	Statistics analysis
	Categories tree	Profile dimensions Intercultural Sensitivity
	Validation categories (Tirangulation researchers + Chen&Starosta Intercultural Sensitivity Model	
	Convergence	Divergence / Discrepancy
	Integration findings with a systematic triangulation of perspect	
	Central themes and categories + Main Narrative / Discourse Findings	

RESULTS

International Experience and Acculturation in the UK

Arrival in the UK and feelings about the move

The participants discussed several motivations for moving to the UK. These generally fall into three main categories: personal experience, professional development and practical reasons.

First, it is the research that they do here that they do not have in other universities; the second thing is the culture because I have always been drawn to English or British culture, I wanted to experience it. In addition, third, I'd say that I was looking to experience living abroad, far from my family, I wanted that personal development (Miguel).

Table 2. Statements about arrival and present moment

	Min	Max	Mean	SD
1. I feel comfortable living in Europe	4	5	4,50	,535
2. I found it easy adapt to living in Europe	1	5	3,75	1,488
3. My move to Europe was how I expected it to be	2	5	3,62	1,061
4. I experienced culture shock when I moved to Europe	2	5	4,00	1,195
5. I feel integrated into European culture and society	2	5	3,50	1,309

The participants had both positive and negative expectations of British people having been told that 'they would be more formal, more polite and more things like that' (Miguel) but that 'they say that English people are cold and that it'll be difficult to find people to help you out or say come with me here or come along there' (Hugo). For most, they were clear that they would be moving somewhere quite different from their country of origin:

> *I knew it would be difficult, but I didn't think it would be so difficult. I mean, I'd say that El Salvador and England are completely different worlds; we don't have anything in common, nothing at all (Diego).*

Most reported positive things about the experience of living in the UK: discovering and learning new things, meeting people (Luis, Miguel, Marcelo, Hugo, Diego) and being shown around and helped out (Miguel, Marcelo). The arrival was often intimidating or uncomfortable but a positive challenge (Antonio). Meeting people from other countries and the international mix of UK universities (Miguel, Marcelo, Hugo) stood out as positive.

On the other hand, some participants reported more negative aspects of their arrival and first impressions of the UK. Some discussed having to leave things behind, such as their family stability, work, partners, and family, and having to adapt (Alicia, Gustavo). They noted that getting used to a new environment took time (Alicia), and they mentioned the difference in climate and food (Gustavo), which left difficult situations at home (Gustavo), and getting used to speaking the language (Gustavo, Hugo, Antonio) as aspects that were initially difficult to manage.

The extent to which the environment was international seemed to have an impact on the first impressions. When there were many nationalities, it was generally a positive thing, even when this was something many had not truly experienced before (Miguel, Marcelo, Hugo). Indeed, having an interest in meeting people from different places and being curious were seen as useful precursors. However, when the environment was less international, owing to the nature of the course or the residence, it was more difficult to adapt with only British people around (Gustavo, Antonio):

> *The majority of the people who studied with me and the ones around me were British, so I felt the issue of the language barrier most of all ... and like it made it harder to adapt very quickly ... it was difficult, the first 2 or 3 weeks, I found it hard and I barely came out of my room and stuff, so it wasn't that pleasant (Gustavo).*

The role of the university was another key factor in terms of teaching styles and the attitudes of staff and fellow students.

> *University is difficult, ... the way of teaching is very different from the Mexican way and more than anything I feel like it is a very lonely process, like they don't make a society, they are very individualistic and it is difficult to communicate with my classmates. (Allia)*

Others felt that they experienced more independence and academic freedom through the teaching style (Marcelo) and that although it was challenging at first, it could lead to more opportunities for working and networking (Gustavo).

In general, these first impressions gave way to different feelings as they began to settle. Some claimed to be 'satisfied with the way of life here' (Miguel) or fulfilling their goals (Alicia, Antonio) (items 1, 2 and 3, Table 2) and reported feeling very happy with their current situation (Alicia, Hugo, Antonio) (item 1, Table 2). Although there were times when some felt frustrated or wondered if all the effort was worth it (Diego) (items 4 and 5, Table 2), most had 'lowered the volume' (Antonio) of their own culture to try to appreciate aspects of their new environment, saying that they felt 'very at home at this stage in my life' (Hugo). Some felt that they had assimilated more because the relationships they had formed and made an effort to understand the culture, and people made them feel more content (Alicia).

Social Relations

Support

The narratives about the support needed to embark on an international experience were broadly similar for most of the participants. Most mentioned their family and often their parents in particular to provide the emotional (and sometimes financial) support that gave them confidence in their ability to study abroad (Luis, Alicia, Gustavo, Hugo).

Some also mentioned their friends from their home country as important sources of support (Luis, Alicia, Gustavo) and financial support from their governments (Miguel). Some commented on the support provided by the University in terms of events (Miguel) and supervisors or tutors (Hugo, Antonio) and meeting people romantically (Alicia), through sport (Gustavo), or have made good friends with housemates (Miguel, Alicia). Most focused on the importance of finding good friends[1] in the UK. Four said that they had made good British friends (Marcelo, Gustavo, Diego, Antonio), but all eight discussed the importance of having friends from around the world. Perhaps this was because they were also navigating an international experience. This emerged as the main theme.

Friendship

For many, having friends who also spoke Spanish helped with the acculturation process (Luis, Marcelo, Gustavo, Hugo, Antonio). Indeed, on a practical level, their proficiency with the language had an impact on how well they initially settled: 'I think that knowing how to speak the language truly well definitely helps with that.' (Marcelo). They claimed not to be nervous (item 9, Table 2) and to have a better attitude (item 8, Table 2) toward interacting with people from other cultures since they moved to the UK, which is a good indicator of a positive process of acculturation and intercultural learning.

---

[1] We are defining a 'friend' as someone they spend time with outside of their timetabled academic study who they have met during their time in Europe.

Table 3: Intercultural Friendships

	Min	Max	Mean	SD
1. I have European friends	2	5	4,38	1,061
2. I have friends from Latin America	4	5	4,88	,354
3. I have friends from my country of origin	1	5	3,86	1,464
4. I have friends from many different countries	5	5	5,00	,000
5. Most of my friends have the same first language as me	2	4	2,88	,641
6. I speak other language (different to my first language) with most of my friends	3	5	4,00	,756
7. I find it difficult to maintain close friendships with people from different cultures to me	1	4	2,25	,886
8. My attitude to people from other cultures has become more positive since I moved here	3	5	4,25	,886
9. I am more nervous about interacting with people from different cultures since I moved here	1	3	1,75	,707

Three themes emerged: the importance of an international environment, the benefits of finding others who share their language and culture and the difficulty of forming relationships with British people.

Shared language and culture

Finding others who shared aspects of their culture or language, at least at the beginning, helped the participants settle (Luis, Marcelo, Gustavo, Hugo, Antonio).

International environment

Some also commented on the role of the university and noted that within the classroom, relationships were fine, but there could be more support for integration outside the classroom (Alicia, Gustavo), which was more difficult. The importance of an international environment and meeting people from around the world had a positive impact on acclimatization (Luis, Miguel, Marcelo, Gustavo, Diego, Antonio). The participants commented that they liked 'that diversity of people' (Antonio), finding it easier to get along with a more international group of people (Gustavo) and finding it 'easier to make friends with other people who also come from far away' (Miguel).

British people

The most dominant theme, however, was the extent to which they were able to establish relationships with British people. In general, the participants claimed that it was more difficult to make friends with local people than with other international students (Luis, Miguel, Diego, Marcelo, Gustavo, Antonio). Most said that they had fewer British friends, in part because they were in an international environment at the University but also because of cultural differences.

They discussed how it takes a long time to make relationships with British people (Antonio), who are 'generally more closed' (Diego), reserved (Antonio) or 'not inclusive' (Gustavo). This may be because there is not a shared sense of humor (Marcelo), because it is difficult to find things in common (Gustavo), or because it is simply difficult to relate to British people because they are established here (Luis, Miguel, Diego). There was a strong perception that British people are not close to their families and that the culture is very individualistic, cold, distant and closed (Miguel, Alicia, Diego, Antonio). Most also identified segregation between groups and that it is difficult to break into a group of British people. For this reason, they missed aspects of Latin American culture (Luis, Miguel, Gustavo, Hugo, Diego). Some speculated on the aspects of the culture that made them feel this distance, and they highlighted the polite, respectful nature of British culture as something that seemed to inhibit close relationships (Miguel, Antonio):

> *I don't believe English people because they are so courteous but so cold at the same time; they are so distant (Antonio)*

Others commented that even when it is possible to make friends with British people, it is seen as because they are not 'typical'—'he is the "least English" English person who I know' (Antonio). There was a lot of stereotyping when it came to judging whether they would relate better to people from different places.

In terms of British culture, participants spoke positively about social class, which they saw as more equal than the vast inequalities of Latin American countries (Alicia, Marcelo, Gustavo). There were also positive comments in terms of security and social organization (Luis, Miguel, Antonio). The transport system was also viewed in positive light for being reliable and efficient (Luis, Alicia) and, importantly, having the freedom to go out, use public transport or walk alone without safety fears (Alicia, Gustavo, Diego, Antonio).

There were negative comments about issues related to food and drink. The participants made comparisons between British and Latin American food, with participants missing the latter (Luis, Miguel, Alicia), and some also lamented the lack of Latin food available (Luis), the cost and quality of food (Alicia) and the social interaction surrounding food culture (Luis). The British drinking culture was also identified as negative (Miguel, Alicia).

There were both positive and negative comments about social attitudes and values. British culture was seen as individualistic, cold, closed minded, distant (Miguel, Alicia, Diego, Antonio), overly correct, reserved and moderated, and therefore false (Miguel, Antonio). Three had experienced discriminatory comments (Miguel, Gustavo, Antonio). On the other hand, many participants saw British culture as responsible and punctual (Hugo), polite and courteous (Alicia, Marcelo, Gustavo, Antonio), and accepting and integrating other cultures (Marcelo) (compared with assimilation policies, which they had seen in France). Several people commented that there was more freedom to behave in ways that you wanted without judgment (Gustavo, Diego, Antonio):

> *What I like most is the freedom that people have; people can do more things than in my country, and it is more accepted. ... there's not as much prejudice in English society; they are more progressive. (Diego)*

Two participants gained insight from partners and their families, who presented new perspectives that they had not seen before, and this new way of seeing things in a different light enabled them to reassess some of their prior assumptions in a way that was very positive (Alicia, Marcelo).

It seemed that it was by forming close relationships that the participants were best able to unlock ideas about culture and begin to see different perspectives in a light that they had not done before and that are not possible virtually or from a distance. The fact that these relationships were hard to find at the outset perhaps meant that they had to do more work to get past the 'polite' and 'cold' exterior of British social relations, but for those that did so, the impact on their understanding and the acculturation process was profound.

Identity development

The participants were asked to define themselves from a list of terms. Most thought of themselves as international students (Luis, Miguel, Diego, Hugo, Antonio), but some selected other terms, including global citizen (Alicia, Hugo), transnational citizen (Marcelo), international citizen (Gustavo), and immigrant (Diego). These labels are often connected with the aspects of their identity that are important to them, which are explored below.

To define themselves, two of them used sociodemographic variables such as their gender, profession, nationality, or domicile (Luis, Miguel), and seven talked about the values and qualities they possessed (Miguel, Alicia, Marcelo, Gustavo, Diego, Hugo, Antonio). These included being responsible, organized, and careful (Miguel, Alicia, Marcelo, Antonio), loyal and friendly (Alicia, Diego, Antonio), happy and fun (Alicia, Gustavo, Diego), hardworking and resilient (Alicia, Diego), knowledgeable and interested in learning (Marcelo, Hugo), curious and open (Gustavo, Hugo), thoughtful (Diego), quiet and slow (Marcelo), idealist (Gustavo), ambitious (Diego), adventurous (Hugo) and anxious (Antonio). One person mentioned the importance of the value of living and letting live (Miguel).

When asked whether this experience has changed how they identify themselves, five of the participants said that there would have been minor changes to the words they used (Luis, Miguel, Hugo, Diego, Antonio), whereas the other three said they would have used the same words but noted that they had changed in terms of the degree of emphasis (Alicia, Marcelo, Gustavo). One participant felt that they had changed a lot as a person since they left their own country 'above all in empathy and kindness' (Diego).

However, for most, this change was incremental, for example, being more confident (Gustavo, Antonio) or more sure of themselves and who they are now (Alicia, Gustavo, Hugo). For some, it was difficult to be themselves at the beginning, but 'as you adapt, you are able to reaffirm who you are' (Gustavo). An important issue was feeling that they were more open, tolerant and less judgmental (Diego, Gustavo, Hugo):

> *However, I wasn't such an open person as I am now to different cultures, to get to know new people and places, that is something that I have acquired this year. (Hugo)*

There was a feeling that even when the words they used to describe themselves were the same, they still felt that there had been a qualitative change in their way of being, for example, picking up traits they saw and liked in British culture, 'like being more polite or complaining less about things' (Marcelo).

They felt that being exposed to more cultural diversity had an impact on their sense of self and who they are (Diego, Alicia, Marcelo, Hugo). Having themselves reflected in another culture was seen as an opportunity to look at their own idiosyncrasies or ideas and consider where they come from. Many reported that they had grown in some way through the experience of living abroad (Diego, Alicia, Marcelo, Gustavo, Hugo). Some thought that these realizations about how they had changed would be stronger once they returned home and had more chances to reflect on what they had done and seen.

> *I think that I am different, perhaps I am not going to truly notice until I get back and I reflect on it .... May be not change as a person, but grow, add more things to my rucksack to put it that way (Hugo)*

Intercultural Sensitivity

Interculturality is generally understood as an interaction or a relationship (Luis, Miguel, Diego, Alicia, Marcelo, Hugo), which involves the capacity to engage with each other and develop a deeper understanding and acceptance of each other's culture and work together (Hugo) when something new arises from the mixing of cultures (Diego) and when there is a genuine connection.

Some participants referred to the system of ideas that underpins different cultures as an important factor in defining both cultural diversity and interculturality (Luis, Marcelo, Hugo, Antonio). The participants said that their understanding of these ideas had broadened since being in the UK, perhaps because of greater cultural differences to which they were exposed (Luis, Miguel, Diego), and even if the understanding was similar, they saw cultural difference as a point of interest for mixing and learning about the 'other', and they felt they had the opportunity to experience and practice the ideas (Diego, Hugo).

Chen Intercultural Sensitivity Model

In this final section, we consider the above findings and relate them to the five dimensions (Table 4) and six characteristics identified by Chen and Starosta (1997) and draw together the findings from the interviews and questionnaires (all the averages that surpass the theoretical medium scores[2]) in considering the extent to which we found evidence of these aspects of IS development in the participants and their experiences.

---

[2] Theoretical scores have been calculated from the number of items of each dimension, as a reference of the minimum, maximum and medium scores (theoretical), scoring 1, 5 or 3 in all items, respectively.

Table 4. Participants' scores and theoretical scores of the intercultural sensitivity scale

	Min	**Max**	**M**	**SD**	***Min Theor SC***	***M Theor SC***	***Max Theor SC***
Interaction Involvement	26	32	28,63	1,92	*7*	*21*	*35*
Respect of Cultural Differences	18	29	24,37	3,70	*6*	*18*	*30*
Interaction Confidence	14	23	18,50	2,82	*5*	*15*	*25*
Interaction Enjoyment	10	15	12,75	1,66	*3*	*9*	*15*
Interaction Attention	10	13	11,25	1,16	*3*	*9*	*15*
ISTotal	87	105	95,5	6,5	*24*	*72*	*120*

The participants noted changes in terms of each of the characteristics of people with high IS identified by Chen and Starosta (1997).

Empathy and interaction enjoyment

Empathy was reflected in the ways they discussed understanding experiences with people who enabled them to see things from different perspectives (Miguel). For some, this learning about themselves reaffirmed who they are and the values they hold (Gustavo).

All the participants mentioned aspects of the experience they had enjoyed; experiencing different perspectives was something motivating and positive (Diego, Alicia, Hugo, Miguel, Antonio), and for some, this was key to underpinning the changes they experienced:

> *I've loved it, doing these things and feeling motivated to learn, to want to share these things .... It has been enriching ... I think that it will change my way of seeing things, seeing life (Hugo)*

Involvement in interactions

The participants noted the importance of an international environment to stimulate involvement in intercultural interactions (Luis, Miguel, Marcelo, Gustavo, Diego, Antonio). They commented on the enriching nature of forming relationships with people of other cultures (Luis, Miguel, Diego, Alicia, Marcelo, Hugo). One key aspect to note was the importance of making contact with others and living, interacting and learning about others (Miguel, Diego, Alicia, Gustavo) to aid in the development of IS:

> *... it's like a driver of this sensibility to live abroad and like this experience of being alone, feeling different .... I think you can do that in your own country, but going abroad is much quicker and more effective. (Antonio)*

Open Mindedness to Differences and Respecting Cultural Differences

The demonstration of open mindedness was a key aspect of the IS noted by many participants (Miguel, Alicia, Gustavo, Hugo, Antonio), and this was often related to how they approached similarity and difference. Many said that they felt that they were more open minded as a result of their experience in the UK (Diego, Gustavo, Hugo). All of the participants said that they felt a difference between themselves and others in the UK (Luis, Miguel, Marcelo, Gustavo, Hugo, Diego, Antonio), which was related to differences in terms of their mentality, language and background (Luis, Marcelo, Hugo, Diego, Antonio):

> *I feel like my mentality is very different from the English mentality (Diego)*

However, most were clear that they felt comfortable managing this difference (Luis, Miguel, Alicia, Marcelo, Gustavo, Hugo, Antonio) (item 3, Table 3) and that they had developed ways to respect, accept, appreciate and embrace difference (Alicia, Hugo, Gustavo):

> *It's where you make an effort to find similarities and appreciate the differences (Alicia)*

Indeed, for many being open, it was often easy to find points of similarity:

> *It's nice, at first when you meet a person from another culture, you feel different, but once those bonds of friendship grow stronger, you realize that we are not that different (Miguel)*

Being open to difference and similarity could be accomplished through taking an interest and asking questions to learn more (Miguel, Gustavo, Hugo, Antonio), for example, having a greater awareness of different cultural practices (Hugo) (item 2, Table 3).

Self-regulation or reflection and interaction attention

The participants were reflective about how the experience had impacted their way of being. They reflected on how they had worked on becoming more intercultural (Antonio, Miguel, Alicia, Hugo, Diego), reflected on their own culture from the outside (Miguel, Alicia, Hugo, Diego, Antonio) and perhaps became less tolerant of negative aspects, such as racist comments or jokes (Miguel, Antonio). However, they also recognized that it is difficult to be intercultural, especially when you love your own culture (Diego, Alicia, Antonio).

Importantly, this reflection was also seen as part of a process (Diego, Hugo, Antonio), and there was a need to keep checking oneself and making an effort (Diego, Antonio, Alicia).

They talked about adopting new habits (Marcelo) or taking care to understand differences better (Gustavo) and, for some, reflecting on their experience had helped to reaffirm who they are (Alicia, Gustavo, Hugo) or how this had impacted their sense of identity (Diego, Alicia, Marcelo, Hugo). For some, reflecting on differences they noticed with their own culture also highlighted positive aspects of the culture of their country of origin (Alicia, Diego).

Self-esteem and Confidence and Interaction Confidence

The development of self-esteem was also evident in many of the participants; they mentioned their personal development or how they had grown in some way (Miguel, Diego, Alicia, Marcelo, Gustavo, Hugo), improvement of language skills (Diego, Gustavo, Hugo), and the confidence they had gained (Alicia, Marcelo, Gustavo, Hugo, Antonio). They talked about having the tools to experience a new culture (Marcelo) and develop confidence in oneself that can open doors (Hugo).

Suspension of judgment

Suspension of judgment, questioning prior assumptions and taking time to understand different perspectives were all parts of how they saw the development of their own IS. Appreciating things for what they are (Miguel, Diego, Gustavo, Hugo, Antonio) was one way that participants had begun to suspend their judgments:

Overcoming prejudice and recognizing their own biases and reflecting on their prior behavior (Antonio, Gustavo, Hugo, Diego) were also mentioned and demonstrated ways in which the participants had become less judgmental about other cultures:

> *I think before I was more, not closed exactly, but I wouldn't be excited about meeting people from other countries, but now I would ... because I hadn't lived it, and when you don't know, often you judge it before getting to know it, and I think now I get to know something and then judge (Hugo)*

They mentioned learning through relationships (Alicia, Marcelo), being open to challenging their assumptions, asking questions and learning before forming opinions (Hugo). They often surprised themselves with the things they liked (Diego, Hugo, Antonio), and they cited this as evidence of the changes taking place in them.

DISCUSSION

Since IS has been highly valued worldwide, several researchers have proposed it as a prerequisite for achieving intercultural competence (Chen and Starosta, 2000; Hammer, Bennet and Wiseman, 2003). In Chen and Starosta's (2000) study, IS was found not only to be crucial for enabling people to become successful global citizens but also to be a predictor of intercultural competence (Wu, 2015).

Numerous empirical studies have revealed that the development of IS is associated with various sociocultural, social–psychological, personality and individual determinants (Rodríguez-Izquierdo, 2022). There is abundant evidence that international experience, such as studying abroad, is a key way in which an IS can be developed (Olson & Kroeger, 2001; Anderson et al., 2006; Tarchi et al, 2019). However, it has long been recognized that it is fully possible to study abroad without truly experiencing culture (Lantz-Deaton, 2017). Unless students' reflective processes are explicitly fostered, their exposure to cultural differences does not necessarily increase their intercultural understanding (Vande et al. 2012). There are many variables that impact IS development, such as initial levels of intercultural competence (Anderson et al. 2006), staff qualifications for an international classroom (Tekkens, 2003) or reflective and meeting opportunities offered by host and local institutions before departure and prereturn (Vande et al. 2012).

The participants, despite their varied backgrounds, share similar experiences, noting that good language skills and prior international exposure facilitate intercultural interactions. Fantini (2019) emphasized that language fluency enhances cultural understanding. Initial experiences can be challenging, often marked by homesickness and the idealization of one's home culture, complicating relationship-building with locals. Personal support from both home and within the host country is critical for positive self-identity development.

Despite this, first moments are often difficult and are especially marked by a disenchantment with what they expected and what they found. There is a tendency to miss home, idealizing and comparing everything: culture, food, and people. Thus, there is a tendency to generalize: "British people are like that...". Once they arrive, forming meaningful relationships is key. Personal support (from home and in the UK) is the most important aspect of achieving a positive perception of the experience abroad and its own role, which impacts positive self-identity development.

Forming close relationships can be hard with British people (perhaps this is specific to Britain, or perhaps it is always harder with the host nation as they are more settled into their lives), so an international environment is fundamental to a positive environment to develop IS. Friendships enable one to 'lower the volume' of one's own culture and be more inclined to make an effort to understand other perspectives. Social support and coping strategies help mitigate acculturative stress (Yeh & Inose, 2003). A diverse environment enhances the overall experience, whereas a lack of cultural partners can hinder adaptation.

The more international or intercultural an environment is, the more positive the feeling about the experience. Being the only international student in a local context complicates cultural differences. Finding people with a shared culture or language at the beginning was another source of help for those who had less prior experience or lower language skills. These "cultural partners" could take on a role, at least at the beginning, as support to interact with the difference.

For participants, universities play an important role in supporting students in finding a community. Universities were seen to be very international places, which was great but also, owing to culture and structures, could be very lonely, and not enough was done to facilitate the making of friends (this tended to be done in informal settings and rarely in the classroom). Mixing with others and lowering the volume of their own culture was a positive step. This idea of self-regulation connects with that of Tabor and Milfont (2019), who reported that students with high levels of emotional intelligence and a growth mindset toward cultural learning exhibited better academic and social adjustment in their studies abroad.

Social relations are not only the main element of good integration but also the most difficult. These are easy to manage on a superficial level, but going deeper is difficult. The fact that these relationships (especially with British people) were hard to find at the outset, perhaps meant that they had to work harder at the experience. This emotional engagement had an important impact on their process of acculturation. This finding aligns with that of Sawir et al. (2008), who examined the experiences of loneliness and social isolation among international students in Australia. This highlights the importance of social networks and extracurricular activities in mitigating feelings of loneliness. Sawir et al. (2008) suggested that universities should provide more opportunities for social interaction and emotional support to help international students integrate better into their new environments. In this sense, it would help if the university took a more active role in promoting interaction between students. However, real change occurs when prejudices are put aside on both sides. When this happens, something clicks, and suddenly, the whole experience takes on a different meaning and results in a new understanding of oneself as well. Self-knowledge and development of identity, maturity toward a feeling of being a global citizen, and development of IS.

There are several important personal factors, including the propensity to ask questions, the desire to learn about other cultures, and the ease of making friendships across cultures. This can be impacted by many factors in the environment. This is related to Gudykunst's dynamic theory of cross-cultural adaptation (2005). This model focuses on the interaction between an individual's cultural identity and the demands of the new environment. Gudykunst & Kim (2017) demonstrated that international students' ability to manage the tensions between their original cultural identity and new cultural expectations is crucial for successful adaptation.

The development of effective acculturation strategies is aided by relationships. The emotional element is fundamental, along with reflection on the role of oneself in the context. Reflection on the meaning of experience and relationships plays a fundamental role in understanding new identities as intercultural people. Not a new identity but a deepening of some values or getting to know yourself better, in different ways, getting to know one's own culture better, and yet increasing self-confidence to face intercultural environments and perhaps broader life challenges. An intercultural environment does not always have a large effect on identity change but rather promotes self-reflection. The participants related that, at first, the other culture "serves" as a constant comparison; if there is a positive change in one's identity, the cultural difference complements who I am. It seems that the development of resilience (Smith & Khawaja, 2021) is a key protective factor that helps students manage loneliness and adapt to academic life abroad.

There is something key to say about the development of confidence as core to the process and the development of openness to difference and becoming less judgmental. Also on reflecting on who they are and their own cultures. This reflection is an important process; whether it happens during the experience or when the person comes back home, it is indispensable. This connects with Deardorff's framework for intercultural competence (2006), which proposes a model of intercultural competence that includes attitudes, knowledge, and skills, emphasizing the importance of self-reflection and evaluation in the development of intercultural competence.

CONCLUSIONS

The issues discussed here highlight the significant social value of addressing the integration of international students, a priority for countries welcoming increasing numbers. Ensuring smooth integration and intercultural experiences is vital for fostering understanding and nurturing global citizens (William et al., 2024). This research emphasizes the often-overlooked affective dimension of intercultural competence (Spitzberg & Changnon, 2009).

Despite extensive research on factors influencing intercultural sensitivity (IS), inconsistent results indicate a need for further investigation (Rodríguez-Izquierdo, 2022). The current literature tends to focus on short-term study abroad rather than long-term settlement experiences, which involve community participation and assimilation as keys to developing IS.

Previous studies have emphasized primarily the cognitive dimensions of acculturation (Sanhuenza & Cardona, 2009), often neglecting the emotional aspects crucial for forming cross-cultural relationships. The development of intercultural competence involves transforming one's identity, values, self-confidence, and perspectives (Arthur, 2000). Qualitative methods should be employed to explore how immigrants navigate their cultural orientations and integrate cultural schemas (Chirkov, 2009; Ward, 2008). It is essential to highlight participants' experiences, as research has often concentrated on dominant cultures (Touraine et al., 2004).

Our study focuses on Latin American students in the UK, aiming to understand their views on status and identity. This evidence can inform the design of programs to enhance affective intercultural competence, improving interactions in culturally diverse environments such as UK higher education.

The results show that emotions significantly influence the study-abroad experience, affecting self-discovery and cultural openness. Building close relationships is vital for acculturation, unlocking new perspectives. While international environments can facilitate this, students often initially gravitate toward familiarity, with deeper learning occurring when they confront their biases.

The study suggests further exploration of the development of intercultural sensitivity among local populations, as the responsibility for integration should not rest solely on newcomers (Qu & Song, 2024). High intercultural competence in international students will not suffice without engagement from host communities.

The findings indicate that Allport's contact hypothesis is insufficient for developing IS. In contrast to the "immersion assumption" (Vande et al. 2012), the presence of cultural diversity on campuses does not automatically lead to intercultural contact (Mostafaei and Nosrati, 2018). This "illusion of internationalization" (Harrison and Peacock, 2010) and "immersion myth" (Jackon, 2018) hinder many international students from establishing relationships with national students. Many international students tend to connect primarily with peers of their own nationality, highlighting the necessity of facilitated interaction, as the literature and our results have shown (He, Lundgren & Pynes, 2017).

In conclusion, the literature and our results demonstrate that emotional regulation is critical for international students, who often face stress, anxiety, and loneliness as they adapt to new cultural and academic environments. Emotional intelligence (of both sides), coupled with a positive attitude toward cultural learning, facilitates better adjustment. Self-regulation and emotional regulation are necessary not only for personal well-being but also for social interaction and academic performance. Educational institutions could foster intercultural competence by incorporating reflective practices and intercultural training programs into their curricula. These orientation programs will be interesting for international and local students and should include components that strengthen resilience and provide specific strategies for coping with loneliness, which are crucial for emotional and social adaptation.

Acknowledgment

We thank the participants and the University of York for funding the transcription assistance. In the preparation of this manuscript, we did not utilize artificial intelligence (AI) tools for content creation.

REFERENCES

Anderson, P. H., Lawton, L., Rexeisen, R. J. & Hubbard, A. C., (2006). Short-term study abroad and intercultural sensitivity: A pilot study. International *Journal of Intercultural Relations, 30*, 457-469.

Arnett, J. J., (2011). Emerging Adulthood(s). The Cultural Psychology of a New Life Stage, in L. A. Jensen (Ed.), *Bridging Cultural and Developmental Approaches of psychology* (pp. 254-275), (University Press).

Arthur, N., (2000). Predictive characteristics of multicultural counseling competence. *Annual conference of the American Educational Research Association*. (Nueva Orleans, LA, abril 24-28) (paper). ERIC#: ED440338.)

Blair, L., (2019). Latin Americans are one of the UK's fastest-growing groups. https://www.newstatesman.com/politics/2019/12/latin-americans-are-one-of-the-uks-fastest-growing-groups-so-why-arent-they-recognized

Downing, J. & Husband Ch., (2002). Comunicación Intercultural, Multiculturalismo y Desigualdad Social. Ponencia presentada en el Congreso de la IAMCR 2002. Barcelona 21-26 de julio 2002.

Eguiluz, I., (2017). Migrantes latinoamericanos en Madrid: percepciones y significados sobre reproducción y sexualidad. http://eprints.ucm.es/42556/.

Creswell, J. W. (2003). *Research Design: Qualitative, Quantitative, and Mixed Methods Approaches* (2ª ed.). Sage Publications.

Chen, G., (1997). A review of the concept of intercultural sensitivity. Biennial Convention of the Pacific and Asian Communication Association, Honolulu

Chen, G. M. & Starosta, W. J., (2000). The development and validation of the intercultural communication sensitivity scale, *Human Communication, 3, 1-15.*

Chirkov, V., (2009). Critical psychology of acculturation: What do we study and how do we study it, when we investigate acculturation?, *International Journal of Intercultural Relations 33*, 94–105.

Converse, M., (2012). Philosophy of phenomenology: How understanding aids research, *Nurse Researcher, 20*(1), 28–32.

Giorgi, A., & Giorgi, B., (2003). P*henomenology* (Sage, California).

Hammer, M. R., Bennett, M. J., & Wiseman, R., (2003). Measuring intercultural sensitivity: The Intercultural Development Inventory, International *Journal of Intercultural Relations, 27*(4), 421–443. https://doi.org/10.1016/S0147-1767(03)00032-4

Harrison, N., & Peacock, N. (2010). Cultural distance, mindfulness and passive xenophobia: using integrated threat theory to explore home Higher Education students' perspectives on 'internationalization at home'. *British Educational Research Journal, 36*(6), 877-902. https://doi.org/10.1080/01411920903191047

He, Y., Lundgren, K., & Pynes, P. (2017). Impact of short-term study abroad program: Inservice teachers' development of intercultural competence and pedagogical beliefs. *Teaching and Teacher Education, 66*, 147-157. https://doi.org/10.1016/j. tate.2017.04.012

Lantz-Deaton, C. (2017). Internationalization and the development of students' intercultural competence. *Teaching in Higher Education, 22*(5), 532-550. https://doi.org/10.1080/13562 517.2016.1273209

Lester, J. N., Cho, Y., & Lochmiller, C. R., (2020). Learning to do qualitative data analysis: a starting point, *Human Resource Development Review, 19*(1), 94–106. https://doi.org/10.1177/1534484320903890.

McIlwaine, C., Cock, J. & Linneker, B., (2011). *No Longer Invisible: the Latin American community in London,* University of London, London).

McIlwaine, C. and Bunge, D. (2016). *Toward Visibility*. QMUL, London.

Mostafaei, M., & Nosrati, F. (2018). Research into EFL teachers' intercultural communicative competence and intercultural sensitivity. *Journal of Intercultural Communication Research,* 47(2), 73-86. https://doi.org/10.1080/1747575 9.2018.1424020

Olson, C.L. & Kroeger, K. R., (2001). Global competency and intercultural sensitivity, Journal of Studies in International Education, 5(2), 116-137.

Passiatore, Y., Pirchio, S., Carrus, G. et al.,(2019). Intercultural practices and inclusive education in Europe: can migration be a resource for individual and societal development?, *European Journal Psychol Education 34*, 209–224. https://doi.org/10.1007/s10212-017-0360-y

Qu, M. & Song, X. (2024). We have to change; they stay the same: Chinese international students' academic experiences at an Australian university. *Journal of International Students, 14*(3), 171-191. https://www.ojed.org/index.php/jis/article/view/6466/2881

Rodríguez-Izquierdo, R.M. (2022). International experiences and the development of intercultural sensitivity among university students. *Educación XX1*, 25(1), 93-117. https://doi. org/10.5944/educXX1.30143

Sanhuenza, S. & Cardona, C., (2009). Evaluación de la sensibilidad intercultural en alumnado de educación primaria escolarizado en aulas culturalmente diversas, Revista de Investigación Educativa, 27(1), 247-262.

Spitzberg, B. H., & Changnon, G., (2009). Conceptualizing intercultural competence., in D. K. Deardorff (Ed.), *The SAGE handbook of intercultural competence* (pp. 2–52), (Sage, California).

Vande, B., Paige, M. & Hemmeng, K., (2012). *Student Learning Abroad: What Our Students Are Learning, What They're Not and What You Can Do About It,* (Virginia: Stylus Publishing).

Vilà, R., (2006). La dimensión afectiva de la competencia comunicativa intercultural en la Educación Secundaria Obligatoria: Escala de Sensibilidad Intercultural, *Revista de Investigación Educativa, 24*(2), 353-372.

Weber, M., (1949). The methodology of the social sciences, (The Free Press).

William, S., Peters, K., & Hegazi, I. (2024). A Qualitative Exploration of Challenges for International Students Enrolled in Health Professional Education Degrees in Australia. *Journal of International Students, 14*(3), 468–490. https://doi.org/10.32674/jis.v14i3.6822

Tarchi, C., Surian, A & Daiute, C., (2019). Assessing study abroad students' intercultural sensitivity with narratives, *European Journal of Psychology of Education, 34,* 873–894 https://doi.org/10.1007/s10212-019-00417-9

Bennett, M. J. (2013). *Basic Concepts of Intercultural Communication: Paradigms, Principles, and Practices.* Intercultural Press.

Tabor, A. S., & Milfont, T. L. (2019). Predictors of Psychological and Sociocultural Adjustment among International Students: Emotional Intelligence, Intercultural Competence, and Resilience. *Journal of Intercultural Relations, 72*, 127-138.

Fantini, A. E. (2019). Intercultural Communicative Competence in Educational Exchange: A Multinational Perspective. Routledge.

Gross, J. J. (2015). Emotion Regulation: Current Status and Future Prospects. *Psychological Inquiry, 26*(1), 1-26.

Gudykunst, W. B., & Kim, Y. Y. (2017). *Communicating with Strangers: An Approach to Intercultural Communication.* McGraw-Hill.

Matsumoto, D., Hirayama, S., & LeRoux, J. A. (2017). Emotion Regulation in Cross-Cultural Contexts. *Handbook of Emotion Regulation* (2nd ed.). Guilford Press.

Smith, R. A., & Khawaja, N. G. (2021). A Review of the Psychological and Social Challenges Faced by International Students: Acculturation, Coping, and Mental Health. *Journal of International Students, 11(*1), 4-20.

Bennett, M. J. (1993). Toward Ethnorelativism: A Developmental Model of Intercultural Sensitivity. In R. M. Paige (Ed.), *Education for the Intercultural Experience*. Intercultural Press.

Deardorff, D. K. (2006). Identification and Assessment of Intercultural Competence as a Student Outcome of Internationalization. *Journal of Studies in International Education, 10*(3), 241-266.

Hammer, M. R., Bennett, M. J., & Wiseman, R. (2003). Measuring Intercultural Sensitivity: The Intercultural Development Inventory. *International Journal of Intercultural Relations, 27*(4), 421-443.

Kim, Y. Y. (2001). *Becoming Intercultural: An Integrative Theory of Communication and Cross-Cultural Adaptation.* Sage Publications.

Lazarus, R. S., & Folkman, S. (1984). *Stress, Appraisal, and Coping*. Springer

Poyrazli, S., Arbona, C., Bullington, R., & Pisecco, S. (2001). Adjustment Issues of Turkish College Students Studying in the United States. *College Student Journal, 35*(1), 52-62.

Sawir, E., Marginson, S., Deumert, A., Nyland, C., & Ramia, G. (2008). Loneliness and International Students: An Australian Study. *Journal of Studies in International Education, 12(*2), 148-180.

Ward, C., Bochner, S., & Furnham, A. (2001). *The Psychology of Culture Shock.* Routledge.

Yeh, C. J., & Inose, M. (2003). International Students' Reported English Fluency, Social Support Satisfaction, and Social Connectedness as Predictors of Acculturative Stress. *Counseling Psychology Quarterly, 16(1*), 15-28.

Author bios

SARAH CARRICA-OCHOA, Pedagogue and Educational Psychologist (2011, University of Navarra, UN) and International Doctorate in Pedagogy (Cum Laude, 2015, UN). I have 2 years of professional experience as an educator in centers for minors in situations of conflict/social risk (Ilundain Haritz-Berri Foundation). Currently, I am a professor at the Faculty of Education and Psychology (University of Navarra). My research line, within social pedagogy, focuses on how to improve—from an inclusive approach centered on achieving social justice—socioeducational care for groups at risk of social exclusion, mainly youth. Email: scarrica@unav.es

ELEANOR JOANE BROWN, Senior Lecturer in Education and Social Justice, has worked in the Department of Education of the University of York since September 2013. My primary research interests are in global development and global citizenship education, social justice and transformative learning, formal and nonformal educational settings, and social movements and communities. I am particularly interested in critical, participative and decolonizing approaches to knowledge and understanding and alternative spaces for learning. Email: eleanor.brown@york.ac.uk

Article

Journal of International Students
Volume 14, Issue 5 (2024), pp. 109-123
ISSN: 2162-3104 (Print), 2166-3750 (Online)
jistudents.org

Navigating the Unknown: College Transitions of Third Culture Individuals

Justin Weller
Michigan State University, USA

ABSTRACT

Research on third-culture individuals (TCIs) is an emerging topic in college student development. However, while emerging literature on TCIs exists, research on TCIs' personal development in postsecondary contexts is still lacking. This literature review addresses this issue. In this review, I argue that the literature predominantly illustrates that TCIs experience a negative transition to college that negatively impacts their personal development. I then synthesize the literature, identifying the background of the research surrounding TCIs. Next, I summarize the four main themes that the literature identifies as struggles that TCIs experience while transitioning into college: family, social connections, mental well-being, and identity construction. I then highlight the important contribution that resilience has to TCIs' lives in college. I conclude by arguing that recommendations from the literature and practice should be adopted by all postsecondary institutions to better support TCIs.

Keywords: Third-culture individuals, identity development, higher education

In 2004, Mark Waters released the award-winning movie *Mean Girls*, a household classic for many Americans. While *Mean Girls* is undoubtedly a comedic film that illustrates how female-identifying high school students navigate the social hierarchy of the "girl world," it is also a story about a third culture individual (TCI)—Cady Heron—transitioning into her parents' culture after living on the African continent for most of her life. Cady experiences several challenges transitioning into high school, such as social isolation, missing cultural context from her peers, and missing friends she made abroad, among other challenges (Waters, 2004).

A woman's experience is not an anomaly. In fact, many TCIs experience similar challenges as they transition from their cultural upbringings to college. In this review, I argue that the literature predominantly illustrates that TCIs experience a negative transition to college that negatively impacts their personal development, utilizing the theoretical framework developed by Purnell and Hoban (2014). I conclude by arguing that institutional recommendations from the literature and practice should be adopted by all postsecondary institutions to better support TCIs.

UNDERSTANDING TCIS: SYNTHESIS OF THE LITERATURE

Background of TCIs

Before I begin discussing the literature, it is paramount that I define who TCIs[1] are. TCIs, as a subpopulation of international students, diverge from the traditional definition of international students because they "are not a monolithic group" (Trimpe, 2022, p. 1023). While there is scholarly debate on who constitutes a TCI, most researchers use Pollack et al.'s (2017) definition of TCIs, which are students who "grow up (or grew up) outside their parents' passport country and culture for many different reasons" (Pollack et al., 2017, p. 4). TCIs are often children of parents who are diplomats, armed service members, missionaries, and work in international business (Pollack et al., 2017). Some researchers have an expansive definition of TCIs, arguing that the definition includes "refugee[s], asylum seeker[s], [and]...migrant[s]" (Murphy-Lejune, 2002, p. 101). Pollack et al. (2017) and Muphy-Lejune (2002) both agree, however, that TCIs are students who are integrated into their parents' passport country after spending significant time abroad, developing multiple identities.

Useem et al. (1963) first coined the term "third culture" to describe how children develop outside of their parents' culture (i.e., the primary world) and the cultures they grow up in (i.e., the secondary world). The term "third culture" describes how TCIs form their own integrated world (i.e., the tertiary world) in relation to their primary and secondary worlds (Useem et al., 1963). Because TCIs often live in several countries and are brought up in many different cultural environments, TCIs often have great social perspective-taking skills (Williams, 2023), which is the ability to take many other perspectives outside of one's worldview (Selman, 1980). TCIs are often interculturally sensitive and open-minded because of their experiences growing up in multicultural worlds (De Waal & Born, 2020). TCIs are also multilinguistic, a skill they develop from living in multiple cultures (Abdalla, 2024; Tannenbaum & Tseng, 2015).

---

[1] While terminology, such as "third culture kid" (TCK), exists, I utilize the term "third culture individual" in this literature review. The term "TCK" may be appropriate in other contexts, but this literature review seeks to understand the experiences of third culture individuals in postsecondary contexts, making the term TCK infantilizing toward the TCI community, as many TCIs function beyond their childhood in their postsecondary status.

Context of Research on TCIs

Despite there being over 200,000,000 TCIs globally (Iyer, 2013), research on TCIs is lacking, primarily because the population is misunderstood and overlooked in the literature (Thurston–Gonzalez, 2009). Much of the literature on TCIs illustrates that TCIs thrive in academic spaces (Tajibayeva et al., 2023; Useem & Cotrell, 1993). However, it is important to note that TCIs are not monolithic and may struggle academically in college. In fact, researchers have found that not only do TCIs stop out of college (Pollock et al., 2017), they do so because they feel that institutions do not understand them and that they do not belong (Smith, 2011). Because belonging is a crucial variable that mediates student persistence in higher education (Gopalan & Brady, 2019; Strayhorn, 2019), it is a topic of primary concern for higher education administrators.

In addition, much of the literature focuses on children of white, Christian missionaries of the Global North. This focus problematizes how applicable research can be applied to TCIs of the global majority, interfaith TCIs, etc. New research must be developed to understand how TCIs of historically minoritized identities develop in college. With that said, emerging research is beginning to develop that is focused on TCIs from the Global South, particularly in Central East, South, Southeast, and Southwest Asia.[2]

Because there is a gap in the literature on how TCIs develop in postsecondary settings, the purpose of this literature review is to understand how TCIs develop in colleges. I do so by reviewing specific elements of TCIs' postsecondary development that have been documented in the literature. Important aspects of TCIs include how TCIs find communities on campus, what support systems TCIs have while in college, and how TCIs identify in college. By understanding how TCIs develop in postsecondary contexts, higher education administrators can better serve this important population.

THEORETICAL FRAMEWORK

The theoretical framework underlying this literature review is the Third Culture Kid Transition into University Model, developed by Purnell and Hoban (2014). In Purnell and Hoban's (2014) original study, the model described the experiences of 12 TCIs transitioning into postsecondary institutions in Australia. This model describes how TCIs transition into colleges, making this model an important framework for this literature review.

This quadripartite model describes how TCIs' childhood and early adult experiences shape their experiences in postsecondary contexts. The first stage is

---

[2] I use the term "Southwest Asia" in this literature review to describe the region formally referred to as the "Middle East." This use of terminology reflects the transition away from the Orientalist linguistic practice of describing the world in relation to the West (i.e., "Far East," "East Indies") (Bishara, 2023). By transitioning away from Orientalist terminology, I offer a decolonial approach to academic discourse.

the preparation stage, in which TCIs begin moving to their parents' country of origin (Purnell & Hoban, 2014). In this stage, TCIs may grieve of the loss of experiences made abroad and begin researching the context of their parents' passport country to prepare them for university (Purnell & Hoban, 2014). The second stage is the initial transition stage, in which TCIs begin navigating their parents' passport country (Purnell & Hoban, 2014). In this stage, the reality of living in their parents' passport country creates culture shocks for TCIs (Purnell & Hoban, 2014). Aside from the natural realities of navigating early adulthood, TCIs may feel that excitement integrates into the populace but disengages from their peers at the institution they attend (Purnell & Hoban, 2014). This stage lasts approximately six months after arrival (Purnell & Hoban, 2014). The third stage is the adaptation stage, in which TCIs begin developing strategies to adjust to their new cultural setting (Purnell & Hoban, 2014). In this stage, TCIs "settled into" their new environment at the university and developed routines in their social life yet still feel disengaged from their peers (Purnell & Hoban, 2014). This stage lasts approximately six months to two years after arrival (Purnell & Hoban, 2014). The fourth and final stage is the stabilization stage, in which TCIs have acclimated to their university experience (Purnell & Hoban, 2014). In this stage, TCIs recognize that while they have found connections in their new environment, the desire to seek connections abroad is alive for TCIs (Purnell & Hoban, 2014). TCIs also begin seeking professional mental health services in this stage (Purnell & Hoban, 2014). This stage lasts approximately two years or more after arrival (Purnell & Hoban, 2014). Overall, this model provides a practical overview sufficient to analyze the developmental experiences of TCIs in postsecondary contexts.

RESEARCH INSIGHTS

While the literature has many different insights applicable to TCIs, I focus on four specific areas that impact TCIs: familial support systems, friendships and social relationships, mental well-being, and identity development. These areas are not the only challenges that affect TCIs in college but are the four most recurring challenges that the literature identifies TCIs face. Moreover, I highlight how resilience plays a role in TCIs' experiences in college.

Family

The first conclusive insight that the literature illustrates is that family plays a critical role in a TCI's life. Family is at the core of TCIs' identity, as their transition from one place to another is centered around familial decisions. Accordingly, TCIs need familial support as part of their transition into college. For example, Huff (2001) reported that family presence is positively correlated with TCI adjustment because parents help prepare their students for the cultural norms of college. Without social preparation from their parents, TCIs find it difficult to navigate collegiate cultural norms (Purnell & Hoban, 2014), just like Cady in Mean Girls found it difficult to understand social cues in high school. Similarly, Lijadi and van Schalkwyk (2014) reported that families play a critical and paramount role in socializing TCIs in college because families provide the most stability in the lives of TCIs. For example, in that study, participants reported that families had been present at critical moments in TCIs' lives, whereas friends and other peers were temporary connections compared with the longevity of familial relationships (Lijadi & van Schalkwyk, 2014). Additionally, Ra et al. (2023) reported that the relationships that TCIs had with their family helped them adapt to their institutional setting. For example, families help prepare TCIs for the college application process (Williams, 2023). Overall, we find that families play a significant role in the lives of TCIs as they transition into college.

Social Connections

With respect to social connections, the literature illustrates divergent findings concerning TCIs' personal development. Choi et al. (2013) identified two main types of friendships that TCIs develop in college: (1) functional connections and (2) social and emotional connections. Functional friendships are friendships that serve a purpose outside of the social and emotional realm (Choi et al., 2013). Conversely, social and emotional friendships are friendships with deeper connections (Choi et al., 2013). TCIs develop functional connections before developing social and emotional connections because doing so serves as a protective strategy (Choi & Luke, 2011). TCIs fear the grief that stems from losing deep friendships, a symptom of past traumatic transitions, and thereby keep friends at a distance to avoid these negative emotions (Choi & Luke, 2011; Lijadi & van Schalkwyk, 2014; Purnell & Hoban, 2014). Additionally, Smith and Kearney (2016) reported that TCIs shift their personalities to the social context they need to serve. TCIs do not form friendships with non-TCIs, as non-TCIs do not share the same experiences with TCIs, thus lacking the affinity necessary to form close attachments (Choi & Luke, 2011; Mizutani & Waalkes, 2023; Firmin et al., 2006). Overall, while TCIs desire friendships, forming intimate connections may be difficult on the basis of their traumatic experiences of cultural transitions abroad (Choi & Luke, 2011; Moore & Barker, 2012).

TCIs who formed social and emotional friendships did so primarily with other TCIs or with students from backgrounds of cultures they experienced in their childhood. For example, researchers have reported positive transitions to college when TCIs bond with other TCIs (Hervey, 2009; Lijadi & van Schalkwyk, 2014; Mizutani & Waalkes, 2023; Smith & Kearney, 2016). In addition, Hervey (2009) reported that TCIs also make rich connections with other students from the countries they lived in during their upbringing. TCIs look for relationships that foster uniqueness and independence, as TCIs are instilled with independence from a young age (Choi et al., 2013; Williams, 2023). By forming connections that foster uniqueness and independence, TCIs are able to grow in close friendships.

However, friendships were not always associated with positivity. For example, Purnell and Hoban (2014) reported that while TCIs did make friendships with other TCIs, some TCIs avoided developing social and emotional intimacy because of the alcohol culture associated with the universities in the study. Moreover, because TCIs prefer independence, they may not desire to form social connections at all, which can contribute to social isolation (Downie, 1976; Gaw, 2000).

Accordingly, social relationships are often a component of engagement in college student development (Astin, 1984). TCIs' level of engagement in college has mixed findings, however. On the one hand, Ra et al. (2023) reported that extracurricular activities and service-learning opportunities were important parts of putting academic coursework into practice and establishing a sense of belonging on campus. Moreover, Tyler (2002) reported that—in the context of high school students—TCIs were able to make friends when they were placed in extracurricular settings that matched similar interests with newly made friends. However, Espada–Campos (2018) reported that TCIs may not seek out cultural extracurricular activities in college because of the stigma of not belonging on campus, especially if TCIs do not share a cultural heritage with a cultural group on campus despite spending extensive time with that culture in their formative years of development. Overall, friendships made in college serve multiple purposes, depending on the context of the situation. In addition, TCIs' involvement in undergraduate activities has a positive effect on their personal development, but perceived barriers may still exist.

Mental Well-Being

Mental well-being is an area of transition in college that TCIs may especially struggle with. As TCIs move from one place to another, the constant state of transition during TCIs' most formative years of identity often causes mental well-being struggles (Melles & Frey, 2014). When TCIs enter college, these mental well-being struggles can persist and may even increase.

The literature shows that TCIs experience mental well-being struggles, such as anxiety and depression, in their transitions into college (Gaw, 2000; Habeeb & Hamid, 2021; Lijadi & van Schalkwyk, 2014; Purnell & Hoban, 2014; Smith & Kearney, 2016). However, the explanations for why students experience these mental well-being struggles are different. One reason is that, for some TCIs, mental well-being struggles are a natural part of the acculturation process, where reverse culture shock, the ability to orient oneself back to one's home culture, causes significant challenges to a TCI's psychosocial health (Gaw, 2000; Hervey, 2009; Huff, 2001; Lijadi & van Schalkwyk, 2014). This may be temporary, in which TCIs eventually adapt and integrate their past experiences into college (Lijadi & Van Schalkwyk, 2014). However, some never recover from reverse culture shock and never reach stable well-being (Purnell & Hoban, 2014).

Another possible explanation for the decline in mental well-being is that some TCIs feel homesick and cannot adapt to the new cultural environment (Hervey, 2009). Homesickness over their past lives involves a significant acculturative challenge where TCIs miss the friends, family, and environments in which they grew up (Hervey, 2009). For other TCIs, adapting to their parents' cultural environment functions as a new culture in which they never grew up, thus causing acculturative challenges. For example, Habeeb and Hamid (2021) reported that the orientation to a Western culture that values individualism from an Eastern culture that values collectivism contributed to TCIs' depressive symptoms.

The last possible explanation documented in the literature is childhood attachment issues that manifest in college. Attachment theory argues that the ability to form social connections in adulthood can be explained by the attachment one has to one's caretaker in childhood and adolescence (Bowlby, 1982). Mortimer (2010) argues that because TCIs grow up experiencing multiple abrupt transitions in life, they develop dismissive-avoidant and fearful-avoidant attachment styles, which, in turn, prevent TCIs from developing secure relationships. These attachment styles may cause TCIs to experience mental well-being struggles where TCIs may strive for deeper connections with others but do not invest in connections in the case of another transition in one's life, increasing psychosocial stress (Hervey, 2009). Finally, Lijadi and van Schalkwyk (2014) reported that moving from one culture to another in early childhood left TCIs with abandonment wounds, thus influencing their experiences with mental well-being in college, such as interpersonal relationship conflict. Overall, the literature has demonstrated that TCIs may experience negative mental well-being struggles in colleges that can persist into adulthood.

Identity Construction

The formation of identity for TCIs transitioning into universities is multifaceted. The literature identifies themes related to the loss of cultural identity, discrimination, and self-identity. Beginning with the loss of cultural identity, researchers have found that TCIs struggle to identify where home is, as TCIs are in constant transition (Downie, 1976; Kortegast & Yount, 2016). As a result, because TCIs cannot identify where home is for themselves, they struggle to identify who they are (Downie, 1976). Moreover, Hervey (2009) reported that TCIs who had difficult and traumatic transitions during their early childhood experiences correlated positively with negative identity development into college. In addition, Fail et al. (2004) reported that TCIs can experience identity confusion in college when they are not well adjusted to institutions. However, recent research has shown that TCIs use acculturative strategies, such as finding elements of experiences abroad in a new environment, to renegotiate where home is for them (Kortegast & Young, 2016).

Research shows that TCIs' identity development can also be hampered by racial discrimination. For example, in Gambhir and Rhein's (2021) study on Indian TCIs in Thailand, TCIs described being questioned by their peers about their linguistic capabilities and racial identity in college. For example, TCIs who were born in India were asked why they spoke Thai so eloquently, which initially caused psychosocial stress but later displayed resiliency after such instances of discrimination (Gambhir & Rhein, 2021). In addition, Smith and Kearney (2016) reported that TCIs were socially excluded from their peers because cultural traditions formed abroad did not translate well into college. Moreover, Firmin et al. (2006) reported that TCIs often face stereotype threat in college. These challenges pose significant obstacles to identify construction and development for TCIs who are already entering a difficult transition in their lives.

While much of the literature has reported overall negative identity development in TCIs' transitions into college, it is also important to acknowledge that TCIs experience positive identity development in college. For example, while TCIs struggle to assimilate the host culture, TCIs identify with a multicultural identity and can communicate cross-culturally (Moore & Barker, 2012; Mortimer, 2010). Moreover, Habeeb and Hamid (2021) reported that TCIs often self-author their identity, often choose to identify outside or in addition to their passport country's heritage, and that self-authorship is crucial for success in college. Overall, identity development is complex and fluid for TCIs, who identify with a multicultural identity in one instance but fail to identify themselves in other instances.

Resilience

However, TCIs develop resilience in postsecondary settings, despite the challenges they face. Resilience in TCIs is associated with an increased sense of adaptability surrounding life transitions, such as beginning postsecondary education, which reduces stressors during these transitions (Jones et al., 2023). In many cases, community and mentorship are critical factors that help TCIs develop resilience. For example, Espada-Campos (2018) and Weigel (2010) reported that TCIs identified communities among international student communities in colleges, fostering a positive peer support system when navigating the cultural transition to their parents' country of origin. In another study, Purnell and Hoban (2014) reported that a virtual mentoring program that centered on personal skill development was crucial for TCIs transitioning into institutions in their parents' passport country. Furthermore, Mizutani and Waalkes (2023) reported that TCIs in their study reported a sense of belonging when they connected with other students in colleges who had similar backgrounds and identities, corroborating literature findings that affinity is a critical necessity to feel a sense of belonging in collegiate settings (Astin, 1984; Cooper, 2009; Hurtado & Carter, 1997; Strayhorn, 2019; Tinto, 1993). In short, TCIs are complex students and develop strategies to cope with the challenges they face when they attend postsecondary institutions.

IMPLICATIONS

The findings from this literature review have several implications for higher education institutional practices. Beginning with the topic of familial support, because researchers have emphasized how crucial the role that family plays in the lives of TCIs, institutions must prioritize a familial approach to student support. Some institutions have taken a familial and collectivistic approach to student support before it has produced tangible results for first-generation college-going (first-generation) students. For example, when Stanford University evolved its approach to support first-generation students, such as sending acceptance letters using collectivistic and family-oriented language, first-generation students' performance in academic classes improved (Stephens et al., 2012). While this study focused on first-generation students, it is reasonable to expect similar results for TCIs, who are more likely to persist and succeed when families are engaged in the college-going process. Moreover, Marrun (2020) argues that, in the context of Latino/a/e/x/* student engagement, institutions should follow the approaches of the University of Illinois, Urbana Champaign (UIUC). UIUC implemented activities such as family weekends and established departmental offices for family engagement, which were successful for Latino/a/x/e/* students (Marrun, 2020). This translates well to TCIs, as families play similar yet critical roles in their students' sense of belonging on campus as Latino/a/x/e/* families do.

Institutions should similarly adopt familial approaches to help TCIs transition into universities. For example, similar to Marrun's (2020) research, institutions could implement family weekends during the semester to emphasize the relevance that families play in TCIs' lives. During these weekends, institutions hold events and informational sessions that emphasize the closeness of family, such as faculty-parent-student events, tours of the institution, and sporting events (Jurich et al., 2015). In addition, new student orientation departments could incorporate families as part of their students' transition into the university, such as designing informational sessions with families and students as opposed to separating families and students. Institutions, such as the University of Michigan (n.d.), have already implemented this approach. Thus, institutions should follow the approaches of the aforementioned institutions to replicate familial support for TCIs.

Another recommendation for institutions to consider is creating affinity spaces for TCIs to interact with other TCIs or international students of backgrounds that TCIs grew up with. The literature has demonstrated that involvement in extracurricular activities is correlated with TCIs' academic success (Ra et al., 2023). Thus, TCIs should be bonded with other TCIs and other international students to increase their sense of belonging on campus (Weigel, 2010). For example, Lewis & Clark College (2023) implemented the "Third Culture Kid Program" in 1992 to help other TCIs on campuses develop meaningful friendships with one another through social engagements, such as English tutoring programs and biweekly dinners. Spangler (2021) also recommends mentorship programs that link newly admitted TCI students with other TCI students at universities to help navigate the transition easier for TCIs. Programs such as this help establish spaces for TCIs to develop friendships with peers during difficult transitions in college that only TCIs can understand (Cranston, 2017). Programs such as these also positively impact TCIs' identity formation by relating to other TCIs who understand the collegiate challenge.

Another consideration for higher education institutions is the efficacy of transition programs for TCIs. Transition programs, or reentry programs, are programs meant to orient TCIs back to their passport country and help alleviate potential challenges TCIs face in their transition into college (Spangler, 2021). Orientation programs such as these significantly increase TCIs' self-efficacy and belonging to other TCIs on campus (Cranston, 2017; Davis et al., 2010). For example, Klemens and Bikos (2009) identified the student organization, Mu Kappa, in their study, which helps TCIs transition into college through programs such as retreats and campus activities. Purnell and Hoban (2014) identified "Sea Change" as the mentoring program for TCIs, which provides virtual mentoring and interpersonal development skills for incoming TCI students. As such, institutions must develop concrete and effective transition programs, such as programs as part of their orientation programs to ameliorate the challenges TCIs face in their transition into college.

Moreover, institutions need to respond to the mental well-being challenges that TCIs experience in college. It is clear from the literature that institutions are failing TCIs. To combat the mental well-being challenges that TCIs face on campus, Stultz (2003) argues that chief student affairs officers should prioritize training student affairs personnel on TCI experiences in college to better respond to TCIs' challenges. Institutions should prioritize diversity training on TCIs. Applied intervention strategies, such as diversity training, have been shown to reduce the prejudice of historically marginalized populations (Hanover & Cellar, 1998) and increase workplace humility (Smith & Silk, 2011). A lack of knowledge about TCIs from student affairs practitioners may lead TCIs to not engage with campus resources (see Pope et al., 2019). In the words of Mead (2021), "It is vital that student affairs divisions measure their effectiveness in helping students from underrepresented backgrounds succeed, while also using outcomes-based assessment to improve these efforts continually" (p. 120). Thus, institutions must train their student affairs personnel in TCI populations.

Ra et al. (2023) argued that institutions should invest in mental health offices on campus. Munn and Ryan (2016) further argued that institutional mental health departments must be trained to understand the mental well-being challenges that TCIs face in college. Spangler (2021) corroborates this, adding that institutional mental health departments need trauma-informed practices for TCIs, an area in which institutions are currently lacking. An example of a trauma-informed therapy practice that is effective for TCIs includes relational-cultural therapy, a therapeutic practice that acknowledges the cultural context of an individual's upbringing and emphasizes building relationships through interdependent growth (Jordan, 2018). In fact, this therapy was effective for TCIs to develop interpersonal relationships following the challenges they experienced in their upbringing (Melles & Frey, 2014). Institutions should employ similar practices in their mental health departments. Without these critical recommendations, TCIs are at risk of stopping college (Quick, 2010; Smith, 2011), causing retention concerns among this historically marginalized population within higher education.

Overall, these multidimensional recommendations are necessary to confront the concrete challenges that TCIs face in college. Without these necessary changes, TCIs will continue to navigate their social and developmental contexts in college with little to no institutional support. TCIs deserve better and more equitable environments in college so that they can thrive during some of the most formative years of their lives. The time has come for institutions to rise to this challenge.

Acknowledgment

This article incorporates content generated by artificial intelligence (AI) tools. The sections where AI tools were employed are the entire work for grammar and spelling review & organizing references. The use of AI tools complied with ethical standards and guidelines for academic integrity. The final content has been thoroughly reviewed and edited to ensure accuracy, relevance, and adherence to academic standards.

REFERENCES

Abdalla, F. M. A. (2024). Belonging as a post-secondary inter/national student. *Journal of International Students, 14*(4), 1047–1063. https://doi.org/10.32674/jis.v14i4.6438

Astin, A. W. (1984). Student involvement: A developmental theory for higher education. *Journal of College Student Personnel, 25*(1), 297–308.

Bishara, A. (2023). Decolonizing Middle East anthropology: Toward liberations in SWANA societies. *American Ethnologist, 50*(3), 396–408. https://doi.org/10.1111/amet.13200

Bowlby, J. (1982). *Attachment and loss* (2nd ed.). Basic Books.

Choi, K. M., Bernard, J. M., & Luke, M. (2013). Characteristics of friends of female college third culture kids. *Asia Pacific Journal of Counseling and Psychotherapy, 4*(2), 125–136. https://doi.org/10.1080/21507686.2013.779931

Choi, K. M. & Luke, M. (2011). A phenomenological approach to understanding early adult friendships of third culture kids. *Journal of Asia Pacific Counseling, 1*(1), 47–60. https://doi.org/10.18401/2011.1.1.4

Cooper, R. (2009). Constructing belonging in a diverse campus community. *Journal of College & Character, 10*(3). https://doi.org/10.2202/1940-1639.1085

Cranston, S. (2017). Self-help and the surfacing of identity: Producing the third culture kid. *Emotion, Space, and Society, 24*, 27–33. https://doi.org/10.1016/j.emospa.2017.07.006

Davis, P., Headley, K., Bazemore, T., Cervo, J., Sickinger, P., Windham, M., & Rehfuss, M. (2010). Evaluating impact of transition seminars on missionary kids' depression, anxiety, stress, and well-being. *Journal of Psychology and Theology, 38*(3), 186–194. https://doi.org/10.1177/009164711003800303

De Waal, M. F., & Born, M. P. (2020). Growing up among cultures: Intercultural competencies, personality, and leadership styles of third culture kids. *European Journal of International Management, 14*(2), 327–356. https://doi.org/10.1504/ejim.2020.10022259

Downie, R. D. (1976). Re-entry experiences and identity formation of third culture experienced dependent American youth: An exploratory study (Publication No. 7627089) [Doctoral dissertation, Michigan State University]. ProQuest Dissertations & Theses Global.

Espada–Campos, S. (2018). Third culture kids (TCKs) go to college: A retrospective narrative inquiry of international upbringing and collegiate engagement (Publication No. 12085378) [Doctoral dissertation, University of Pennsylvania]. University of Pennsylvania Doctorate in Social Work (DSW) Dissertations

Fail, H., Thomson, J., & Walker, G. (2004). Belonging, identity and third culture kids: Life histories of former international school students. *Journal of Research in International Education*, *3*(3), 319–338. https://doi.org/10.1177/1475240904047358

Firmin, M., Warner, S., & Lowe, A. (2006). Social adjustment among students growing up in foreign mission-field contexts. *Christian Higher Education*, *5*(2), 115–124. https://doi.org/10.1080/15363750500182711

Gambhir, R., & Rhein, D. (2021). A qualitative analysis of the repatriation of Thai-Indian third culture kids in Thailand. *Asian Ethnicity*, *22*(3), 464–480. https://doi.org/10.1080/14631369.2019.1661770

Gaw, K. F. (2000). Reverse culture shock in students returning from overseas. *International Journal of Intercultural Relations*, *24*(1), 83–104. https://doi.org/10.1016/S0147-1767(99)00024-3

Gopalan, M., & Brady, S. T. (2019). College students' sense of belonging: A national perspective. *Educational Researcher*, *49*(2), 134–137. https://doi.org/10.3102/0013189x19897622

Habeeb, H., & Hamid, A. A. R. M. (2021). Exploring the relationship between identity orientation and symptoms of depression among third culture kids college students. *International Journal of Instruction*, *14*(3), 999–1010. https://doi.org/10.29333/iji.2021.14358a

Hanover, J. M. B., & Cellar, D. F. (1998). Environmental factors and the effectiveness of workforce diversity training. *Human Resource Development Quarterly*, *9*(2), 105–124. https://doi.org/10.1002/hrdq.3920090203

Hervey, E. (2009). Cultural transitions during childhood and adjustment to college. *Journal of Psychology and Christianity*, *28*(1), 3–12.

Huff, J. L. (2001). Parental attachment, reverse culture shock, perceived social support, and college adjustment of missionary children. *Journal of Psychology and Theology*, *29*(3), 246–264. https://doi.org/10.1177/009164710102900307

Hurtado, S., & Carter, D. F. (1997). Effects of college transition and perceptions of the campus racial climate on Latino college students' sense of belonging. *Sociology of Education*, *70*(4), 324–345. https://doi.org/10.2307/2673270

Iyer, P. (2013, June). *Where is home* [Video]. TED Conferences. https://www.ted.com/talks/pico_iyer_where_is_home/transcript?language=en

Jones, E. E., Reed, M., Meyer A., H., Gaab, J., & Ooi, Y. P. (2023). Stress, mental health and sociocultural adjustment in third culture kids: Exploring the mediating roles of resilience and family functioning. *Frontiers in Psychology*, *14*. https://doi.org/10.3389/fpsyg.2023.1093046

Jordan, J. V. (2018). *Relational-cultural therapy* (2nd ed.). American Psychological Association. https://doi.org/10.1037/0000063-000

Jurich, J. A., Leite, R., & Chabot, J. (2015). Student perceptions of inappropriate parent behavior on "moms" and "dads" weekends. *Marriage & Family Review*, *51*(8), 730–752. https://doi.org/10.1080/01494929.2015.1085481

Klemens, M. J., & Bikos, L. H. (2009). Psychological well-being and sociocultural adaptation in college-aged, repatriated, missionary kids. *Mental Health, Religion, & Culture*, *12*(7), 721–733. https://doi.org/10.1080/13674670903032629

Kortegast, C., & Yount, E. M. (2016). Identity, family, and faith: U.S. third culture kids transition to college. *Journal of Student Affairs*, *53*(2), 230–242. https://doi.org/10.1080/19496591.2016.1121148

Lewis & Clark College. (2023). *Third culture kids/global nomads*. https://www.lclark.edu/offices/international/third_culture_kids/

Lijadi, A. A., & van Schalkwyk, G. J. (2014). Narratives of third culture kids: Commitment and reticence in social relationships. *The Qualitative Report*, *19*(49), 1–18. https://doi.org/10.46743/2160-3715/2014.1213

Marrun, N. A. (2020). "My mom seems to have a *dicho* for everything!": Family engagement in the college success of Latina/o students. *Journal of Latinos and Education*, *19*(2), 164–180. https://doi.org/10.1080/15348431.2018.1489811

Mead, R. (2021). Student affairs assessment: Measuring the effectiveness of assessment plans designed to shrink the academic equity gap. *Journal of Student Affairs*, *17*, 109–122. https://files.eric.ed.gov/fulltext/EJ1337101.pdf

Melles, E. A., & Frey, L. L. (2014). "Here, everybody moves": Using relational cultural therapy with adult third-culture kids. *International Journal for the Advancement of Counselling*, *36*, 348–358. https://doi.org/10.1007/s10447-014-9211-6

Mizutani, Y., & Waalkes, P. L. (2023). Experiences of Confucian Asian college students with third-culture-kid backgrounds. *International Journal for the Advancement of Counselling*. https://doi.org/10.1007/s10447-023-09533-0

Moore, A. M., & Barker, G. G. (2012). Confused or multicultural: Third culture individuals' cultural identity. *International Journal of Intercultural Relations*, *36*(4), 553–562. https://doi.org/10.1016/j.ijintrel.2011.11.002

Mortimer, M. (2010). Adult third culture kids: Common themes, relational struggles and therapeutic experiences (Publication No. 3428760) [Doctoral dissertation, Alliant International University, San Diego] ProQuest Dissertations & Theses Global.

Munn, S. K., & Ryan, T. G. (2016). An examination of mental health promotion within international schools and current reform practices that can benefit third culture kids. *International Journal of Educational Research*, *25*(2), 170–191. https://doi.org/10.1177/105678791602500204

Murphy-Lejune, E. (2002). An experience of interculturality: Student travellers abroad. In G. Alred, M. Byram, & M. Fleming. *Intercultural experience and education* (pp. 101–113). Multilingual Matters. https://doi.org/10.21832/9781853596087-010

Pollack, D. C., van Rekken, R. E., & Pollack, M. V. (2017). *Third culture kids: Growing up among worlds* (3rd ed.). Nicholas Brealey Publishing.

Pope, R. L., Reynolds, A. L., & Mueller, J. A. (2019). *Multicultural competence in student affairs: Advancing social justice & inclusion.* (2nd ed.). Jossey-Bass.

Purnell, L., & Hoban, E. (2014). The lived experiences of third culture kids transitioning into university life in Australia. *International Journal of Intercultural Relations, 41*(1), 80–90. https://doi.org/10.1016/j.ijintrel.2014.05.002

Quick, T. L. (2010). *The global nomad's guide to university transition.* Summertime Publishing.

Ra, Y., Ko., H., Cha, I., & Kim, H. (2023). A qualitative exploration on repatriate experiences of South Korean third culture kids in college. *Current Psychology*. https://doi.org/10.1007/s12144-023-04654-6

Selman, R. (1980). *Growth of interpersonal understanding: Developmental and clinical analysis.* Academic Press.

Smith, V. J. (2011). Third culture kids: Transition and persistence when repatriating to attend university (Publication No. 3495996) [Doctoral dissertation, Oklahoma State University] ProQuest Dissertations and Theses Global.

Smith, V. J., & Kearney, K. S. (2016). A qualitative exploration of the repatriation experiences of US third culture kids in college. *Journal of College Student Development, 57*(8), 958–972 https://doi.org/10.1353/csd.2016.0093

Smith, B. D., & Silk, K. (2011). Cultural competence clinic: An online, interactive, simulation for working effectively with Arab American Muslim patients. *Academic Psychiatry, 35*(5), 312–316. https://doi.org/10.1176/appi.ap.35.5.312

Spangler, K. R. (2021). The impact of repatriation on third culture kids and the role higher education institutions play in supporting repatriating students: A transcendental phenomenological study (Publication No. 3280) [Doctoral dissertation, Liberty University] Doctoral Dissertations and Projects.

Stephens, N. M., Fryberg, S. A., Markus, H. R., Johnson, C. S., & Covarrubias, R. (2012). Unseen disadvantage: How American universities' focus on independence undermines the academic performance of first-generation college students. *Journal of Personality and Social Psychology, 102*(6), 1178–1197. https://doi.org/10.1037/a0027143

Strayhorn, T. L. (2019). *College students' sense of belonging: A key to educational success for all students* (2nd ed.). Routledge. https://doi.org/10.4324/9781315297293

Stultz, W. (2003). Global and domestic nomads or third culture kids: Who are they and what the university needs to know. *Journal of Student Affairs, 12*(1), 81–90. https://citeseerx.ist.psu.edu/document?repid=rep1&type=pdf&doi=758a210d4b4c810fb4c92536b7ebc808a5a1af3f

Tajibayeva, Z., Nurgaliyeva, S., Aubakirova, K., Ladzina, N., Shaushekova, B., Yespolova, G., & Taurbekova, A. (2023). Investigation of the psychological, pedagogical and technological adaptation levels of repatriated university students. *International Journal of Education in Mathematics, Science, and Technology*, *11*(3), 755-774. https://doi.org/10.46328/ijemst.3336

Tannenbaum, M., & Tseng, J. (2015). Which one is Ithaca? Multilingualism and sense of identity among third culture kids. *International Journal of Multilingualism*, *12*(3), 276–297. https://doi.org/10.1080/14790718.2014.996154

Tinto, V. (1993). *Leaving college: Rethinking the causes and cures of student attrition.* (2nd ed.). University of Chicago Press.

Thurston–Gonzalez, S. J. (2009). *A qualitative investigation of the college choice experiences and reentry expectations of U.S. American third culture kids* (Publication No. 3367137) [Doctoral dissertation, Loyola University Chicago] ProQuest Dissertations & Theses Global.

Trimpe, M. L. (2022). Reimagining a model for international students' college readiness and transition. *Journal of International Students*, *12*(4), 1019–1025. https://doi.org/10.32674/jis.v12i4.4162

Tyler, M. P. (2002). The military teenager in Europe: Perspectives for health care providers. In M. Ender. *Military brats and other global nomads: Growing up in organization families* (pp. 25–34). Praeger.

University of Michigan. (n.d.). *Parents & family members.* Office of New Student Programs. https://onsp.umich.edu/orientation/parents-family-members

Useem, R. H., & Cotrell, A. B. (1993). TCKs four times more likely to earn bachelor's degrees. *Newslinks*, *12*(5). http://www.tckworld.com/useem/art2.html

Useem, J., Useem, R. H., & Donoghue, J. D. (1963). Men in the middle of the third culture: The roles of American and non-Western people in cross-cultural administration. *Human Organization*, *22*(3), 169–179. https://doi.org/10.17730/humo.22.3.5470n44338kk6733

Waters, M. (Director). (2004). *Mean girls* [Film]. Broadway Video; M. G. Films; Paramount Pictures.

Weigel, D. (2010). Third-culture students: An exploratory study of transition in the first year of college (Publication No. 3404298) [Doctoral dissertation, University of South Carolina] ProQuest Dissertations and Theses Global.

Williams, S. R. (2023). U.S. third culture kids' identity and college success. *International Journal of Intercultural Relations*, *94*(1), 101801. https://doi.org/10.1016/j.ijintrel.2023.101801

Author bio

Justin Weller is a second-year graduate student in the College of Education at Michigan State University, USA. His major research interests lie with international students, particularly with third-culture individuals, student activism, and global higher education policy review. Email: weller10@msu.edu

Article

Journal of International Students
Volume 14, Issue 5 (2024), pp. 125-140
ISSN: 2162-3104 (Print), 2166-3750 (Online)
jistudents.org

Internationalization in Architecture Higher Education: A Strategy of Studio Immersion from the Student Perspective

Rully Damayanti
Petra Christian University, Indonesia

Elvina Wijaya
Petra Christian University, Indonesia

Bram Michael Wayne
Petra Christian University, Indonesia

Apiradee Kasemsook
Silpakorn University, Thailand

Kuowei Eleazar-Godfrey Chiu
Tunghai University, Taiwan

ABSTRACT

Internationalization has become a requirement of higher education to adequately train future practitioners, including architects, in the global world. Studio immersion is an experimental type of curriculum and teaching where the studio is prepared, operated, and evaluated by educators and students from joined universities. In this paper, we investigate the perspective of students who have performed studio immersion, which consists of three Asian universities in batches 2022 and 2023, with a total of 147 students from Indonesia, Thailand, and Taiwan. We used mixed methods research to identify real obstacles and challenges and to determine to what extent this study benefits students. The results show that the students experience a progressive understanding of personal development, a broader meaning of architecture beyond technical and aesthetic systems but social and cultural, and an understanding of architecture as a multifaceted profession. The students reported their dissatisfaction with the pursuit of the university's reputation, studio dynamics, and uncertainty in the assignment's limitations. English interaction among students is not affected by their early exposure to English for their generation. This type of studio immersion could create a new studio culture that is unique to a global learning experience.

Keywords: Internationalization, higher education, school of architecture, studio immersion, studio culture

INTRODUCTION

Internationalization of Higher Education Institutions

The term internationalization in higher education (HE) is currently complicated, whether ad hoc or fragmented since many purposes and educational players are involved. HE institutions see internationalization as a large time and resource commitment, but it is necessary to prepare future practitioners for a globalized society (Dupre, 2022; Ostwald & Williams, 2008; Yeravdekar & Tiwari, 2014). Almost all universities mention this term as their strategy not only to attract international students but also to show that they are part of global education (Wit, 2020). It has also evolved into a commercial term to inform the public that the quality of their learning is global or world-class (Bamberger & Morris, 2023). The strategy goes beyond student mobility, as its early intention of internationalization, but includes international accreditation, international programs, international exposure, or international recognition (Zolfaghari et al., 2009). HE institutions have developed strategies that involve diverse educational activities that involve educators and students from different countries, which are becoming more international, intercultural and global (Knight, 2008; Knight & de Wit, 2018). It is also intended to achieve the HE vision or mission of becoming a global university. There is currently an increasing number of internationalization activities since the use of technology for distance learning (Dupre, 2022; Hou & Kang, 2006; Knight & de Wit, 2018).

Given the various internationalization activities carried out by HE, the question arises whether this provides direct benefits to students. On the basis of earlier studies related to students' perspectives, several benefits were found. The benefits include increased awareness and comprehension of various national and international issues, networking opportunities, the development of social and emotional intelligence, and the creation of income for the future (Hayle, 2008; Trinh & Conner, 2019). In brief, the students believe that internationalization can help them become more globally competent in fostering inclusivity and diversity. Furthermore, the primary barrier to internationalization implementation, particularly in Asia, is the low proficiency of instructors and students in English (Sutrisno, 2019; Tek et al., 2023; Trinh & Conner, 2019). It is believed that internationalization can reinforce Western-centric education by ignoring the differences and cultural diversity of each nation's educational system (Ng, 2012).

The success of internationalization in HE is determined from two directions: one that is strategic from the government and university authorities and the second from educators (Dupre, 2022). The authority factor includes regulation, financial, administrative, and infrastructure support from the university. Educators require leadership in terms of their ability and willingness to carry out internationalization (Dupre, 2022). Furthermore, the skills of educators and students are important for starting internationalization (Salama, 1999). A Cambodia-based study indicates that institutional leadership, policies, human resources, and institution type affect university internationalization achievement. Competency, networking opportunities, a sense of belonging, the nature of the profession, and demographic characteristics all influence educators' success levels (Tek et al., 2023). Data from Cambodia indicate that issues at the educator level and English ability were the cause of the internationalization handicaps.

Since the 1980s, internationalization in HE has become one of the strategies used to improve the awareness of students toward international exposure and strengthen the research and product knowledge of institutions in Asia Pacific. For example, in Indonesia, internationalization is accommodated by government regulations stated in the Constitution for Indonesia Higher Education Article 5 no. 12/2012 as a legal basis. The principles of internationalization include equality, respectfulness, the promotion of technological science, and human values, which refer to the interaction and integration of international dimensions in academic activity without losing their characteristic Indonesian values. The main strategy is to increase mobility in people, programs, and institutions (Mali, 2020). Although research on internationalization in Indonesian HEs has not been conducted much (Ota, 2023), it has practically been shown that educators' characteristics play a significant role in the successful implementation of internationalization in HE.

Internationalization in Architecture Education

Architecture education is a highly regulated sector internationally and nationally. To address professional, social, and cultural considerations, architecture education must have specific curriculum objectives, as mandated by the International Union of Architects/Union Internationale des Architects (UIAs). The primary goal of the UNESCO-UIA Charter for Architectural Education 2023 is to establish a global network of architectural education to address the challenges of the contemporary world ("UNESCO-UIA Charter for Architectural Education (Updated July 2023)," n.d.). At the national level, for example, the Indonesian Institute of Architects (IAI), a member of the UIA, must abide by UIA regulations, particularly those for educational goals. The goal is to equip young architects with nationally, regionally, and globally recognized competencies (*Berita IAI*, n.d.).

The core of the architecture curriculum is architectural design studio courses, which offer students continuously and progressively more advanced skills and integrated knowledge in architecture design during their studies. The design studio courses are key components where students practically apply design principles, spatial/form theory and techniques in defining architectural solutions. A studio is traditionally known as a place for students to apprentice to professional architects so that philosophical thoughts and ways to design can be shared with the apprentice (Hacihasanoglu, 2021; Webster, 2008). Currently, professional architects play their role as tutors, reviewers or jurors with the same function, which is to conduct the way of thinking of students.

This shift in professional architects' role is to respond to the contemporary approach of learning, which involves placing students at the center of learning, while teachers play the role of facilitators (Crowther, 2013). This situation makes students independent learners when the world is widely open in front of them (Yeravdekar & Tiwari, 2014). In addition, to respond to the behavior and characteristics of students, which are changing drastically, especially in the globalization era and information technology advancement (Crowther, 2013), the learning process in the design studio needs to be more flexible and dynamic. This approach occurs when students actively engage with the learning process while teachers provide support, resources and guidance, which contrasts with the traditional operation of the architecture design studio (Ostwald & Williams, 2008).

The internationalization strategy in design studios often creates a dilemma for the schools of architecture. On the one hand, the school has a rigid curriculum in terms of a list of competencies to respond to certain requirements of international UIA and national standards, for example, IAI in Indonesia or the Architects Council of Thailand Regulation. The school has the responsibility to teach and train the students to become professional architects through the learning process that dominantly occurs in the design studio, which has international/national competencies and is implemented in the design studio activities.

On the other hand, while internationalization is something that must be undertaken in the studio, it could bring a dynamic architectural pedagogy with shifting methods and approaches. This internationalization studio is somewhat difficult to apply, especially because it involves international educators or students with different backgrounds (Munasinghe, 2008), since students are still learning the ability to design step by step, depending on the level of their design studio courses and the curriculum of the home institutions. The dynamic design of the studio could gradually omit the uniqueness of the studio in terms of the studio culture and method of design (Dupre, 2022). This uniqueness is the strength of a specific studio or the master architects, as in the traditional definition of a studio (Gray, 2013). Therefore, internationalization tends to generalize to studio culture.

Architecture Studio Immersion

Studio immersion is one experimental type of internationalization used in architecture learning to overcome the main challenge of the curriculum when it initially needed to match the studio syllabus among joined universities. Studio immersion is prepared, operated, and evaluated by educators from joined universities. The studio assignment and schedule were prepared together, and the studio group consisted of a mix of students and teachers, as well as project sites located in the city where the joined universities are located. In the case of this research, the students and teachers had a chance to visit the sites and do studio work together and then continue the discussion and the studio critics online. Educators who are friends find it simpler to establish trust to build a new studio culture, and they are prepared to take on the roles of both teachers and organizers.

Starting in 2022, the architecture programs at Petra Christian University, Indonesia (PCU), and Silpakorn University, Thailand (SU), decided to implement an internationalization strategy through a type of studio immersion, and in 2023, Tunghai University (TU) started to join. Since 2024, the study of studio immersion has continued. The study involved is the first semester of the final year of each curriculum. SU and TU engage the studio in year five, whereas PCU does so in year four. In the studio, there are two assignments: one is group-based master planning design, and the other is individual work on architecture building design. Students work in groups of two or three mentors who serve as studio facilitators for the course of two assignments. The methods, approaches, management, operations and schedules of previous studies have changed as a result of this immersion study at PCUs and SUs becoming the first international study.

As shown in Figure 1, the studio immersion activities are related not only to the assignments but also to site visits, architectural excursions and social gatherings with colleagues and friends. Students and educators/tutors are mixed into 4 and 5 groups, with 5:5:1 numbers of PCU, SU and TU tutors in 2023, and the ratio of PCU, SU and TU students is 61:78:8.

site visit to Bangkok and Surabaya

studio discussion in Bangkok and Surabaya

Figure 1: Documentation of the studio immersion 2023

The purpose of this study is to identify students' perceptions in terms of their learning skills and architectural experiences, which include three universities from three Asian countries: Indonesia, Thailand, and Taiwan. The article aims to answer the research question of whether internationalization activity adds knowledge about architecture and provides skills for future careers. The research identifies the benefits, shortcomings, and challenges from the student's point of view. In the future, teachers and schools of architecture could respond better to the challenges that students face during the process of internationalization. This research will help Asian HE in identifying the best type of international involvement, especially for the school of architecture.

METHOD

This research was conducted with mixed quantitative and qualitative methods to explore the opinions of PCU, SU and TU students who are involved in this immersion study. The mixed method used in this study is an explanatory sequential design that consists of two phases (Creswell, 2014). First, the research starts with the quantitative methods that are followed second by the qualitative assessment to purposely choose respondents to confirm the trends found in the prior quantitative assessment. This mixed method has been proven to be effective in behavioral studies (Lopez-Fernandez & Molina-Azorin, 2011).

The main research question is whether internationalization activity adds knowledge about architecture and provides skills for future careers. Data were obtained through a Google form questionnaire distributed to all the students who participated in the immersion study in 2022 and 2023, with a total of 147 students. After the questionnaire was distributed, it was followed by interviews with specific students and educators. Descriptive analysis is used to analyze the questionnaire data, which are then divided into two categories: the Studio Operational category, which evaluates the students' agreed-upon implementation of studio management and development of soft skills during the studio, and the Comprehensive Understanding category, which evaluates the students' perceptions of their knowledge of architecture and their comprehension of architects as professionals after they finish the study.

RESULTS AND DISCUSSION

Studio Operational

The primary barrier to conducting studio immersion found in this research is in contrast to the previous findings determined to be language as a medium of teaching? between the students and the educators (Ostwald & Williams, 2008; Tek et al., 2023). According to this research, language limitations do not prevent students from interacting and communicating (Figure 2).

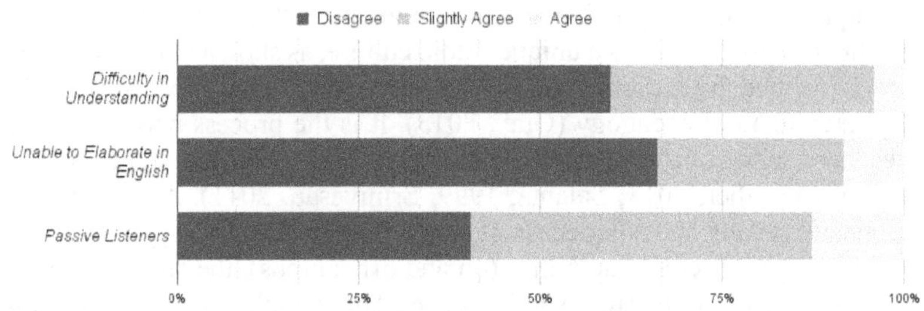

Figure 2: Language barriers

Not all students' involvement in studio immersion occurs through English language proficiency selection; only the PCU requires the equivalent of TOEFL 450. This is because PCU students participate in larger batches than SU and TU students do, necessitating selection to determine the student ratio. The graph demonstrates that student interaction and communication are unaffected even when students' English language proficiency is not comparable (as measured by language certificate scores).

In the tutorial activities between the students and tutors, almost half of the students perceive that their tutors place them as passive listeners due to their limited language skills (Figure 2). This result shows the lower power of the students to discuss and argue in English during the design jury (*The Analytics of Power: Re-Presenting the Design Jury on JSTOR*, n.d.). This contrasts with the previous table, where students are confident in their English to communicate and interact with other students. According to the interviews, this is because the tutors give out spoon-fed answers during the tutorial to limit the time of discussion, and then, the students feel that the tutors view them as passive listeners.

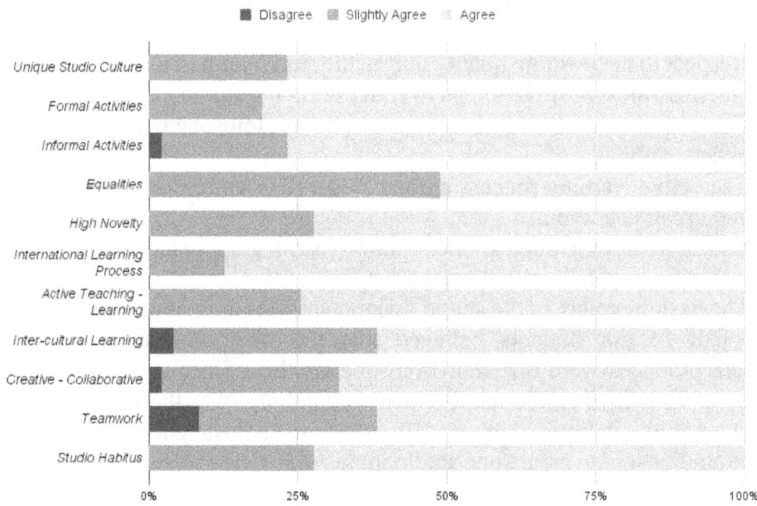

Figure 3: Student's perspective on Studio immersion

Compared with their previous studios, more than 70% of the students believe that studio immersion creates a unique studio culture, as shown in Figure 3. Studio culture is formed by beliefs, experiences, and places that are accommodated through architectural pedagogy (Gray, 2013). It is the process between students and teachers, when the educators are the providers while the students are the recipients (Crowther, 2013; Salama, 1999; Srinivasan, 2011). According to the questionnaire results, the uniqueness of studio immersion is clearly shown by the structured and unstructured activities (on and off campus), the variety of applied teaching methods, and the studio assignments. These could provide opportunities for students to explore the knowledge freely and provide their experience to the new type of studio (see Figure 3). More than 70% of the students believed that both structured and unstructured interactions with other students in their group significantly contributed to the success of the studio tasks (see Figure 3). Structured activities consist of scheduled studio discussions and site visits, specifically to Bangkok and Surabaya, by studio assignments. Unstructured activities are student-led activities that take place offline and online. In addition to the schedule of site visits, the students gather by themselves, as well as during online activities. Students also strongly agree with several studio-related activities that help them become more tolerant, cooperative, and adaptive (see Figure 3).

As the two cities selected as the locations for the studio's projects, Bangkok and Surabaya were visited by the students from the three universities. Together with the educators, the students completed the site survey, which focused on architecture as a dynamic to social and cultural change in contemporary society (Salama, 2021; *Un-Working,* n.d.). The students also engage in additional social activities unrelated to their studio tasks, such as going to movies, shopping and karaoking (see Figure 3). After the visit, the students engage in online social activities such as group gaming sessions or lighthearted conversations on Discord. This is what fosters student cooperation to facilitate engagement and communication (Webster, 2008).

With respect to the learning quality during the studio immersion, the students identified the four most positive things overall during the studio, namely:

- The experience of an international learning atmosphere with a global understanding
- The active learning process among students to understand architecture and urban conditions
- Educators have applied an intercultural learning approach in practice to make it more realistic and comprehensive.
- The design project in the studio assignments has high novelty value

Over half of the students believed that the three universities' studio management practices were different from one another. Since each studio has contributed to its unique studio management and culture over the years, named uniqueness or studio habitus (Gray, 2013), it requires adjustment and alteration when three studios join to create one studio immersion. The students felt unequal in their studio immersion management among the three universities. Since two universities conducted the first studio immersion in 2022 and the third university was added the following year, not all students experienced a strong sense of equality among the studios from the three universities. The first two universities have the most influence over studio management and tasks, but all three universities have equal access to lectures and discussions.

Sixty percent of the students believed that teamwork with different backgrounds was more challenging than studio assignments were. Previous research has shown that the greatest problem faced by internationalization in studios is not cultural differences but the structure of the studio, communication and resources (Dupre, 2022). The students agreed that their efforts in maintaining good networks and communication within the group outweighed the difficulty of the studio assignments, particularly the first assignment, which was to propose a master plan. This is because the master plan is the first group assignment for the half-semester, meaning it is the first time working together on an assignment when you do not know your group members in advance. Nearly every student experienced this difficulty, but by the end of the study, they believed that their ability to interact and communicate with others had enabled them to overcome this difficulty (Figure 2).

The table 2 shows two types of opinions from the students: one focuses on satisfaction, whereas the other focuses on dissatisfaction (Figure 4). Students expressed satisfaction in terms of enhanced self-confidence, the ability to interact, and a sense of pride. The students also highlighted their dissatisfaction with the pursuit of the university's reputation, studio dynamics, and uncertainty in the assignment's limitations. Instead of fostering the students' architectural skills, the students believe that the university is using the studio immersion program to improve its standing among other universities internationally. It is parallel with the opinion that internationalization only follows the market lead, with less reaching the full potential of the students (Dupre, 2022).

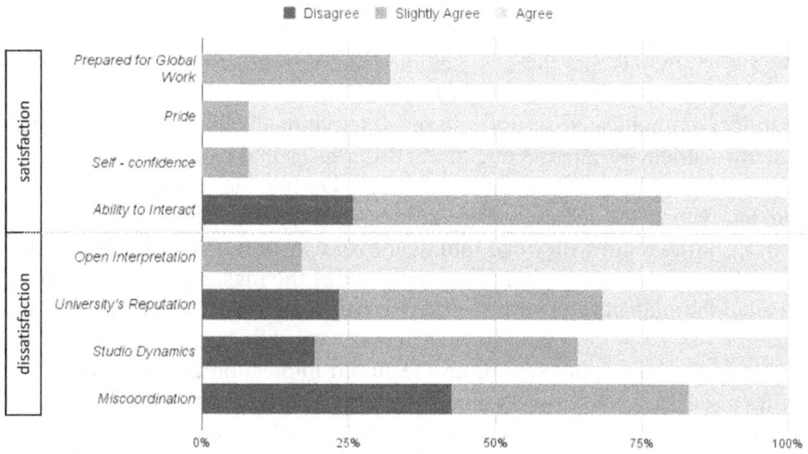

Figure 4: Studio Dynamics

Nearly half of the students agreed that the studio dynamics bring feelings of uncertainty/ambiguity that are particularly related to the project descriptions and limitations (Figure 4). Some researchers believe that internationalization studies make the curriculum overcome the disintegration of the planned curriculum (Dupre, 2022; Mostafa & Mostafa, 2010; Ostwald & Williams, 2008). The students feel that the studio is too dynamic, so it is not integrated with the school curriculum. This dynamism is due to the changes that occur in the studio, for example, changes in details related to assignment products and meeting schedules with the tutors. Students felt that these changes moved the studio further away from the original curriculum design.

According to the interviews, the three universities' worth as studio management educators admitted that this was a result of the limited time available to complete preliminary coordination for studio planning. As shown in previous research, internationalization should be carefully and thoroughly planned to achieve more coordination regarding the applied pedagogy (Munasinghe, 2008). Preliminary online talks are held to address the project's primary issues and find comparable sites (in terms of potential, challenges, and area) and then have less time to discuss in more detail, such as the brief narrative of the project, which includes the limitations, the drawing products and the per-group discussion time table. At the beginning of the study, students had difficulty adjusting to the level of dynamics of the studio immersion; however, in the end, they were able to understand that managing the immersion studio required special management regarding budgets, academic schedules and site visits from the three universities that sometimes could not fit all the students' expectations.

Comprehensive Understanding

Following the completion of the studio immersion, more than 90% of the students expressed pride in their participation and the quality of their work. Although it is obvious that there is a cultural difference between them (Killick, 2018), students now feel more confident in themselves because they have successfully communicated across cultures. Internationalization in the studio has faced many challenges in terms of cultural differences that could lead to tensions as well as focus (Gray, 2013; Salama, 2021). During the master plan design assignment, which is completed in groups, students are aware of cultural differences, but in reality, they can find their own way or methods to interact and even negotiate the design during the assignment of the master plan. In addition, almost all of the students feel very prepared to face the global world in their future careers.

Students are aware that setting up the studio immersion is more work than setting up a standard academic studio. The internationalization studio is exposed to a highly diverse range of architectural paradigms, real-world environments, and architectural theories (Crowther, 2013; Dupre, 2022; Salama, 2021; Srinivasan, 2011). Over 90% of the students thought that the success of this international study can be attributed to positive relationships between the three universities, particularly between educators who are involved in the studio and support from various entities, such as the international office and university/department leaders, concerning internal administration, scheduling, finances, career development of the educators and the fulfillment of the strategic plan of the institutions.

After the studio immersion, the students have a deeper comprehension of what architecture means, which are the three most important thoughts from the students:

- Architecture is viewed as the result of social and cultural integration rather than just the aesthetics of buildings
- The sociocultural context of modern society, in which buildings are designed, can be used to understand architecture
- The studio provides assignments in a real societal context so that it helps interpret sociocultural conditions as an architectural background.

In addition, 90% of the students reported that they are becoming more aware that the architect profession is a multifaceted career that involves aspects from the technical and sociocultural domains as well as aesthetics. Students believe that they have a deeper understanding of critical thinking, which they may use for future self-improvement rather than only finishing the assignment in the studio. In previous research, the internationalization of design studies has revealed various architectural theories, in which educators need to apply the constructivist approach to communicate across cultures, whereas the learning experience urgently needs intercultural skills to understand contemporary society (Crowther, 2013; Salama, 2021; Srinivasan, 2011; *Un-Working*, n.d.).

Summary

This research aims to investigate the perceptions of students who finished their studies in 2022 and 2023. The goal is to determine whether internationalization activity adds knowledge about architecture and provides skills for future careers. According to the research findings, studio immersion broadens students' understanding of architecture to include the sociocultural context of contemporary society in addition to technical and aesthetic systems. Therefore, the profession of an architect is understood as a multifaceted profession. With respect to their future careers in an increasingly globalized world, students are confident in their capacity to overcome cultural differences. Their struggle to adjust to the new friends, teachers, and studio culture was demonstrated, and it was overcome by social interaction and communication, both formal and informal, which can foster networking and trust. The students believe that studio immersion has helped them become more confident, global and intercultural learners.

According to the findings, in regard to communication in the studio, students initially struggle with their English but eventually gain the confidence to engage with their peers. Their confidence is growing, especially through online informal activities, such as online gaming. Owing to their early exposure to English, the students are conversant in both English and worldwide communication via the internet and online gaming. Even though their English proficiency is not comparable, the interaction among students is not affected.

CONCLUSIONS

The question of identity and uniqueness of education becomes the greatest challenge for internationalization in HE as well as in schools of architecture. Some scholars have argued that internationalization could reinforce Western-centric education by ignoring the differences and cultural diversity of each nation's educational system (Jones, 2022; McAllester, 2024). However, HE acknowledges that despite the significant time and resource commitments needed, internationalization is a modern necessity to train future practitioners in a globalized society.

There is an opportunity for the school of architecture to implement internationalization in the learning process, especially in the studios. This is because the school is regulated internationally under UIA requirements for architecture curriculum goals, which means that all schools of architecture match in terms of the learning skills provided. The internationalization of studios is becoming more feasible for application in the modern world, where students encounter no boundaries in learning and engagement and more student-centered learning. Nonetheless, it is challenging to alter the studio culture that has grown over the years at each institution, as it has become unique in that it adds value to the entire educational process. The master architect, who primarily directs the design approach and style of the studio assignment, is credited with having expertise in the architecture project. As the spirit of collaboration is the foundation of the studio, the new studio culture that will be built over time will fulfill the main purpose, which is to be more relevant and connected in the increasingly independent world.

This type of studio offers a new strategy for architecture schools to apply internationalization, which is typically regarded as unachievable. Research immersion creates a unique characteristic in terms of its challenges, handicaps, benefits and shortcomings, whereas it also needs various types of support. The university's internationalization-supporting policies and strategies, as well as the instructors' openness to fostering a new studio culture, are crucial to the studio immersion program's success. The chance to study various national contexts and cultures that produce architecture is provided to the students to help them with their assignment.

The definition of internationalization in HE includes the meaning of process as well as strategy; it is not a target but rather how to pursue a common purpose together by undertaking specific actions/strategies that differ from one institution to another (Knight, 2008). It is possible that certain institutions are better suited for the type of studio immersion than others strongly depend on resources are; all have a common purpose of improving HE quality and tolerance in a world where people are more independent and connected (Knight, 2008; Knight & de Wit, 2018).

This research is limited to the perspective of the students only, but in the future, it could be expanded to the perspective of the leaders since this strategy of studio immersion initially to answer the global need to be equal and relevant. Additionally, the difference in internationalization in Asian compared with non-

Asian HE could be highlighted to allow for a more thorough analysis and implementation of the best possible strategy.

REFERENCES

Bamberger, A., & Morris, P. (2023). Critical perspectives on internationalization in higher education: Commercialization, global citizenship, or postcolonial imperialism? *Critical Studies in Education*, *0*(0), 1–19. https://doi.org/10.1080/17508487.2023.2233572

Berita IAI. (n.d.). Retrieved from https://iai.or.id/berita/menyetarakan-pendidikan-arsitektur-indonesia-dengan-standar-internasional-ikatan-arsitek-indonesia-mendorong-terbentuknya-program-pendidikan-profesi-arsitek-ppar

Creswell, J. W. (2014). *Research Design: Qualitative, Quantitative, and Mixed Methods Approaches*. SAGE.

Crowther, P. (2013). Understanding the signature pedagogy of the design studio and the opportunities for its technological enhancement. *Journal of Learning Design*, *6*(3), Article 3. https://doi.org/10.5204/jld.v6i3.155

Dupre, K. (2022). International experiments in the Australian architecture curriculum: An educator's perspective. In *The Routledge Companion to Architectural Pedagogies of the Global South*. Routledge.

Gray, C. (2013). *Informal peer critique and the negotiation of habitus in a design studio. 12*. https://doi.org/10.1386/adch.12.2.195_1

Hacihasanoglu, O. (2021). *Terms and Concepts on Design Studio in the Research Articles of 2010's* (SSRN Scholarly Paper 3838218). https://papers.ssrn.com/abstract=3838218

Hayle, E. M. (2008). *Educational Benefits of Internationalizing Higher Education: The Students' Perspectives*. https://library-archives.canada.ca/eng/services/services-libraries/theses/Pages/item.aspx?idNumber=1032974527 Last Modified: 2022-09-01

Hou, J., & Kang, M.-J. (2006). Differences and Dialogic Learning in a Collaborative Virtual Design Studio. *Open House International*, *31*(3), 85–94. https://doi.org/10.1108/OHI-03-2006-B0011

Jones, E. (2022). Problematizing the Idea of Curriculum 'Internationalization.' *Journal of International Students*, *12*(1), Article 1. https://doi.org/10.32674/jis.v12i1.4592

Killick, D. (2018). Critical Intercultural Practice: Learning in and for a Multicultural Globalizing World. *Journal of International Students*, *8*(3), Article 3. https://doi.org/10.32674/jis.v8i3.64

Knight, J. (2008). *Higher Education in Turmoil: The Changing World of Internationalization*. https://doi.org/10.1163/9789087905224

Knight, J., & de Wit, H. (2018). Internationalization of Higher Education: Past and Future. *International Higher Education*, 2. https://doi.org/10.6017/ihe.2018.95.10715

Lopez-Fernandez, O., & Molina-Azorin, J. F. (2011). The use of mixed methods research in the field of behavioural sciences. *Quality & Quantity*, *45*(6), 1459–1472. https://doi.org/10.1007/s11135-011-9543-9

Mali, M. G. (2020). Internasionalisasi kampus sebagai strategi perguruan tinggi dalam menghadapi era revolusi industri 4.0. *Jurnal Manajemen Publik Dan Kebijakan Publik (JMPKP)*, *2*(1). http://jurnal.umb.ac.id/index.php/JMPKP/article/view/4518

McAllester, K. (2024). Transposed identity negotiation: A new conceptual framework. *Journal of International Students*, *14*(3), Article 3. https://doi.org/10.32674/jis.v14i3.6132

Mostafa, M., & Mostafa, H. (2010). How Do Architects Think? Learning Styles and Architectural Education. *Archnet-IJAR*, *4*, 310–317. https://doi.org/10.26687/archnet-ijar.v4i2/3.139

Munasinghe, H. (2008). Architectural education and design studio tradition. *7*.

Ng, S. W. (2012). Rethinking the mission of internationalization of higher education in the Asia-Pacific region. *Compare: A Journal of Comparative and International Education*, *42*(3), 439–459. https://doi.org/10.1080/03057925.2011.652815

Ostwald, M., & Williams, A. (2008). *Understanding Architectural Education In Australasia. Volume 1: An Analysis of Architecture Schools, Programs, Academics and Students.*

Ota, L. T. T., Tracy X. P. Zou, Hiroshi (Ed.). (2023). *East and Southeast Asian Perspectives on the Internationalisation of Higher Education: Policies, Practices and Prospects*. Routledge.

Salama, A. (1999). *Incorporating Knowledge about Cultural Diversity into Architectural Pedagogy* (pp. 135–144).

Salama, A. (2021). *Transformative Pedagogy in Architecture and Urbanism.* https://doi.org/10.4324/9781003140047

Srinivasan, B. (2011). Three holy myths of architectural education in India. *Archnet-IJAR*, *5*. https://doi.org/10.26687/archnet-ijar.v5i1.227

Sutrisno, A. (2019). Internationalization of Indonesian Higher Education: Recent Initiatives and their Problems. *International Higher Education*, *97*, Article 97. https://doi.org/10.6017/ihe.2019.97.10941

Tek, M., Nok, S., & Chea, P. (2023). What makes academics (in)active in higher education internationalisation: Evidence from Cambodia. *Journal of Higher Education Policy and Management*, *0*(0), 1–15. https://doi.org/10.1080/1360080X.2023.2288731

The Analytics of Power: Re-presenting the Design Jury on JSTOR. (n.d.). Retrieved April 30, 2023, from https://www.jstor.org/stable/40480704

Trinh, A. N., & Conner, L. (2019). Student Engagement in Internationalization of the Curriculum: Vietnamese Domestic Students' Perspectives. *Journal of Studies in International Education*, *23*(1), 154–170. https://doi.org/10.1177/1028315318814065

UNESCO-UIA Charter for Architectural Education (n.d.). *International Union of Architects.* https://www.uia-architectes.org/en/resource/unesco-uia-charter-for-architectural-education-revised-july-2023/

Un-Working: New Tactics for Architectural Pedagogy: Journal of Architectural Education (n.d). https://www.tandfonline.com/doi/abs/10.1080/10464883.2019.1633208

Webster, H. (2008). Architectural Education after Schön: Cracks, Blurs, Boundaries and Beyond. *Journal for Education in the Built Environment*, *3*(2), 63–74. https://doi.org/10.11120/jebe.2008.03020063

Wit, H. de. (2020). Internationalization of Higher Education: The Need for a More Ethical and Qualitative Approach. *Journal of International Students*, *10*(1), Article 1. https://doi.org/10.32674/jis.v10i1.1893

Yeravdekar, V. R., & Tiwari, G. (2014). Internationalization of Higher Education and its Impact on Enhancing Corporate Competitiveness and Comparative Skill Formation. *Procedia - Social and Behavioral Sciences*, *157*, 203–209. https://doi.org/10.1016/j.sbspro.2014.11.023

Zolfaghari, A., Sabran, M., & Zolfaghari, A. (2009). Internationalization of Higher Education: Challenges, Strategies, Policies and Programs. *Online Submission.*

Author bios

RULLY DAMAYANTI, PhD (Corresponding author), Assistant Professor in the Architecture Department at Petra Christian University, Indonesia. The major research interest is in architecture and urban spatiality, spatial temporality and urban design history and theory. Email rully@petra.ac.id
https://orcid.org/0000-0001-8409-1760

ELVINA WIJAYA, M.T., is a Lecturer in the Department of Architecture at Petra Christian University, Indonesia. The major research interest in the area of building technology, focusing on building and occupant interaction to enhance health, comfort and well-being. Email: elvinawijaya@petra.ac.id
https://orcid.org/0009-0003-5851-7985

BRAM WAYNE, M.Ars., is a Lecturer in the Department of Architecture, Petra Christian University. He currently studies on Biophilic Factor and walkability in the city. Email: bram.wayne@petra.ac.id

APIRADEE KASEMSOOK, Ph.D., is an Associate Professor in the Department of Architecture, Silpakorn University, Thailand. Her major research interests lie in the area of spatial morphology of buildings and settlements, transnational spatial culture, and environmental philosophy.
Email: KASEMSOOK_A@su.ac.th

KUO-WEI CHIU, Ph.D., Assistant Professor and Director of Regenerative Earth and Anthropocene Design Lab, Department of Architecture at the Tunghai University. His major research interests lie in the areas of sustainable urbanism, urban design, urban morphology, ancient urbanism, biomimicry, extreme environment, and interplanetary space architecture. Email: kc@thu.edu.tw

Article

Journal of International Students
Volume 14, Issue 5 (2024), pp. 141-158
ISSN: 2162-3104 (Print), 2166-3750 (Online)
jistudents.org

Gender Differences in the Acculturative Stress of International Students: A Meta-Analysis

Rawan Alzukari
Mississippi State University, USA

Tianlan Wei
Mississippi State University, USA

ABSTRACT

This meta-analysis examines gender differences in acculturative stress among international students. Despite numerous studies on cultural adjustment, inconsistencies persist regarding gender differences in acculturative stress. This study synthesizes findings from 12 empirical studies. Comprehensive searches across databases, including institutional libraries, Google Scholar, PsycINFO, ScienceDirect, and ResearchGate, were conducted. Studies were categorized by geographic location, publication type, sample size, instruments, and participant age. The meta-analysis revealed no significant differences in acculturative stress levels between male and female international students. These findings suggest the need for further research on gender differences and other variables related to acculturative stress. Understanding these variables could enhance interventions and support international students' well-being and adaptation.

Keywords: Acculturative stress, culture, gender differences, international students, meta-analysis

Thousands of international students travel from different parts of the world yearly to complete their studies abroad and obtain degrees from universities and colleges. According to the *Open Doors* Report, over 1 million international students were enrolled in U.S. institutions during the 2022/2023 academic year, marking a 12% increase from the prior academic year. Additionally, new international student enrollments grew by 14%, with 298,523 new students joining U.S. institutions, as seen in the most recent data (IIE, 2023). This contributes to diversity, enriching the learning experience for both local and international students and fostering a more inclusive and globally aware academic environment. However, international students face challenges and difficulties adapting to the new culture. These challenges include but are not limited to, language, customs, financial difficulties, academic pressures, homesickness, and others. Consequently, anxiety, depression, and culture shock can occur (Oyeniyi et al., 2021).

Acculturation refers to the wide range of changes that occur when there is contact between cultures (Lee,2014). Acculturation can be defined as the process of cultural change and adjustment to a new culture, which happens to people when they interact with the new culture (Gibson, 2001). It also refers to changes in the behavior and values of people due to their interactions in a new culture (Kagan & Cohen, 1990). In addition, acculturation stress is considered one of the most threatening problems faced by international students and negatively affects them academically, socially, and psychologically. Acculturative stress is defined as "one kind of stress in which the stressors are identified as having their source in the process of acculturation, a particular set of stress behaviors that occur during acculturation, such as lowered mental health status (especially confusion, anxiety, depression), feelings of marginality, and alienation, heightened psychosomatic symptoms and identity confusion" (Berry, 1995, p. 479). Furthermore, Berry and colleagues (1987) described acculturative stress as the poor physical and psychosocial health of people adjusting to a new culture and interacting in an environment that lacks the strength of their usual cultural connections, status, and social support. Experiencing pressure to adapt to a different culture can cause acculturative stress. In academic settings, international students may view the new culture as a threat to their previous way of life. For example, using a new language, adapting to a new educational system, practicing new cultural behaviors, and perhaps abandoning previous cultural beliefs and values can pose difficult and challenging situations for international students engaging with other cultures (Ayoob et al., 2011).

Several students' demographic characteristics, such as gender, marital status, age, and educational status, can be associated with their acculturative stress levels. Gender is one of the most prominent of these factors. The results related to gender and acculturative stress are mixed and not yet well-established (Gebregergis, 2018). It has been suggested that males and females differ in how they perceive acculturative stress (Ayoob et al., 2011). Gender plays a significant role in the stress process, affecting both the perception of a situation as stressful, coping responses, and health outcomes resulting from stress reactions (Matud, 2004). Overall, understanding demographic factors, including gender, and their impact on acculturative stress is essential for designing effective interventions and support systems to help people overcome cultural adjustment difficulties and enhance their well-being.

However, the literature on international student adjustment remains inconsistent regarding gender differences in adjustment problems, especially acculturative stress. Thus, more studies are needed to explore gender differences and acculturative stress among international students. Therefore, the present study investigates gender differences in acculturative stress among international students within the host context. To bridge the gap in the previous literature, a meta-analysis was conducted using 12 retrieved empirical studies to explore gender differences in acculturative stress across various study feature variables, including geographic locations, instruments, sample sizes, and mean age.

Research Questions

The following research questions were proposed:

> RQ_1: Are there gender differences in the experience of acculturative stress among international students within the host context?
>
> RQ_2: To what extent do these variables (geographical location, instrument used, sample size, and average age) influence gender differences in acculturative stress among international students?

LITERATURE REVIEW

Acculturative Stress Factors of International Students

Acculturative stress is one of the prominent challenges faced by international students. Some of these stressors can be caused by rejection and identity threats, which constitute social obstacles that prevent them from adapting or acculturating.

Yu et al. (2014) conducted a study on 567 international students at universities in Wuhan to explore the acculturative stress of international students in China and its influential factors. The results revealed external and internal sources of acculturative stress. The external sources consist of three components linked to each other: deprivation of opportunities, identity threat, and rejection. The internal sources include the conflict between cultural values and the lack of self-confidence and cultural competence. In addition, Iorga et al. (2020) argued that there are many factors associated with acculturative stress. They conducted research on 265 international students at a public medical university in Romania to determine these factors. One of the leading factors associated with acculturative stress is comfort level in terms of language, climate, and food. The study also revealed that hatred, rejection, and fear are significantly associated with low levels of comfort, causing acculturative stress and perceived discrimination.

Moreover, social and demographic factors may be a significant source of acculturative stress. Gebregergis (2018) investigated the main sources of acculturative stress and their associations with sociodemographic factors. The results revealed that age, previous travel experience, language proficiency, interaction with local students, educational level, and financial support were significantly related to international students' acculturative stress levels. This means that younger international students and students with previous travel experience less acculturative stress. International students who are able to engage with local students and use the language efficiently in communication are less likely to experience acculturative stress. The educational level also plays a role in the acculturation process, as the results revealed that international graduate students (master's and doctoral) have a higher level of acculturative stress than undergraduate students do. This may be due to the difference in the number of academic tasks required of graduate students. Similarly, Talwar et al. (2022) conducted a study of 208 international students at a Malaysian university to examine acculturative stress levels and discover sociodemographic factors associated with acculturative stress. The results revealed that acculturative stress levels were high among most international students who reported feelings of discrimination, rejection, homesickness, and fear. The results also revealed that family support, year of study, and poor language proficiency were essential factors related to cultural stress among students. The length of stay or number of years the student has spent in the host country also plays a role in cultural adaptation to a new environment. Thus, as the length of stay increases, students gain greater knowledge of the environment and culture in the host country, which can lead to a decrease in acculturative stress levels.

Xie and Ridley (2024) explored three-way interactions between Chinese international students' acculturative stress, proactive coping, and future time perspective in predicting their subjective well-being. The participants were 198 undergraduate and graduate students attending U.S. universities who completed an online survey. The study results indicated that acculturative stress is negatively associated with subjective well-being. In addition, the analysis of the subscales of acculturative stress indicated that language insufficiency, social isolation, and academic pressure were significantly correlated with well-being. These findings suggest that individuals who have low levels of stress in these aspects are likely to have more positive emotions, such as excitement and satisfaction. However, not all studies have reported a significant relationship between acculturative stress and academic performance. For example, Yun and Greenwood (2021) reported no significant associations between acculturative stress and sleep quality or between acculturative stress and academic performance in international students. They suggested that international students, particularly those with greater academic ability, may have developed coping mechanisms or received adequate academic support, which could explain the lack of a significant relationship in their studies. These findings contrast with earlier research identifying a strong link between acculturative stress and academic difficulties. In addition, Soufi Amlashi et al. (2024) conducted a systematic review and meta-analysis on the relationship between acculturative stress and psychological outcomes among international students. Their synthesis of 29 studies, with a combined sample size of 7,247 participants, revealed that higher levels of acculturative stress are significantly linked to increased symptoms of anxiety, depression, and overall psychological distress. The authors emphasize the need for targeted interventions to mitigate these stressors and enhance the well-being of international students.

Furthermore, Desa et al. (2012) studied postgraduate students at the School of Psychology and Human Development, University Kebangsaan, Malaysia. Their study aimed to explore the type of acculturative stress that most international students experience. Four aspects of acculturative stress, namely, social, attitudinal, family, and environmental, were measured. The results indicated that the environment and attitudes were the international students' most common sources of acculturative stress. With respect to the environment, many international students face challenges and difficulties related to adapting to a new environment and educational system. In addition, international students' negative attitudes toward the host country affect their acculturative stress levels, leading to difficulty adjusting and feelings of discomfort and dissatisfaction. However, positive attitudes are often linked to better adjustment and a reduced level of stress.

A longitudinal study conducted by Koo et al. (2021) on first-year international college students was conducted to examine their experiences with acculturative stress and adjustment during their first year of enrollment in the U.S. The results revealed that social interactions and English language proficiency are the main factors associated with acculturative stress among international students. Acculturative stress and difficulties adapting were also negatively associated with social interactions and the use of the English language.

In summary, the findings of the previous study emphasize several factors impacting acculturative stress levels among international students. Notably, social interactions and English language proficiency are significant factors in this stress. Additionally, demographic factors, such as age and educational level, along with travel experiences, length of stay, attitudes, and the environment, were explored as essential elements impacting the acculturation process. Additionally, self-confidence, adequate intercultural communication skills, and the avoidance of conflicting values play a protective role against acculturative stress.

Acculturative Stress between Genders

Although there are mixed results in previous studies on gender differences in acculturative stress, the results of some studies have shown that there are statistically significant differences between the genders. One of these studies by Castillo et al. (2015) focused on 1,004 Latino college students in the United States. The participants completed the Multidimensional Acculturative Stress Inventory (MASI; Rodriguez et al., 2002) to measure their levels of acculturative stress. The results showed that both males and females suffered from acculturative stress. However, Latino male students have higher levels of acculturative stress than female students do. The authors of the study mentioned that one possible explanation for this is socialization in Latino culture and the sense of shame that males may feel when asking for help. Therefore, seeking help is linked to their weakness, which may hinder them from adapting to the new environment and culture. Similarly, another study by Mahmood and Burke (2018) investigated acculturative stress levels and certain demographic factors among 413 international students in a nonmetropolitan university environment in the United States. The results revealed that male students had higher acculturative stress scores than females did. Thus, males are more likely to be prone to sociocultural adaptation difficulties and face more challenges in adjusting to the academic environment. In addition, Talwar et al. (2022) examined the levels of acculturation stress among 208 international students enrolled in a Malaysian university. The acculturative Stress Scale for International Students (ASSIS; Sandhu & Asrabadi, 1994) was administered. The results indicate that male students had significantly higher ASSIS scores than females did. Finally, Koo et al. (2021) conducted a longitudinal study to examine the acculturative stress and adjustment experiences of international students during their first year of enrollment in the U.S. The findings indicate that male students with lower socioeconomic backgrounds had higher levels of acculturative stress than their female peers did at the end of their first year.

In contrast, some previous studies have shown that female international students experience a higher level of acculturative stress than males do. Ayoob et al. (2011) carried out a study to examine gender differences in Acculturative Stress and Health among 219 Kashmiri graduate students in India. Their acculturative stress levels were measured via the Social, Attitudinal, Familial, and Environmental Scale (SAFE-SF; Mena, Padilla, & Maldonado, 1987). The results indicated that there was a significant difference between genders in acculturative stress, and female students experienced greater accurate stress than male students did. Accordingly, compared with male students, female students reported high levels of anxiety, insomnia, and depression. The researchers stated that these results can be explained by the fact that female students in the Indian cultural context may have more cultural restrictions, less freedom, and less insecurity than male students. In addition, Kefayati (2016) examines the predictors of acculturative stress in international students studying at Eastern Mediterranean University, Cyprus. The participants were 174 Iranian and Nigerian international students aged 18--35 years. The study revealed that female students experienced more acculturative stress than male students did. One possible explanation for these results is that female students have a greater level of homesickness and guilt and, therefore, greater difficulty adapting to the new environment than males do. Nigerian female students also reported higher levels of perceived discrimination. Another study by Hahn (2010) on 511 international students studying at a northeastern university in the USA investigated the levels of stress and coping experienced by gender. The results indicate that female students experienced greater cultural stress than male students did. Finally, Cong et al. (2024) explored the impact of various factors, including gender, on the acculturative stress experienced by Asian international students in the United States and compared these stress levels before and during the COVID-19 pandemic. Using data from 204 students across ten universities and colleges, the study revealed that English proficiency and gender were significant predictors of acculturative stress. Higher perceived English proficiency was associated with lower acculturative stress, whereas female students reported higher stress levels than their male counterparts did. Moreover, the pandemic exacerbated feelings of sadness and perceived discrimination among these students. The authors suggested that a possible reason for this difference is that females may be more vulnerable during acculturation because of their lower social status and multiple role expectations, leading to cultural conflicts and maladaptation. Additionally, females are more expressive and efficient in processing emotions, especially negative emotions, making them more likely to report stress.

On the other hand, other studies suggest that there are no statistically significant differences between genders in acculturative stress. Misra et al. (2003) conducted research on 143 international students in the USA to examine whether there are gender differences in life and academic stress. The findings indicated that there was no significant difference in cultural adjustment or academic stress by gender. The participants reported some difficulties regarding cultural adjustments, such as American food, social interactions, cultural norms, and some racial discrimination. The results also indicated that female students had greater behavioral, emotional, and physiological reactions to stressors than male students did. Another study by Gebregergis (2018) was conducted on 506 international students in China. The aim of this study was to investigate whether students' levels of acculturative stress differ on the basis of their sociodemographic characteristics. However, the study revealed no statistically significant differences in the scores of males and females. Similarly, Gholamrezai (1995) carried out research recruiting 173 international students from 11 nationalities in Australia to explore the role of sociodemographic factors in international students' acculturative stress. The researcher compared males' and females' acculturative stress scores and found no statistically significant differences. The researcher argued that gender is not a valid explanatory factor for observed differences in acculturative stress because it is confounded with other background characteristics.

While much research has explored the factors contributing to acculturative stress, the findings regarding gender differences have been notably inconsistent. The results of studies investigating gender differences in acculturative stress have been mixed, with some research suggesting that male students experience greater acculturative stress, whereas others indicate the opposite or report no significant difference at all. These inconsistencies can be attributed to several factors, which are important to understand when interpreting both the literature and the findings of this meta-analysis. One key factor is the role of cultural contexts and societal gender norms, which may shape how males and females experience acculturative stress. In some cultures, traditional gender roles impose stricter expectations on one gender, contributing to heightened stress during the process of acculturation. For example, research indicates higher levels of acculturative stress among male international students, often attributed to social norms, shyness in seeking help, and socioeconomic challenges (Castillo et al., 2015). Conversely, in societies where women face greater cultural restrictions, female students may encounter more challenges in adapting to a new culture because of limited freedoms or societal expectations, resulting in higher levels of acculturative stress. These increased levels of acculturative stress among female students are often linked to cultural restrictions, homesickness, guilt, and discrimination (Ayoob et al., 2011). The differing cultural norms regarding gender roles may explain the variation in findings across studies conducted in different countries.

Variations in coping mechanisms between genders may also account for some of the mixed findings. For example, men and women often use different coping strategies when dealing with acculturative stress, with women more frequently seeking social support, whereas men may be less likely to ask for help, especially in cultures where doing so is stigmatized for males (Mahmood & Burke, 2018). Such differences in coping approaches can significantly affect the levels of reported acculturative stress, as those who seek social support often experience lower stress levels than individuals who internalize their struggles.

Another important factor is the methodological differences between studies, which may contribute to the inconsistencies in the reported results. The instruments used to measure acculturative stress, such as the Acculturative Stress Scale for International Students (ASSIS) and other scales, might capture the nuances of stress differently, depending on the context. Additionally, sample sizes and participant demographics, such as level of education, length of stay, and age, can influence the outcomes. Smaller studies with more homogeneous samples may report gender differences than larger, more diverse studies do not (Gebregergis, 2018; Talwar et al., 2022). Research also indicates that gender is not a critical factor in the differences between acculturative stress levels, as other social and background characteristics play essential roles (Gebregergis, 2018).

Therefore, conducting a meta-analysis would help clarify these discrepancies and contribute to a deeper understanding of the role of gender in acculturative stress among international students.

The rationale for conducting a meta-analysis lies in its ability to provide a more holistic and statistically rigorous examination of gender differences in acculturative stress among international students, even in the absence of clear indications from previous studies.

METHOD

A comprehensive search was conducted across multiple databases, including Google Scholar, PsycINFO, ScienceDirect, and ResearchGate, using combinations of keywords such as "Acculturative Stress," "International Students," "Gender Differences," and related terms. Initially, 19 studies that met the general scope of the meta-analysis were retrieved.

After an initial screening of titles and abstracts, studies that did not meet the inclusion criteria were excluded. For inclusion in this meta-analysis, studies had to meet the following criteria:

1. Published in peer-reviewed journals or dissertations.
2. Focused specifically on international students.
3. Acculturative stress was measured via validated instruments (e.g., the Acculturative Stress Scale for International Students [ASSIS]).
4. Reported gender as a variable in their analysis of acculturative stress.

Studies were excluded if they:

1. Focused on nonstudent immigrant populations or other groups such as expatriates.
2. Did not provide sufficient information on gender differences in acculturative stress.
3. Addressed acculturative stress in the context of other demographic factors (e.g., age or marital status) was the primary focus of the study.

4. The acculturative stress score means (M) and standard deviations (SD) for gender comparisons were not reported.

After this screening process, 12 studies that met all the inclusion criteria were selected for full-text review and ultimately included in the final meta-analysis.

Coding process

After the studies were retrieved, each one was systematically coded to investigate the gender differences in the acculturative stress of international students. The coding process involved identifying key study features, including the following:

1. Author and year.
2. Geographic location: USA or other countries.
3. Publication type: Peer-reviewed articles or dissertations.
4. Sample sizes: Small ($N \leq 300$ students) or large ($N > 300$ students).
5. Instruments used: ASSIS or other instruments.
6. Participants' mean age: Below 24 years (e.g., 20, 21, 23) or 24 years and above (e.g., 24, 25, 27, 28).

The coding process was conducted step by step under the guidance of an expert instructor, ensuring consistency through discussions and resolving any discrepancies.

Effect size calculations and statistical analyses

In general, the effect size for each study was calculated as the difference between the mean acculturative stress scores for males and females, divided by the pooled standard deviation. The effect size (*ES*), standard error (*SE*), and weight (*w*) for each study were calculated via Excel software. To ensure accuracy in the calculations, the results were then verified via SPSS, and an additional researcher independently checked the calculations. SPSS was used to conduct all the statistical analyses after individual effect sizes (*ESs*), standard errors (*SEs*), and weights (ws) were calculated for all 12 qualifying studies. These analyses included calculating overall effect sizes, *Q* statistics, degrees of freedom (*df*), and both fixed and mixed effects models. The mixed-effects model for the meta-analysis was conducted via SPSS, with alpha values of .05, .01, and .001 used for all the statistical tests.

RESULTS

In this meta-analysis of gender differences in acculturative stress among international students, findings from 12 studies were synthesized. The retrieved articles presented mixed results, with some studies reporting no significant difference between genders in acculturative stress (Gebregergis, 2018; Gholamrezai, 1995; Misra et al., 2003), whereas others have suggested that either males (Castillo et al., 2015; Koo et al., 2021; Lee, 2014; Mahmood & Burke,

2018; Misra & Castillo, 2004; Talwar et al., 2022) or females (Ayoob et al., 2011; Hahn, 2010; Kefayati, 2016) experience greater stress in acculturation.

However, this meta-analysis revealed no significant differences in acculturative stress between male and female international students. The overall random effects model effect size (*ES*) for gender differences in acculturative stress among international students, on the basis of a meta-analysis of 12 studies, was 0.017 (*SE* = 0.075), 95% CI [-0.132, 0.165]. The test of the mean (*Z*) yielded a value of 0.219, indicating that the mean effect size is not significantly different from zero. Therefore, the meta-analysis did not find a statistically significant difference in acculturative stress between genders among international students.

Table 1: Summary of major meta-analyses on gender differences in the acculturation stress of international students

Study ID	Author, Year	ES	SE	W	Geographic Location	Publication Type	Sample Sizes	Instruments	Mean Age
1	Misra & Castillo (2004).	.32	.21	23.70	US	Peer-reviewed article	Small (n=143)	Others	24
2	Misra, Crist & Burant (2003).	-.08	.17	35.09	US	Peer-reviewed article	Small (n=143)	Others	24
3	Mahmood & Burke (2018).	.21	.10	92.69	US	Peer-reviewed article	Large (n=413)	ASSIS	24
4	Castillo et al., (2015)	.16	.07	185.27	US	Peer-reviewed article	Large (n= 1004)	Others	20
5	Ayoob, Singh & Jan (2011).	-.41	.14	53.56	Others (India)	Peer-reviewed article	Small (n=219)	Others	23
6	Lee (2014).	.61	.29	12.20	Others (Ireland)	Dissertation	Small (n=75)	ASSIS	24

Study ID	Author, Year	ES	SE	W	Geographic Location	Publication Type	Sample Sizes	Instruments	Mean Age
7	Gebregergis (2018).	.12	.09	123.74	Others (China)	Peer-reviewed article	Large (n=506)	ASSIS	27
8	Talwar et al., (2022).	.30	.15	43.13	Others (Malaysia)	Peer-reviewed article	Small (n=208)	ASSIS	21
9	Yu et al., (2014).	.03	.09	129.69	Others (China)	Peer-reviewed article	Large (n=336)	ASSIS	23
10	Gholamrezai, (1995).	.00	.15	43.21	Others (Australia)	Dissertation	Small (n=173)	ASSIS	27
11	Kefayat, (2016).	-.63	.16	41.36	Others (Cyprus)	Dissertation	Small (n=174)	ASSIS	24
12	Hahn, (2010).	-.17	.09	127.30	US	Dissertation	Large (n=511)	Others	24

Table 2: Overall effect size

Study ID	*K*	*ES*	*SE*	95% CI		Test Of mean	Test of heterogeneity in effect sizes	
				Lower	Upper	*Z*	*Q*	*Df*
1	--	0.32	0.20	-0.08	0.72	1.56	--	--
2	--	-0.08	0.16	-0.41	0.24	-0.48	--	--
3	--	0.21	0.10	0.01	0.41	2.06*	--	--
4	--	0.16	0.07	0.01	0.30	2.20*	--	--
5	--	-0.40	0.13	-0.67	-0.13	-2.96*	--	--
6	--	0.61	0.28	0.05	1.17	2.14*	--	--
7	--	0.12	0.08	-0.05	0.29	1.36	--	--
8	--	0.29	0.15	-0.003	0.59	1.93	--	--
9	--	0.02	0.08	-0.14	0.19	0.30	--	--
10	--	0.001	0.15	-0.29	0.29	0.008	--	--
11	--	-0.63	0.15	-0.93	-0.32	-4.05***	--	--
12	--	-0.16	0.08	-0.34	0.006	-1.88	--	--
Overall effect size								
1.fixed	12	0.027	0.0331	-0.038	0.092	0.811	50.28***	11
2. Random	12	0.017	0.075	- 0.132	0.165	0.219		

Note. k = number of studies; *ES* = effect size; *SE* = standard error; CI = confidence interval. **p*< .05. ***p* < .01. ****p* < .001.

Table 3: Subgroup analysis: mixed-effects results

Study Features	K	ES	SE	95% CI		Test Of mean	Test of heterogeneity in effect sizes	
				Lower	Upper	Z	Q	Df
By Geographic Location								
1.USA	5	0.07	0.09	-0.10	0.25	0.83	12.99**	4
2.Others	7	-0.02	0.12	-0.26	0.21	-0.21	35.36***	6
Total Between (Q_B)							0.44	1
By Publication								
1.Peer-reviewed article	8	0.08	0.06	-0.05	0.21	1.15	20.30**	7
2.Dissertations	4	-0.10	0.18	-.046	0.26	-0.55	17.53***	3
Total Between (Q_B)							0.85	1
By Sample Sizes								
1.Large	5	0.07	0.06	-0.05	0.20	1.06	11.26**	4
2.Small	7	-0.01	0.15	-0.31	0.28	-0.09	34.22***	6
Total Between (Q_B)							0.25	1
By Instruments								
1.ASSIS	7	0.06	0.10	-0.14	0.27	0.60	28.82***	6
2.Others	5	-0.04	0.11	-0.28	0.18	-0.38	19.75***	4
Total Between (Q_B)							0.48	1
By Mean Age								
1.Below 24	4	0.02	0.12	-0.21	0.26	0.19	16.05**	3
2.At or above 24	8	0.01	0.10	-0.19	0.22	0.15	33.42***	7
Total Between (Q_B)							0.003	1

Note. k = number of studies; ES = effect size; SE = standard error; CI = confidence interval. $*p < .05$. $**p < .01$. $***p < .001$.

Although significant heterogeneity was found within each subgroup, the overall effect size (*ES*) remained nonsignificant across all subgroups. Given that the *Qb* is consistently nonsignificant for all study feature analyses, it appears that no study feature can explain the lack of significance.

In summary, the subgroup analyses did not reveal statistically significant differences in acculturative stress between genders across different categories. However, there was notable heterogeneity in effect sizes within each subgroup, indicating variability in the findings across studies.

DISCUSSION

The results of the present meta-analysis did not yield statistically significant differences in acculturative stress according to sex. These findings suggest that gender may not be a substantial factor in acculturative stress among international students. These findings support several previous studies that reported no significant gender differences in acculturative stress among international students (Gebregergis, 2018; Gholamrezai, 1995; Misra et al., 2003). For example, Mustaffa and Ilias (2013) indicated that gender is not a distinguishing factor for cross-cultural success. Another study revealed that male and female international students do not differ in terms of both sociocultural and psychological adjustment (Rujipak & Limprasert, 2016). However, the results of this study contrast with those of other studies that indicated that either male or female students experienced higher levels of acculturative stress (Castillo et al., 2015; Koo et al., 2021; Lee, 2014; Mahmood & Burke, 2018; Misra & Castillo, 2004; Talwar et al., 2022; Ayoob et al., 2011; Hahn, 2010; Kefayati, 2016). These discrepancies highlight the complexity of the factors influencing acculturative stress and the need for further investigation.

One possible explanation for the lack of significant gender differences in acculturative stress among international students could be the development of differing cultural norms and gender roles in diverse cultural contexts. Cultural norms refer to the social expectations and behaviors caused by cultural contexts. For example, in some cultures, traditional gender norms may view women's roles as caregivers and homemakers who endure extreme sacrifices, whereas in other cultures, they may promote more equal views where men and women share responsibilities equally. These norms can affect various aspects of life, including gender roles, family dynamics, and social interactions (Castillo et al., 1015). As societies become more developed and globalized, traditional gender roles and expectations may change, leading to equal stressors and coping mechanisms between male and female international students. In addition, support services and resources offered by educational institutions and host countries to international students can help relieve stressors and reduce observed gender differences in acculturative stress levels (Gebregergis, 2018). For example, student affairs services could launch initiatives to promote social justice and inclusion among international students. These initiatives should be led by counseling centers, international student services, and offices dedicated to diversity, equity, and inclusion, with additional support from faculty members (Xie & Ridley, 2024). All these developing social dynamics emphasize the need for continued research to understand and address cultural stress among international students.

However, acculturative stress is a complex and multifaceted phenomenon influenced by several factors and is not limited to gender alone. Cultural context, social support networks, language proficiency, academic requirements, and experiences of discrimination can significantly influence an international student's level of acculturative stress. In addition, the measures used in previous studies and self-report questionnaires may not include the full range of these influential factors, leading to the inability to detect significant associations. Moreover, the characteristics of the participants, including their diverse cultural backgrounds and individual coping strategies, may have contributed to the nonsignificant results with respect to gender. International students can alleviate this stress by enhancing their English skills, developing self-compassion, maintaining a positive outlook, and engaging in meaningful activities (Le & Huyen-Nguyen, 2024). Additionally, social support plays a crucial role in mitigating acculturative stress, acting as a protective factor against life stressors and increasing overall health and wellness (Fedolina & Saptandari, 2024).

Implications

The findings of this study not only contribute to our understanding of acculturative stress among international students but also have significant implications for supporting their well-being within academic institutions. By recognizing that gender may not be a substantial factor in acculturative stress, institutions can develop comprehensive support systems that address the broader needs of all students, regardless of gender. This includes implementing inclusive policies, providing culturally sensitive counseling services, offering orientation programs with language assistance, and organizing diverse cultural events. These initiatives would help relieve acculturative stress and better support overall well-being and academic success.

Longitudinal studies with more comprehensive assessments of acculturative stress and its determinants could provide a deeper understanding of the role of gender and other factors in predicting acculturative stress among international students over time. Exploring additional factors such as cultural identity, discrimination, coping strategies, and social integration could further enhance the understanding of acculturative stress dynamics.

In conclusion, while the study did not find significant gender differences in acculturative stress among international students, the complex interaction between factors indicates the need for continued research to support international students' well-being. By addressing limitations and considering different variables influencing acculturative adjustment, future research can usefully contribute to interventions and policies to enhance the acculturation experience of international students.

Acknowledgments

We received the Humane Letters Grant for this publication. No artificial intelligence (AI) tools were used to create content in the preparation of this manuscript. The authors wrote, reviewed, and edited the entire work, adhering to ethical standards and guidelines for academic integrity.

REFERENCES

Ayoob, M., Singh, T., & Jan, M. (2011). Gender difference in acculturative stress and health among college students. *Indian Journal of Psychology*, *1*(2), 1-8. https://www.researchgate.net/publication/349367955_Gender_Difference_in_Acculturative_Stress_and_Health_among_College_Students

Berry, J. W. (1995). 20. Psychology of acculturation. *The culture and psychology reader, 457.*

Berry, J. W., Kim, U., Minde, T., & Mok, D. (1987). Comparative studies of acculturative stress. *International Migration Review, 21*(3), 491–511. https:// doi.org/10.2307/2546607

Castillo, L. G., Navarro, R. L., Walker, J. E., Schwartz, S. J., Zamboanga, B. L., Whitbourne, S. K., Weisskirch, R. S., Kim, S. Y., Park, I. J., Vazsonyi, A. T., & Caraway, S. J. (2015). Gender matters: The influence of acculturation and acculturative stress on Latino college student depressive symptomatology. *Journal of Latina/o Psychology*, *3*(1), 40–55. https://doi.org/10.1037/lat0000030

Cong, M., Dong, Y., & Chao, R. (2024). Acculturative stress of Asian International Students before and during the COVID-19 pandemic. *Journal of Comparative & International Higher Education*, *16*(1). https://doi.org/10.32674/jcihe.v16i1.4918

Desa, A., Yusooff, F., & Kadir, N. B. (2012). Acculturative stress among international postgraduate students at UKM. *Procedia - Social and Behavioral Sciences*, *59*, 364–369. https://doi.org/10.1016/j.sbspro.2012.09.287

Fedolina, B. F., & Saptandari, E. E. W. (2024). Perceived Social Support as Predictor of Acculturative Stress Among Indonesian Exchange Students in Europe. *Jurnal Psikologi Integratif, 12*(1), 83-101. https://ejournal.uin-suka.ac.id/isoshum/PI/article/view/2951

Gebregergis, W. T. (2018). Major causes of acculturative stress and their relations with sociodemographic factors and depression among international students. *Open Journal of Social Sciences*, *06*(10), 68–87. https://doi.org/10.4236/jss.2018.610007

Gholamrezai, A. (1995). Acculturation and self-esteem as predictors of acculturative stress among international students at the University of Wollongong. [Unpublished doctoral dissertation]. University of Wollongong, Australia. http://ro.uow.edu.au/theses/2153/

Gibson, M. A. (2001). Immigrant adaptation and patterns of acculturation. *Human Development, 44* (1), 19-23. https://www.jstor.org/stable/26763493

Hahn, Z. L. (2010). Coping with acculturative stress and depression among international students: A cultural perspective [Doctoral dissertation]. University of Pennsylvania. https://search.proquest.com/openview/9d10c36c21448f0a0c24b0552cbcd6c8/1?pq-origsite=gscholar&cbl=18750

Institute of International Education. (2023). *Open Doors report on international educational exchange: International students.* https://opendoorsdata.org/annual-release/international-students/#data-highlights

Iorga, M., Soponaru, C., Muraru, I.-D., Socolov, S., & Petrariu, F.-D. (2020). Factors associated with acculturative stress among international medical students. *BioMed Research International*, *2020*, 1–9. https://doi.org/10.1155/2020/2564725

Kagan, H. & Cohen, J. (1990). Culture adjustment of international students. *Psychological Science, 1* (2), 131-137. https://doi.org/10.1111/j.1467-9280.1990.tb00082.x

Kefayati, E. (2016). The relationship between acculturative stress, perceived social support, and perceived discrimination in international students [Master's thesis]. Eastern Mediterranean University EMU. http://i-rep.emu.edu.tr:8080/xmlui/handle/11129/4145

Koo, K., Baker, I., & Yoon, J. (2021). The first year acculturation: A longitudinal study on acculturative stress and adjustment among the first year international college students. *Journal of International Students*, *11*(2). https://doi.org/10.32674/jis.v11i2.1726

Le, T. T.-K., & Huyen-Nguyen, T. T. (2024). Stressors and solutions: A preliminary examination of acculturative stress among international students. *Journal of Comparative & International Higher Education*, *15*(5(S)). https://doi.org/10.32674/jcihe.v15i5(s).5838

Mahmood, H., & Burke, M. G. (2018). Analysis of acculturative stress and sociocultural adaptation among international students at a non-metropolitan university. *Journal of International Students*, *8*(1). https://doi.org/10.32674/jis.v8i1.166

Matud, M. P. (2004). Gender differences in stress and coping styles. *Personality and Individual Differences*, *37*(7), 1401–1415. https://doi.org/10.1016/j.paid.2004.01.010

Misra, R., & Castillo, L. G. (2004). Academic stress among college students: Comparison of American and international students. *International Journal of Stress Management*, *11*(2), 132–148. https://doi.org/10.1037/1072-5245.11.2.132

Misra, R., Crist, M., & Burant, C. J. (2003). Relationships among life stress, social support, academic stressors, and reactions to stressors of international students in the United States. *International Journal of Stress Management*, *10*(2), 137–157. https://doi.org/10.1037/1072-5245.10.2.137

Mustaffa, C. S., & Ilias, M. (2013). Relationship between students adjustment factors and cross cultural adjustment: A survey at the Northern University of Malaysia. *Intercultural communication studies*, *22*(1). https://www-s3-live.kent.edu/s3fs-root/s3fs-public/file/19-Che-Su-Mustaffa-Munirah-Ilias.pdf

Oyeniyi, O., Smith, R. L., Watson, J. C., & Nelson, K. (2021). Comparison of first-year international students' adjustment to college at the undergraduate and graduate level. *Journal of Comparative & International Higher Education, 13*(2), 112–131. https://doi.org/10.32674/jcihe.v13i2.2584

Rujipak, V., & Limprasert, S. (2016). International students' adjustment in Thailand. *ABAC Journal*, *36*(1), 34-46. http://www.assumptionjournal.au.edu/index.php/abacjournal/article/view/2278

Soufi Amlashi, R., Majzoobi, M., & Forstmeier, S. (2024). The relationship between acculturative stress and psychological outcomes in international students: A systematic review and meta-analysis. *Frontiers in Psychology, 15*. https://doi.org/10.3389/fpsyg.2024.1403807

Talwar, P., Rethinasamy, S., Abd Ghani, K., Tan, K. W., & Yusoff, N. F. M. (2022). Sociodemographic determinants of acculturation stress among International University students. *EDUCATUM Journal of Social Sciences*, *8*(1), 23-30. https://doi.org/10.37134/ejoss.vol8.1.3.2022

Xie, S., & Ridley, C. R. (2024). Acculturative stress, Chinese proactive coping, future time perspective, and subjective well-being among Chinese international students in the U.S.: A moderation model. *Journal of Comparative & International Higher Education, 16*(2), 180-195. https://ojed.org/jcihe

Yu, B., Chen, X., Li, S., Liu, Y., Jacques-Tiura, A. J., & Yan, H. (2014). Acculturative stress and influential factors among international students in China: A structural dynamic perspective. *PLoS ONE, 9*(4). https://doi.org/10.1371/journal.pone.0096322

Yun, C. T. P., & Greenwood, K. M. (2021). Stress, sleep and performance in international and domestic university students. *Journal of International Students*, *12*(1). https://doi.org/10.32674/jis.v12i1.3299

Author bios

Rawan Alzukari is a PhD graduate in Educational Psychology from Mississippi State University. Her research interests focus on academic self-efficacy, achievement motivation, and the acculturative stress experienced by international students, with a focus on their academic success.
Email: rawanzkri@gmail.com

Tianlan Wei is an Associate Professor of Educational Psychology at Mississippi State University. Her expertise is grounded in her educational psychology background and extensive research in social science domains, and her research interests span a wide spectrum, encompassing developmental trajectories, mathematics education, psychological assessment, and gender equity studies.
Email: ewei@colled.msstate.edu

Article

Journal of International Students
Volume 14, Issue 5 (2024), pp. 159-175
ISSN: 2162-3104 (Print), 2166-3750 (Online)
jistudents.org

Motivations of International Students from Indonesia, Thailand, and the Philippines in Selecting Teacher Education Programs

Fihris *
Nasikhin
Naifah
Sofa Muthohar
Universitas Islam Negeri Walisongo Semarang, Indonesia

ABSTRACT

In this study, we examined the motivations of students from Indonesia, Thailand, and the Philippines in choosing to pursue undergraduate teacher education programs. Through a narrative inquiry approach, we collected data using focus group discussions with international student representatives from the three countries. Findings show that the common motivation of students from the three countries in choosing a teacher education study program was to improve the quality of education in their home countries and form a better next generation. However, there is a fundamental difference in the motivation behind their choices. Filipino students view teaching as a challenging and dynamic job, whereas Indonesian students are driven by religious calling, parental encouragement, and attractive work-hour flexibility. Thailand students, on the other hand, are more motivated by economic factors, the promise of increased self-esteem, and respect from society. This study provides valuable insights into understanding the motives for choosing a teacher education major for international students.

Keywords: motivation, teacher education program, international students, Indonesia, Thailand, Philippines

* *Corresponding author*

INTRODUCTION

The issue of the teaching profession has become the focus of significant discussion in the ASEAN region (Postlethwaite et al., 2014). In Thailand, for example, the inequality of access to education between urban and rural areas and the gap in the quality of education between regions are the main obstacles faced by educators (Supakit Wittayasin, 2017). Moreover, in the Philippines, the lack of educational facilities and low teacher salaries are the main obstacles to retaining qualified teachers (Lorraine Pe Symaco, 2013). Indonesia, the world's fourth-most populous country, faces similar challenges. The number of teachers is not proportional to needs, especially in remote areas, and the difference in the quality of education between islands is a critical issue (Jakhongir Shaturaev, 2021). In addition, in each country, the application of educational technology and the lack of support for the development of the teaching profession significantly affect the quality of education at the national level (Ab Halim bin Tamuri & Norfaizah binti Othman, 2012).

Although the teaching profession in the ASEAN region faces several challenges, the loyalty of the community to educate children in teacher study programs in higher education remains high (Widiati Utami & Nur Hayati, 2016). This can be seen from the results of research by Kawuryan et al. (2012), which revealed an increase in the number of teacher education students in Indonesia every year. In addition, Sirait Swando's research succeeded in revealing a strong desire for high school graduates to pursue teacher education (Sirait Swando, 2016). Data from Stephen Raudenbush's study also show that universities with teacher training programs in Thailand often reject applicants because their quota has been met (Sinaga Bornok, 2021). This shows that the interest of the ASEAN community in studying teacher training programs remains high, despite the limitations in access to such education. In line with Bornok Sinaga's research, further efforts are needed to improve the quality of teacher education to meet the demands of the times and prepare prospective teachers with relevant competencies (Stephen Raudenbush, 2021).

Although the teaching profession in ASEAN countries has become the focus of attention, few studies have analyzed the comparative motivation of ASEAN students in choosing a teaching study program (Thongphukdee Chayapol, & Thanin Ratana O Larn, 2021). In fact, research comparing three countries with different religious characteristics, such as Indonesia, Thailand, and the Philippines, is still very limited. Radcliffe Brown (1945) highlighted that the differences in the majority of religions are unique because there are unique factors that influence students' motivation to choose to teach, including cultural and religious influences. Therefore, further research on differences in motivation in choosing a teacher study program is important to provide deeper insights into the factors that motivate students to choose the teaching profession in ASEAN countries.

This study aims to analyze the various motivations of students from Indonesia, Thailand and the Philippines in choosing a training teacher as their study program. International students from these three countries are selected with special consideration to explore the unique perspectives of each cultural context (Bob Scribner, 1982). The importance of this research lies in its contribution to understanding the factors that influence international students' decisions to choose the field of teacher education, with the hope of improving cross-cultural understanding in the context of education (Vance Randall, 2013). The study began with an in-depth description of how international students from Indonesia, the Philippines, and Thailand made the decision to join a teacher training program. Furthermore, it is critically analyzed to reveal reflections on the experiences of international students from all three countries.

Literature Review

Researchers have paid considerable attention to the potential of teacher education programs create meaningful lives for the community. For example, Amzat Ismail et al. (2017) reported the tendency of Malaysian students to choose the teaching profession as a step to gain respect in society. The analysis of Malmberg Lars-Erik (2006) also shows that the teaching profession in Finland is considered a dream because it offers promising income for teachers. Candidus and Cummins, highlighted the psychological influence of increasing the number of applicants for teacher training programs in Nigerian universities (Candidus Nwakasi & Phyllis, 2018). This reflects the complexity and diversity of considerations that motivate individuals to choose a career path in education.

In their study, Robert and Gao concluded that there is a relationship between a person's motivation to become a teacher and Abraham Maslow's pyramid of basic needs (Robert Taormina, & Jennifer, 2013). Maslow's pyramid of needs organizes the hierarchy of human needs into five levels, ranging from physical needs to self-actualization needs (Saul McLeod, 2007). The relationship between Maslow's pyramid of needs and a person's motivation to become a teacher can be explained through the fulfillment of social needs and the need for self-actualization (Adiele & Nath Abraham, 2020). Asteachers, one has the opportunity to positively influence their students, build meaningful social relationships and feel valued in the educational community (Aspy David, 1969). By meeting these social needs, a teacher can feel personal satisfaction and full achievement as an educator (Joseph Gawel, 2019). In addition, teaching and educational activities also provide opportunities to understand the deep meaning and purpose of life, in accordance with the level of self-actualization needs in Maslow's pyramid.

The pyramid of basic needs presented by Maslow was used as the basis for Dolman et al. in compiling motivational indicators. This includes a number of factors that can describe a person's level of drive or enthusiasm in achieving a goal or doing an activity (Dohlman Lena, 2019). Dolman et al. explained that key indicators of motivation involve an individual's level of interest and inclination toward a task or goal, the extent to which a person feels competent or confident in performing an activity, and the extent to which the results of the effort are considered valuable and meaningful. Similarly, Osemeke Monday and Samuel Adegboyega developed a motivation framework based on the level of determination and resistance to obstacles, and a focus on achieving goals is also a relevant motivational indicator (Monday Osemeke, & Samuel Adegboyega, 2017). Toni Watson asserts that internally motivated individuals tend to have a stronger and more consistent drive in pursuing their goals, whereas external factors such as social support, recognition, or rewards can also play an important role in maintaining a person's motivation level (Tony Watson, 1996).

METHOD

This study adopts a qualitative research approach with focus groups as the main instrument for data collection (Norman Denzin & Katherine, 2007). The selection of in-depth focus group interviews was chosen because of the advantages of the approach, which allowed the researcher to detail and understand the respondents' frame of mind in a more holistic way. This decision is based on the superiority of methods that can provide a rich and in-depth context, enriching the understanding of the phenomenon being studied (Manju Gundumogula, 2020). Therefore, it facilitates the capture of more nuanced and complex views of the focus group, opening up opportunities for more in-depth and interpretive analysis. The collected data were then analyzed with the help of Chat GPT. 4.0 to help find the right word and sentence arrangement while still being guided by the data presented by the research participants.

The focus group members we selected to outline their motivations for choosing a teaching major were third-year students with good English language skills, which is considered a critical stage in their academic journey. Students at this stage are believed to have developed a mature understanding of their field of study from the beginning of their university journey (Saunders, 2012). The twelve respondents involved in this study were from three different countries, with 4 Indonesia students from Walisongo State Islamic University Semarang, 4 Filipino students from the University of Technology Malaysia, and 4 Thailand students from Walisongo State Islamic University Semarang. All the selected respondents were students of the teacher study program at their respective institutions. The selection of focus group members is based on the need to obtain representative and diverse data on their motivations in the context of education in different countries (Hoepfl Marie, 1997).

Table 1: Demographic of Participants

No	Initials	Country of Origin	Places of Study	Age
1	I1	Indonesian	UIN Walisongo Semarang	24
2	I2	Indonesian	UIN Walisongo Semarang	23
3	I3	Indonesian	UIN Walisongo Semarang	24
4	I4	Indonesian	UIN Walisongo Semarang	21
5	F1	Philippines	Universiti Teknologi Malaysia	25
6	F2	Philippines	Universiti Teknologi Malaysia	27
7	F3	Philippines	Universiti Teknologi Malaysia	26
8	F4	Philippines	Universiti Teknologi Malaysia	23
9	T1	Thailand	UIN Walisongo Semarang	25
10	T2	Thailand	UIN Walisongo Semarang	26
11	T3	Thailand	UIN Walisongo Semarang	23
12	T4	Thailand	UIN Walisongo Semarang	22

Focus group discussions were conducted face-to-face in three sessions, each lasting 60–70 minutes for each country involved. After consent was obtained to record nonverbal expressions, each participant's response was recorded. A moderator guided the discussion, the focus of which was to explore students' motivation for choosing teacher training programs in the context of education in Indonesia, the Philippines and Thailand. Efforts are made to ensure that discussions cover only the main aspects that are relevant to the research objectives and avoid discussing unrelated matters. The data are recorded, and transcription is performed with the guidance of the moderator. The collected data were validated with a member checking and triangulation model. The data analysis process following the Miles and Huberman model includes three main steps: data reduction, data presentation, and conclusion drawn/verification. First, the data collected through focus group discussions (FGDs) were reduced, namely, selecting, focusing, and simplifying information according to the research objectives. Second, the data that have been reduced are presented in the form of matrices, tables, or narratives, making it easier to analyze further. Third, the researcher draws conclusions on the basis of patterns, themes, or relationships found in the data and verifies them to ensure the validity of the findings. This process takes place iteratively and continuously throughout the research. (Salmona & Kaczynski, 2024). Artificial intelligence (AI) is used to help compose more detailed and organized sentences and paragraphs through the Chat GPT. 4.0, while the research data are obtained directly according to the research rules described in the research methods section. By using Chat GPT 4.0, we have made every effort to maintain scientific ethics.

RESULTS

Motivation of Indonesian students in participating in teacher education programs

This study shows that the motivation of Indonesian students to participate in teacher training programs is based on social, religious, and patriotic motives. Informant I1 explained that the reason for choosing the teacher study program was to carry out a religious order. In the Islamic view, every individual is required to be able to provide benefits to others. I1 emphasized that being a teacher is considered an implementation of religious command because it involves aspects of teaching and mentoring that are considered positive in Islam. Thus, his decision to pursue this profession was not just a career choice but also a form of obedience to the religious teachings he believed. This can be interpreted as a representation of his personal commitment to religious values, which is reflected in his career choice as a teacher. It is said

> "My religion (Islam) teaches khoirunnas anfauhum linnas, the best human being is a person who is beneficial to others. I think being a teacher truly represents this teaching because teachers teach knowledge that is very useful for our students".

I1's expression is in line with the reasoning given by informant I2. He explained that being a teacher is a noble profession because it can guide other people's careers to be better. This is also the reason why parents of I2 informants always encourage their children to become teachers since their children are still in junior high school. According to her, the encouragement and blessing of her parents to become a teacher convinced her that this profession was the best choice for her. This phenomenon highlights the deep-rooted view of the public that the teaching profession in Indonesia has an important role in shaping the future of children. Informant I2 said that his parents always taught him that the decision to become a teacher was not only a job but also a vocation and dedication to educate and shape the next generation. This understanding reflects the values of care, responsibility and dedication inherent in the profession in Indonesia. I2 revealed,

> "There are many reasons why I chose the teaching program as my place of study, including the support and encouragement from my parents. They have been telling me about the glory of the teaching profession since I was in junior high school, about eight years ago. I agree with my parents that being a teacher is not just a job but also a vocation and dedication to educate and shape the next generation".

Moreover, informant I3 explained that the most important reason for him to study in the teacher study program was job opportunities, which provided less working time than other jobs did. He believes that teachers work only Monday--Friday and still have two days off a week. Informant I3 explained that teachers have clear working time between the mornings at approximately 7:00 and 16:00. This provides an advantage because it makes it possible to maintain a balance between work and personal life. In addition, working hours that provide breaks are important for absorbing learning experiences, developing creativity, and maintaining mental and physical health. He emphasized that teacher training programs not only offer exciting career opportunities but also provide opportunities for individuals to achieve a healthy balance of life. I3 explained,

> "The teacher program will take me to become a teacher. This is interesting because teachers' working hours are ideal in Indonesia because middle-level teachers work only during the day, Monday-Friday. It allows me to develop my potential".

The I4 informants had different reasons for choosing the teacher training program, which aimed to express their patriotic spirit. For him, taking a vocational program is not only about acquiring teaching skills as a teacher but also as a form of participation in developing the education sector in this country. He believes that through teaching, he can make a significant contribution to shaping the golden generation through the education system. In addition, a strong drive to prosper in society by applying good manners is a key factor that encourages him to choose this profession. This belief is in line with the goals of Indonesia's National Education, which emphasizes the importance of shaping the character and intelligence of the younger generation as the foundation for the nation's progress. Informant I4 explained,

> "I took the teacher study program to have good teaching skills. This is important so that I can help the country create a quality generation through good teaching skills. It is important to achieve national education goals in Indonesia"

In response to the I4 informant's answer, the other participants strongly responded to his statement. In response, informant I2 gave his support by stating, "This is a very important reason, because a good generation will be born from quality teachers." This statement reflects the belief in the central role of education and the presence of competent educators in shaping a quality future. This view is in line with the perspective of the I1 informant, who emphasized that the challenges expressed by I4 must be overcome by the development of an effective teacher education program. I1 highlights the need for universities to provide programs that are able to improve students' teaching skills so that the teachers produced truly have the qualities needed to educate future generations.

In this context, the I5 informant added a relevant social dimension by stating that the desire to create a good generation through education is in line with community service efforts. I5 stated, "Teaching is a very influential part of community service; Without education, a country will find it difficult to develop." This statement emphasizes the close relationship between education and social progress, where the role of teachers as agents of social change is becoming increasingly significant. As such, the participants' serious response to the I4 statement reflected an awareness of the complexity of educational challenges and the need for collaboration in addressing them, underscoring the critical role of education in shaping a sustainable and competitive future.

Motivation of Thailand students in participating in teacher training programs

This study successfully shows that the motivation of Thai students to major in teaching is related to respect and price, economic motives, and the need for self-actualization. The T1 informant, in a detailed interview, revealed that his decision to choose a teacher training program was not solely based on his love for education but rather on his aspiration to achieve a respected position in society. In this context, he expressed his belief that the teaching profession in Thailand has a highly valued reputation and is placed at a high level of social status. For T1, being a teacher is not only a job but also a path to recognition and respect from the community. This positive outlook on the teaching profession provides additional motivation for T1 to pursue higher education, with the hope that his investment in learning will lead him to a respected and recognized role in Thailand's social fabric. T1 revealed,

> "I want to be a teacher, that is why I joined this program. Of course not without reason, but because in Thailand, in almost every district, teachers have a very honorable and highly valued position".

Meanwhile, the T2 informant said that the reason for participating in the teacher education program is closely related to the guarantee of teacher professional income in Thailand. On the basis of the discussion he had with his parents, who are also teachers, informant T2 explained that the salary of teachers in Thailand reached 21,950 THB or approximately 625.29 USD (2024 exchange rate) in one month. This far exceeds the average teacher income in various

ASEAN countries, such as Cambodia, Laos and even Indonesia. In addition to the basic salary, this income does not include overtime pay, bonuses, or honorariums for administering exams, which can be a significant addition for teachers in Thailand. The T2 informant emphasized that economic security provides stability and certainty, which in turn makes it easier for a person to achieve happiness in daily life. This finding shows that the motivation of Thailand students to participate in teacher training programs is driven not only by an interest in education but also by the aspiration to achieve economic prosperity, which can bring happiness to their lives.

> "It needs to be said honestly that my main motive for teaching is the security of the income of the teaching profession in Thailand. My parents are teachers and earn approximately 21,950 THB per month. This is important for me to pay attention to because economic security will have a great impact on a person's happiness level."

For the same reason, the T3 informant admitted that his main goal in choosing the teacher study program was related to career opportunities and the ease of obtaining a job: "I took this major because I needed a promising job in the future". However, he did not deny that other reasons related to the desire to devote themselves to the community were very high. He explained that his religion (Buddhism) teaches that humans living in this world can provide benefits, at least for the people around them. This is also encouraged by the teachings of his parents, who emphasize that their children always teach virtue to anyone. On this basis, he feels that taking a teacher education program is a choice that is in accordance with his vision and mission in life. Informant T3 said,

> "Being kind is a religious commandment, my parents always said that we can teach kindness to anyone. I feel that the teaching profession is a choice that is in line with my vision and mission in life".

Meanwhile, informant I4 gave different reasons from his three friends. He stated that the decision to take a teaching study program is related to the need for self-actualization. It has to do with the drive of the individual to reach maximum potential in his field, gain personal satisfaction, and pursue deep interests. Informant I4 expressed the importance of embracing passion in determining the path of education, along with acknowledging that choosing a major is not only about meeting the demands of the job market but also embracing personal values and interests for the formation of personal identity and happiness.

> "The choice of teacher study program is related to self-actualization; I feel free to make choices, and I find this freedom in my life purpose to become a teacher".

In response to T4's expression, T2's informant described his views on his religious teachings, Buddhism, as the path to happiness in life. According to him, choosing this path is a wise decision because it can lead individuals to freedom that goes hand in hand with happiness without violating religious norms. This view reflects a deep understanding of how religious teachings can guide the achievement of happiness, taking into account spiritual and moral values. On the other hand, the response of the I1 informant highlighted another aspect of life, namely, the role of a teacher. I1 emphasized that being a teacher is not only about self-actualization but also about one's readiness to become a role model for one's students. This statement shows an understanding of the moral and social responsibilities inherent in the role of an educator, which not only shapes a career but also shapes positive character and values in the next generation.

Motivation of Filipino students in participating in teacher education programs

On the basis of the results of in-depth discussions with teacher students from the Philippines, this study shows that the motives of Filipino teacher students in taking a teacher study program are focused on the aspects of meeting psychological needs, the desire to contribute to improving the welfare of Filipino society, and career motives to find a job that is not monotonous. The F1 informant explained that he was interested in participating in the teaching program because he was motivated by elementary school teachers in the past. She saw that her female teacher looked happy when interacting with young students. According to him, this happens because the interaction has a positive impact because it can help support children's development, creating a supportive and fun learning environment. Experiences such as this are the basis for why F1 informants want to become teachers because, according to him, being a teacher makes it easier to find happiness in life through a positive contribution to children's growth and learning. In addition, being a teacher gives him the opportunity to continue learning and develop personally, enriching his knowledge in the field of education.

> "I chose the teacher study program because it truly helped me find happiness. " I like children because of their innocence and cute faces; by becoming a teacher, I will meet them often".

The F2 informant firmly stated that his decision to join the teacher study program had a strong background. According to him, this ambition does not come from personal desires but is part of his determination to contribute to improving the quality of education in the Philippines. With the belief that the role of teachers is the main key in shaping human quality, F2 believes that if teachers have good quality, the overall quality of education will improve. According to him, this is the basis for creating a superior and quality generation. In terms of the quality of education, F2 feels encouraged to participate in efforts to improve the quality of education in the environment where he or she lives. In addition, her strong desire to educate children who have skipped school is an additional encouragement that motivates her to pursue her dreams. The F2 educational journey is aimed not only at personal achievement but also at a real commitment to play an active role in creating positive change in the Philippine education system. F2 revealed,

> "It is important for me to pay attention to children who drop out of school, either due to economic factors or a messy family. " The teacher program will help me provide capital to become a good education, which can provide opportunities for them to stay educated".

For different reasons, the F3 informant explained that his goal in taking the teacher study program was an opportunity to find a job that was not monotonous. According to him, being a teacher is a very dynamic job because it involves continuous interaction with students who have various characters and learning needs. The F3 informant imagines that every day, a teacher is faced with new challenges that require creativity and adaptability to create an effective learning environment. In addition, the teaching process involves preparing relevant and interesting learning materials, understanding students' learning styles, and developing teaching methods that are appropriate for student development. From practical field experience, the F3 informant concluded that teachers act as guides, advisors, and motivators, helping students overcome learning obstacles and inspiring them to reach their best potential. This diversity of duties and responsibilities is what makes the job of a teacher interesting and challenging every day. F3 explained,

> "Being a teacher is fun and not boring. From my experience taking part in teaching practice in high school, I find it fun because there are always different challenges every day. This is closely related to the different characteristics and dispositions of students".

In response to F3's argument, the F4 informant expressed his agreement by saying "finding a job that is not monotonous has great relevance in improving one's quality of life and job satisfaction." F4 informants emphasized that nonmonotonous work involves a variety of tasks and challenges that can stimulate professional growth and creativity. In a dynamic work environment, individuals have the opportunity to develop a wide range of skills, expand their knowledge, and increase their resilience to change. According to him, being a teacher can help prevent fatigue and boredom, which can result in a decrease in motivation and productivity. By providing variety in daily tasks, a teacher can feel more engaged in their work, increase their sense of accomplishment, and foster a passion for sustainable development. In conclusion, F3 and F4 informants explained the importance of finding a job that provides space for exploration, challenges and personal growth so that a person can achieve success and happiness in their career.

At the end of the discussion session, the F1, F3, and F4 informants agreed that the teacher study program they took was closely related to the social, geographical, and religious context. The Philippines, as a culturally and ethnically diverse country, encourages students to choose a teaching path as a way to contribute to the development of their society. Social conditions involving economic and educational inequality can be a major trigger, where the desire to inspire future generations and reduce educational disparities is a strong motivation. In addition, the geography of the Philippines, which often consists of hard-to-reach rural areas and has limited access to high-quality education, encourages students to teach in hopes of helping improve the educational situation in the area. In a religious context, strong religious values can also be a driving factor, with the belief that being an educator is a way to serve society and achieve spiritual goals.

DISCUSSION

This study shows that students from the Philippines, Thailand, and Indonesia have the same motivation in deciding to participate in teacher training programs. This unity of purpose is seen in their aspirations to improve the quality of education in their respective countries, which reflects a shared desire to shape the next generation better and achieve the educational goals of each country. The informants from the three countries agreed that choosing a teacher training program is not only a career choice but also a manifestation of a deep desire to make a positive contribution to society. This decision can be considered a tangible manifestation of their service to society, signaling that their commitment to play an active role in creating positive change through education (James Mayall, 1990).

The similarity of reasons for students from Indonesia, Thailand, and the Philippines choosing teacher education programs can be explained by the similar geographical, social, and cultural conditions in these ASEAN countries (Mie Oba, 2019). Geographically, these three countries have regional contexts that tend to affect educational needs and challenges. In addition, similarities in social and cultural structures in ASEAN create a uniform mindset among students, sparking their interest in pursuing teacher education programs (Busapathumrong Pattamaporn, 2012). These factors shape the common needs and social conditions of the surrounding community (Stefan Rother, 2012), making the decision to choose teaching as a relevant study program option and in accordance with the demands of the same regional context.

Despite these similarities, there are different motives that explain why students from the Philippines, Thailand, and Indonesia choose to participate in teacher education programs. Filipino students see teaching as a dynamic and nonmonotonous job, which presents the potential for self-development through new challenges every day. For them, being a teacher also means undertaking entertaining tasks, interacting with children who have unique characters every day (Juncal Cuñado and Fernando Pérez, 2012). On the other hand, Indonesian students are inspired by their religious vocation and the high value placed on the teaching profession in the eyes of God. Encouragement from parents, low working hours, and free time are important factors in their decisions. Moreover, Thai students choose teacher training with economic motives because the teaching profession is rewarded with a decent income, a sense of self-esteem, and respect from society, which is also a form of self-actualization (Juul, 1959).

The results of this study reinforce the findings of Vesamavibool (2015). Studies have shown that the high salary level of teachers in Thailand has a positive effect on people's interest in sending their children to teacher training colleges. Research by Daungkaew, Ratana, and Annop Jeenawathana revealed that the average income of teachers in Thailand reaches 9.5 million rupiah per month, almost double the income of public teachers in Indonesia (Agustina Pitriyani, et al., 2012). In addition to the financial aspect, Gurevichnoted that Robert (1975) also supported this research by highlighting the high prestige that Thailand society gives teachers. This shows that teachers in Thailand are highly valued, a concept that is in stark contrast to reality in Indonesia, as explained by Agi et al., where teachers are faced with honorary status with minimal salaries, creating a situation where teachers are often ridiculed by society because of their profession (Agi Septina Nugraheni &Wiwien Dinar, 2019).

Although some of the findings are in line with previous research, this study highlights significant differences from the analysis of Kongcharoen et al. (2020), which showed that teachers in Thailand are faced with a high workload, including taking exams and other responsibilities in school. In contrast, this study shows that students in Thailand remain motivated to choose a teaching major because they feel that the teaching profession there provides freedom and convenience to actualize themselves through career development.

In the context of education in Indonesia and the Philippines, this study confirms the analysis of David Morgan (2012) that adherence to divine values makes people want to be useful to others. This study challenges the findings of Assagaf et al., (2015) that low salaries can make teacher education programs lose interest in Indonesia. Instead, the study suggests that parents' incentive to send their children to teacher education programs is a stronger reason than salary considerations alone. The findings also reveal a similarity in motivation between Indonesian and Filipino teacher education students, who emphasize comfort at work rather than salary. This result also contrasts with the findings of Majorsy Ursa (2011), who highlighted that salary is the main factor in choosing a job whereas this study shows that comfort also plays an important role in work rather than salary. These findings contrast with previous research that showed that the main factor in choosing a job was income/salary, not convenience.

The results of this study can be attributed to Maslow's theory of basic needs, which organizes the hierarchy of human needs from the most basic to the highest. The motivation of students from these three countries reflects the fulfillment of different levels of needs in this hierarchy. Filipino students who view teaching as a dynamic job can be associated with the need for self-actualization or the fulfillment of personal potential, which is at the top of the hierarchy (Joseph Gawel, 2019). Indonesian students, who are inspired by religious vocations and parental encouragement, describe the need for affiliation and security (Lena Dohlman, 2019). On the other hand, more economically motivated Thai students reflect the fulfillment of physical and security needs, which are at a lower level in Maslow's hierarchy (Anjanaben Trivedi & Amit Mehta, 2019). Thus, the findings of this study suggest that the choice of teacher training program can be understood through the lens of Maslow's basic needs theory, highlighting the complexity of the factors that motivate individuals to continue their education.

The results of this study have significant implications for the development of education in these three ASEAN countries. For Indonesia, it is recommended that the government prioritize increasing teachers' wages to increase the prestige of the profession in society. This is considered a strategic step to restore public interest in sending their children to teacher training programs (Qonitah Cahyaning Tyas, 2023). In addition, Indonesia's educational institutions must integrate more religious elements and moral values into the curriculum because religious elements are the main motivation for students to choose teacher training programs (Meiliyani & Puspita, 2021). For the Philippine government, it is important for educational institutions to provide learning experiences that reflect the dynamics of the teaching profession, emphasizing the challenges and uniqueness of the profession to spread the welfare of teachers to remote villages. For Thai students, institutions need to maintain a focus on the economic and social rewards of teacher study programs, providing practical insights into the financial benefits and social rewards that can be earned as teachers. This approach is expected to create an educational environment that supports a variety of student motives, ensuring that they feel connected to the values on which their professional choice in teaching is based (Arman et al., 2023).

CONCLUSION

The study revealed that students from the Philippines, Thailand, and Indonesia have the same motivation in choosing a teacher training program. They are united in their determination to improve the quality of education in their home countries, which reflects a shared desire to shape a better next generation. The three countries agreed that choosing a teacher training program is not only a career choice but also a manifestation of a deep desire to make a positive contribution to society. This decision signifies their commitment to play an active role in creating positive change through education. Despite these similarities, different motives explain why students from the Philippines, Thailand, and Indonesia choose teacher training programs. Filipino students see the teaching profession as a dynamic job that is not monotonous, providing opportunities for self-development through new challenges every day. For them, being a teacher also means doing entertaining tasks and interacting with children who have unique characters every day. In contrast, Indonesian students are inspired by religious callings. In addition, encouragement from parents, low working hours, and leisure time are also important factors in their choice. Moreover, Thailand students choose teacher study programs with economic motives because their teachers are rewarded with a decent income, a sense of self-esteem, and respect from society, as well as a form of self-actualization.

Although this study succeeded in finding differences in motivation for choosing teacher education majors in Indonesia, Thailand, and the Philippines, it has several limitations that need to be considered. First, the limited number of countries involved in this study may reduce the generalizability of the findings, given that contextual variations between countries can have a significant effect on the motivation to choose a teacher training major. In addition, data collection methods through in-depth discussions are sometimes susceptible to respondent bias and are difficult to measure objectively. For this reason, future research is recommended to expand the scope of the countries studied, use more structured and measurable data collection methods, and consider broader contextual factors. A deeper understanding of motivational variability at the global level can contribute more substantially to the development of more effective and inclusive education policies.

Acknowledgment

This research was supported by Walisongo State Islamic University Semarang, Indonesia, and "Beasiswa Indonesia Bangkit" in collaboration with the Lembaga Pengelola Dana Pendidikan (LPDP) of the Republic of Indonesia. In preparing this manuscript, we used artificial intelligence (AI) tools to help compose more detailed and organized sentences and paragraphs through Chat GPT.

REFERENCES

Adiele, E. E., & Abraham, N. (2013). Achievement of Abraham Maslow's hierarchy of needs theory among teachers: Implications of human resource management in the high school system in Rivers State. *Journal of Curriculum and Teaching, 2* (1), 140-144. https://doi.org/10.5430/jct.v2n1p140

Amzat, I. H., Don, Y., Fauzee, S. O., Hussin, F., & Raman, A. (2017). Determining motivator and hygiene factors among superior teachers in Malaysia: The experience of confirmatory factor analysis. *International Journal of Educational Management, 31* (2), 78-97. https://doi.org/10.1108/IJEM-03-2015-0034

Aspy, D. N. (1969). Maslow and teachers in training. *Journal of Teacher Education, 20*(3), 303-309. https://doi.org/10.1177/002248716902000310

Assagaf, S. C. Y., & Dotulong, L. O. (2015). The influence of discipline, motivation and work spirit on the work productivity of employees of the regional revenue office of Manado City. *EMBA Journal: Journal of Economics, Management, Business and Accounting Research, 3* (2), 1-10.

Bin Tamuri, A. H., & binti Othman, N. (n.d.). Challenges and solutions of higher education institutions in Asia in the face of the ASEAN economic community (AEC). *International Advisory Board, 8* (8), 1-10.

Busapathumrong, P. (2012). Challenges and trends toward the integration of humanities and social sciences research with an emphasis on the ASEAN socio-cultural community blueprint within the ASEAN community. *Humanities and Social Sciences Research, 2* (5), 10-19.

Cuñado, J., & De Gracia, F. P. (2012). Does education affect happiness? Proof for Spain. *Social Indicators Research, 108* (1), 185-196. https://doi.org/10.1007/s11205-011-9874-x

Daungkaew, R., & Jeenawathana, A. (2015). The state of teacher practice is based on work performance standards and behavioral standards in Thailand. *59th, 15th, 366th World Assembly.*

Denzin, N. K., & Ryan, K. K. (2007). Qualitative methodology (including focus groups). *SAGE Social Science Methodology Handbook*, 578-594.

Dohlman, L., DiMeglio, M., Haji, J., & Laudanski, K. (2019). Global brain drain: How can Maslow's motivational theory improve our understanding of physician migration? *International Journal of Environmental Research and Public Health, 16* (7), 1182. https://doi.org/10.3390/ijerph16071182

Gawel, J. E. (2019). Herzberg's theory of motivation and Maslow's hierarchy of needs. *Assessment, Research, and Practical Evaluation, 5*(1), 11-18.

Gundumogula, M., & Gundumogula, M. (2020). The importance of focus groups in qualitative research. *International Journal of Humanities and Social Sciences (IJHSS), 8* (11), 299-302. https://doi.org/10.1080/00224499.2020.1856462

Gurevich, R. (1975). Teachers, rural development and civil service in Thailand. *Asian Survey, 15 (*10), 870-881.

Hoepfl, M. C. (1997). Choosing qualitative research: Primary for technology education researchers. *Volume 9 Issue 1* (Fall 1997), 1-10.

Juul, P. M. (1959). Pelatihan guru di Thailand. *International Journal of*

Educational Science, *5*(1), 109-115.

Kawuryan, S. P., Sayuti, S. A., & Dwiningrum, S. (2021). Teacher quality and educational equity achievement in Indonesia. *Journal of International Teaching, 14* (2), 811-830.

Kongcharoen, J., Onmek, N., Jandang, P., & Wangyisen, S. (2019). Stress and motivation of primary and secondary school teachers. *Journal of Applied Research in Higher Education, 12* (4), 709-723. https://doi.org/10.1108/JARHE-08-2018-0105

Majorsy, U. (2011). Job satisfaction, work spirit and organizational commitment to the teaching staff of Gunadarma University. *Journal of Psychology, 1* (1), 1-10.

Malmberg, L. E. (2006). Teacher orientation and motivation among teacher applicants and student teachers. *Teacher Teaching and Education, 22* (1), 58-76. https://doi.org/10.1016/j.tate.2005.07.015

Mayall, J. (1990). Nationalism and the international community. Cambridge University Press.

McLeod, S. (2007). Maslow's hierarchy of needs. *Simply Psychology, 1* (1), 1-18.

Meiliyani, R., Fitria, H., & Puspita, Y. (2021). The effect of teacher certification and performance on student learning achievement. *Journal of Education Research, 2* (1), 6-14.

Morgan, D. L. (1996). Focus group as qualitative research (Vol. 16). *Wise Publications*.

Nugraheni, A. S., & Prastiti, W. D. (2016). The relationship between social support and psychological well-being in regional honorary teachers (Doctoral dissertation, University of Muhammadiyah Surakarta).

Nwakasi, C. C., & Cummins, P. A. (2018). Teacher motivation and job satisfaction: A case study of northwestern Nigeria. *Global Journal of Educational Research, 17* (2), 103-112. https://doi.org/10.4314/gjedr.v17i2.5

Oba, M. (2014). ASEAN and the creation of regional communities. *Asia-Pacific Review, 21* (1), 63-78.

Osemeke, M., & Adegboyega, S. (2017). A critical review and comparison between Maslow, Herzberg and McClelland's theory of needs. *Funai Journal of Accounting, Business and Finance, 1* (1), 161-173.

Pitriyani, A., Sanda, Y., Remi, S. N., Yesepa, Y., & Mulawarman, W. G. (2022). Compensation system in ensuring the welfare of honorary teachers in state junior high schools. *Journal of Basicedu, 6* (3), 4004-4015.

Postlethwaite, T. N., & Thomas, R. M. (Eds.). (2014). Schools in the ASEAN region: Primary and secondary education in Indonesia, Malaysia, the Philippines, Singapore, and Thailand. *Elsevier*.

Puteh, M., Che Ahmad, C. N., Mohamed Noh, N., Adnan, M., & Ibrahim, M. H. (2015). The physical environment of the classroom and its relation to the comfort level of teaching and learning. *International Journal of Social Sciences and Humanities, 5 (*3), 237-240.

Radcliffe-Brown, A. R. (1945). Religion and society. *Journal of the Royal Institute of Anthropology United Kingdom and Ireland, 75* (1/2), 33-43.

Randall, E. V. (2013). Culture, religion, and education. In *Religion and Schools in Contemporary America* (pp. 59-81). Routledge.

Raudenbush, S. W., Bhumirat, C., & Kamali, M. (1992). Predictors and consequences of primary school teachers' sense of efficacy and students' perceptions of the quality of teaching in Thailand. *International Journal of Educational Research, 17* (2), 165-177.

Robinson, O. C. (2014). Sampling in interview-based qualitative research: A theoretical and practical guide. *Qualitative Research in Psychology, 11* (1), 25-41. https://doi.org/10.1080/14780887.2013.801543

Rother, S. (2012). Wendt meets East: ASEAN culture of conflict and cooperation. *Cooperation and Conflict, 47* (1), 49-67.

Salmona, M., & Kaczynski, D. (2024). Qualitative data analysis strategies. In *How to Conduct Qualitative Research in Finance* (pp. 80-96). Edward Elgar Publishing.

Saunders, M. N. (2012). Select research participants. In *Qualitative Organizational Research: Core Methods and Current Challenges* (pp. 35-52).

Scribner, B. (1982, October). Religion, society and culture: Reorientation of reformasi. In *History Workshop* (pp. 2-22). Editorial Collective, History Workshop, Ruskin College.

Shaturaev, J. (2021). Education in Indonesia: Financing, quality challenges and academic outcomes in primary education. *Архив научных исследований.*

Sikes, P. (2013). The realities of teachers' work in a developing country. In *The Realities of Teachers' Work* (pp. 201-220). Routledge.

Silverman, D. (2015). *Doing qualitative research.* SAGE Publications.

Simanjuntak, R. (2020). Implementation of the ASEAN framework for promoting teacher mobility. *International Journal of Education Development, 12*(5), 45-65.

Sin, T., & Sin, H. (2020). The effectiveness of teamwork on teachers' performance at high schools in Taiwan. *Educational Research Journal, 13* (2), 1-8.

Sinyo, J., & Natsir, M. (2020). Stress of the honorary teacher and its relation to teaching profession. *Journal of Educational Research, 5* (2), 112-125.

Smith, K., & Dawes, L. (2007). Teaching motivation: A systematic review of teacher development literature. *International Journal of Teaching Research, 6* (5), 1-14.

Sunarni, H. (2017). The effect of teacher motivation on student learning outcomes. *Journal of Educational Research, 5* (2), 40-55.

Tamtam, A., Gwiliza, N. T., & Chacha, P. B. (2022). Teacher motivation and student performance in secondary schools in Tanzania. *International Journal of Education Research, 10* (3), 69-75.

Author bios

Fihris, Dr. M. Ag (In the field of Islamic education) is located at the Faculty of Education and Teacher Training, Walisongo State Islamic University Semarang. Her research interests include Islamic education evaluation, social education science, and international students' international students' academic adaptation. Email: fihris@walisongo.ac.id

Nasikhin, M. Pd (in the field of Islamic Studies) is a Doctoral student at the Faculty of Postgraduate Studies, Walisongo State Islamic University Semarang. Her research interests include teacher education, Islamic education, and socialization of international student academics.
Email: NASIKHIN@walisongo.ac.id

Naifah, Dr. M. Ag (In the field of Arabic language education) is an expert in language research methodology at the Faculty of Education and Teacher Training, Walisongo State Islamic University Semarang. His research interests include foreign language studies for international students.
Email: naifah@walisongo.ac.id

Sofa Muthohar, Dr. M. Ag (In the field of Islamic education) is located at the Faculty of Education and Teacher Training, Walisongo State Islamic University Semarang. Her research interests include Islamic education evaluation, social education science, and international students' international students' academic adaptation. Email: sofamuthohar@walisongo.ac.id.

Article

Journal of International Students
Volume 14, Issue 5 (2024), pp. 177-196
ISSN: 2162-3104 (Print), 2166-3750 (Online)
jistudents.org

The Impact of the COVID-19 Pandemic, Perceived Stress, and Self-Regulation of Chinese International Students

Siu-Man Raymond Ting
Zhiqi Liu
North Carolina State University, USA

ABSTRACT

In this study, we explore the perceived stress and self-regulation of four Chinese international students (CISs) at a public research university in the southeastern United States (U.S.) during the COVID-19 pandemic through individual semi-structured interviews. The identified themes include travel restrictions and delayed required tests, mixed experiences after arrival, differences in education systems, inadequate English preparation and performance, cultural and living adjustments, and limited self-care and coping strategies. The implications of these findings emphasize the importance of self-regulation, a deeper understanding of the challenges faced by international students, and considerations for related policy and practice, as well as directions for future research.

Keywords: international students, COVID-19, perceived stress, self-regulation, student adjustment.

The continued growth of international students not only internationalizes higher education institutions but also has a significant positive economic impact on the U.S. (Abdullah et al., 2013; IIE, 2023). Due to the impacts of COVID-19, in 2020–2021, 914,095 international students were pursuing higher education in the U.S., representing a 15% decrease from the previous academic year (IIE, 2023). Although the quarantine policy for COVID-19 was lifted in many countries after 2021, total enrollment in 2022/2023 was 1,057,188, increasing by 11.5% from the previous year—yet this number remained below pre-pandemic levels (IIE, 2023). Additionally, international students contributed $33.8 billion in revenue to the U.S. economy through tuition and living expenses in 2021–2022, reflecting a 33% decrease from the pre-pandemic figure of 45 billion in 2018 (IIE, n.d.; NAFSA, 2022).

The presence of international students in the U.S. not only contributes to the economy but also enriches academic and cultural experiences within higher education institutions and local communities (NAFSA, 2022). However, the COVID-19 pandemic has introduced unique challenges for international students (Zhai & Du, 2020), including feelings of isolation, reduced engagement, difficulties in maintaining connections with their home country, and experiences of discrimination (Kerr, 2022; Maleku et al., 2021; Song et al., 2021). These challenges can significantly impact the self-regulation of international students, affecting their academic and personal performance in the U.S.

LITERATURE REVIEW

The substantial and, in some cases, irreversible effects of the COVID-19 pandemic on students underscore the importance of researching mental health issues among international students during this time (Zhang, 2022). Research has indicated that self-regulation significantly influences students' psychological well-being and related outcomes prior to the COVID-19 pandemic (Balkis & Duru, 2016; Chen & Lin, 2020; Mattern & Bauer, 2014; Singh & Sharma, 2018). However, there has been limited research on how COVID-19-related stress affects student self-regulation. Given that Chinese students constitute 27.4% of the U.S. international student population in 2022/2023 (IIE, 2023) and their substantial cultural and economic impact on American higher education institutions, understanding the experiences of this demographic is particularly crucial. Chinese international students (CISs) face unique challenges exacerbated by cultural and linguistic differences, as well as sociopolitical tensions between China and the U.S., making their experiences indicative of broader issues among international students during the COVID-19 pandemic. Therefore, this study aims to analyze these specific challenges and examine the relationship between stress and self-regulation among CISs in the U.S. during the pandemic.

Adjusting to Life in the U.S.

Adjusting to life in the U.S. presents significant challenges for CIS, particularly with respect to academic performance and acculturation, even before the COVID-19 pandemic (King & Bailey, 2021). Many CISs studying in the U.S. represent their first exposure to American culture. They often embark on this journey alone, lacking immediate family support, established community networks, or long-standing peer relationships (Chai et al. 2020; Lorenzetti et al., 2023). This isolation can exacerbate the difficulties they face, as they lack familiar support systems that provide emotional comfort and practical assistance during stressful times (Lorenzetti et al., 2023). Consequently, the CIS must navigate the dual challenge of excelling academically in unfamiliar higher education institutions while coping with loneliness and cultural disorientation, all without the benefit of established support structures and while trying to build new social connections in an unfamiliar environment.

Recent research has further illuminated these challenges. Huang et al. (2024) examined the difficulties encountered by students placed on academic probation during their first year of college. The study revealed that these students struggled with adapting to new daily routines, managing reduced adult supervision, overcoming inadequate high school preparation focused mainly on test scores, and coping with limited involvement in the college application process (Huang et al., 2024). Additionally, since English is often a second language for international students, proficiency in English is crucial for their success in completing their degrees in an English-speaking country (Li et al., 2010).

Moreover, previous research highlights the importance of academic integration for success. Rienties et al. (2011) reported that academic integration has a positive effect on academic performance. Interestingly, while non-Western and Western international students exhibited similar study performances, those from non-Western backgrounds were found to be less integrated than their Western counterparts were (Rienties et al., 2011). This finding underscores the complex relationships among cultural background, integration, and academic success for international students.

Although studying abroad benefits language acquisition, cultural integration, and enhanced competitiveness in the job market, it also involves challenges due to the culturally different environments (Cao et al., 2017). Presbitero (2016) examined international students' cultural intelligence in relation to culture shock and reported that culture shock was significantly but negatively related to psychological and sociocultural adaptation. Higher levels of cultural intelligence that international students achieve are associated with less impact of psychological and social adjustment on adapting to different cultures (Presbitero, 2016). Additionally, Yuan et al. (2024) reported that cultural empathy and advice satisfaction significantly influence international students' sense of belonging in U.S. institutions, whereas advisor-advisee rapport does not. Their study emphasized the importance of cultural empathy in helping international students feel connected and supported, thereby improving their overall sense of belonging and aiding their adjustment process.

Challenges during the COVID-19 Pandemic

The COVID-19 pandemic has exacerbated the challenges faced by international students. First, COVID-19-related policies and social, political, and historical contexts have led to increased discrimination (e.g., "Xenophobia" and "Sinophobia") against international students. For example, former president Donald Trump's frequent reference to COVID-19 as the "Chinese virus" or "China virus" contributed to the unfair treatment of Asian international students, particularly those from China, who were unfairly perceived as potential carriers of the virus (Fallows, 2020). This misconception has heightened the discrimination faced by these students. (Zhao, 2020). Zhang et al. (2023) investigated the relationship between perceived discrimination and self-reported overall health among international students and reported that higher levels of perceived discrimination during the pandemic were linked to lower levels of positive emotions and perceived social support (Zhang et al., 2023). Consequently, approximately 37.5% of 261 Chinese international student respondents reported moderate to severe posttraumatic stress disorder (PTSD) symptoms (Song et al., 2021).

COVID-19-Related Factors Affecting Mental Health

COVID-19-related factors such as isolation, a lack of campus services, policy regulations, depression, anxiety, and uncertainty have significantly impacted the mental health of Chinese international students (CIS), leading to increased psychological distress (Fischer & Whatley, n.d.; Kerr, 2022; Maleku et al., 2021; Serafini et al., 2020; Song et al., 2021; Xiong et al., 2022). The abrupt shift to remote learning has further distanced students from their campus communities, exacerbating these issues. Interestingly, Paul et al. (2023) reported that international students demonstrated stronger beliefs in adaptability, malleability, and better mental health than domestic students did during the pandemic. However, this study had a small sample size (n=98) and a modest effect size (7% variance explained). Despite these findings, there remains a critical need to explore the complex relationships among the COVID-19 pandemic, perceived stress, and self-regulation. Mental health was found to mediate the relationship between international student status and involvement (Paul et al., 2023), underscoring the importance of considering both perceived stress and self-regulation strategies in understanding and supporting student well-being during crises.

Perceived Stress and Self-Regulation

Self-regulation is a learning process involving goal-directed behavior that enables individuals to delay gratification in the short term to achieve desired outcomes in the future (Carey et al., 2004; Chen & Lin, 2020; Etkin, 2018). The goal of studying self-regulation among students is to equip them with tools to maintain focus, calmness, and alertness, thereby enhancing their psychological well-being (Etkin, 2018). Research has shown that self-regulation directly affects academic stress, with a negative and significant relationship (Arabzadeh et al., 2012). While investigations have investigated the connections between stress and self-regulation (Brock, 2016; Chen & Lin, 2020), few studies have focused specifically on the impact of COVID-19-related stress on self-regulation.

Cultural factors also play a significant role in shaping attitudes toward self-regulation. In Chinese culture, parental attitudes and practices significantly influence students' social and academic adjustment. Academic achievement is highly valued for future economic security and family honor (Luo et al., 2013). Authoritarian parenting, which involves setting strict guidelines and emphasizing obedience and respect, can place substantial pressure on students even after they enter college. Research indicates that authoritarian parenting is associated with greater learning problems and negatively impacts self-regulation (Pinquart, 2016; Shen et al., 2018). Consequently, authoritarian parenting may contribute to challenges faced by international Chinese students, potentially impeding their academic motivation and achievement.

Miller and Brown (1991) developed the 63-item Self-Regulation Questionnaire (SSRQ) to measure various aspects of self-regulation. Chen and Lin (2018) validated this tool with a sample of 1,998 college students in Taiwan and adapted it into the TSSRQ, a 22-item version with five factors: goal attainment (GA, seven items), mindfulness (MF, seven items), adjustment (AD, three items), proactiveness (PA, three items), and goal setting (GS, two items). These five factors explained 54% of the total variance in self-regulation.

The Study

The current study investigated the impacts of COVID-19 and adjustments on Chinese international students (CIS). The research questions were as follows:

1. How did COVID-19 impact the adjustment of international Chinese students?
2. How did the CIS adjust to a new campus during the COVID-19 pandemic?

METHOD

We used a qualitative multiple-case study (Creswell, 2014). This approach examines multiple cases to identify patterns or make comparisons (Crewell, 2014). After the approval of the Institutional Review Board, the first author contacted an Intensive English Program (IEP) at a public major research university in the southeastern U.S. There were approximately thirty students in the program. Volunteers from this program participated in the study and completed the consent form. In November 2022, the second author conducted individual, semi-structured interviews at the program office. The interviews were audio recorded, transcribed by the second author, and subsequently analyzed collaboratively by the authors.

Participants

There were four participants in the study. Their profiles are summarized below with pseudonyms:

Rose

An 18-year-old female was from a northern province of mainland China with an interest in computer science. She was enrolled in the Intensive English Program (IEP) and arrived on campus in August 2022 after graduating from a public high school. Rose described herself as independent and curious about new experiences.

Billy

A 19-year-old male was also interested in computer science. He came from a southwestern province of mainland China and had been on campus for three months at the time of the interview. Before arriving, Billy attended a bilingual international high school (Chinese and English) in China.

Xiao

A 20-year-old male pursued a major in soil science and crops, he was a volunteer assistant at the IEP. He arrived in the U.S. a year ago and recently transferred to this university. Xiao described himself as dedicated to his studies and expressed enjoyment in living here.

Yan

An 18-year-old male with an interest in mathematics. Yan described himself as an introvert but optimistic. He began attending the IEP in the fall and previously studied at a bilingual international high school in China. He came from a province on the east coast of China.

Data Analysis

We utilized Creswell's (2014) qualitative case methodology to analyze the data. The process began with organizing and preparing the raw data, which included verbatim transcripts from the interviews. We then read through all the data, coded it manually, and developed categories and themes on the basis of the codes. The final step involved interpreting the meanings of these themes and descriptions.

In the coding process, we adhered to Tesch's (1990) eight-step framework. Each of the four cases was reviewed by two authors following these steps:

1. Get a Sense of the Whole Data: Each author read the transcriptions of their assigned cases and made initial notes.
2. Pick One Interview: An in-depth review of one interview was conducted to generate preliminary insights.
3. Review More Interviews: Additional interviews were reviewed to compile a comprehensive list of topics.
4. Abbreviation of Topics as Codes: Topics were condensed into codes.
5. Development of Categories from Topics: Codes were organized into categories.
6. Abbreviation for Each Category: Categories were further abbreviated.
7. Assemble Data Material by Category: Data were organized according to each category.
8. Recode Data as Necessary: Existing data are recoded if needed.

Initially, each author reviewed the transcriptions for two cases, taking detailed notes. They then focused on one case to identify key themes by asking questions such as "What is this about?" and examining the underlying meaning of the information. Notes were compiled into a list of topics, which were subsequently grouped into similar categories. These categories were abbreviated into codes, which were then annotated next to relevant text segments.

The authors convened to discuss their notes, compare ideas, and conduct member checking to minimize individual subjectivity. After agreeing on the preliminary codes and categories, each author independently reviewed and coded the second case, following the same steps.

Upon completion of the analysis for all cases, the authors met to review and finalize the categories and codes. Initially, fifteen categories/themes were identified, which were then refined and consolidated into eight main categories/themes. The final step involved making definitive decisions on the abbreviations for each category/theme and arranging them into codes. The coding process facilitated the generation of a comprehensive description of the respondents and categories/themes.

Trustworthiness and Creditability

To ensure trustworthiness and credibility in their qualitative research, the authors followed Gibbs's (2007) recommendations for team research reliability procedures. Initially, the second author transcribed the interviews. The first author then reviewed the transcripts to verify their accuracy and correct any transcription errors. Following this, the authors convened to discuss their coding processes. This meeting allowed them to review definitions of codes, discuss any disagreements, and adjust the wording or codes as needed. By comparing individual analyses and reviewing meeting notes, including cross-checking topics and codes developed independently by each author, the authors enhanced the validity of their data analysis.

The authors also addressed potential biases in the research findings (Creswell, 2014). Both authors are Chinese: one from the Hong Kong Special Administrative Region and the other from mainland China. Throughout the data analysis, they engaged in self-reflection to ensure an open and honest narrative. During meetings, they discussed how their backgrounds—such as gender, race, culture, traditions, socioeconomic status, and personal perspectives—shaped their interpretations of the findings. This reflective process helps mitigate subjectivity and bias.

Additionally, the authors employed a rich, thick description to present their findings, enhancing the validity of their results (Creswell, 2014). They provided detailed descriptions and interpretations of the setting and the unique challenges faced by the students. For example, they offered diverse perspectives and experiences related to themes such as mixed initial experiences, contributing to a more comprehensive and realistic portrayal of the study's outcomes.

RESULTS

Eight themes were identified and reported below.

Motivation for Overseas Studies

The primary motivation for CIS pursuing education in the U.S. was the pursuit of higher-quality education. Billy explained, "My motivation is about opportunities for better education. My academic background was not strong, so I could not get into top universities in China." The students recognized the differences in education systems and the U.S. Billy elaborated,

> I can learn new thinking skills here through small group discussions in class or other situations, which I cannot experience in China...This knowledge I cannot learn from textbooks...Education in China does not encourage thinking. Instead, it is focused on textbooks and results and lacks practical application. It is not helpful for my future life... I want to apply what I learn into real life.

Another student, Rose, said, "The study environment is better here," whereas Yan mentioned, "I want to experience a broader world and reach my potential."

Some students aspired to live in the U.S. after graduation. Rose shared, "My parents want me to work and live here after my graduation.... I applied to study the U.S. during the COVID-19 pandemic. My father has thought about this for a long time." Xiao stated, "My goal is to find internship and research opportunities through my department." These motivations reflect broader trends of migration from China, with an overseas education pathway to future opportunities.

At present, the students' immediate goal is to complete the Intensive English Program or degree. Yan remarked, "My goal is now to pass the IEP although I am not particularly interested in English." The necessity of passing the English program before progressing to the degree program was acknowledged by all the students.

Travel Restrictions and Delayed Required Tests

All the students reported being delayed due to travel restrictions and taking the required tests. Many challenges were reported, ranging from applying for travel documents to being delayed by the restrictions of the quarantine policy. The issues included challenges in applying for passports, taking the TOEFL, and arranging flights. Billy said:

> Yes, some difficulties. In the application process, I went to different places. I found tutorials for TOEFL; I took TOEFL 10 times. My school helped me with my college application. I also got help from private consulting agencies...I cannot take the SAT/TOEFL as I can in a normal situation (because of COVID-19). I had to go to another province to take the test.

The students also encountered delays in passport applications, although the video applications were generally smooth. Billy noted, "The visa application process was smooth, probably because my parents own a business and are not government workers."

Travel from China to the U.S. was particularly challenging. Billy recounted, "Flying to the U.S. was difficult; I had to take an indirect route with stops in two cities in China before reaching the U.S." Rose added:

> The pandemic created both practical and psychological problems for me. The pandemic is a barrier. I faced big problems. My TOEFL was delayed, and finally, for one whole year. In addition, I broke down, so upset. Finally, I did not take the test and I came... My passport application was also delayed by the authorities, unless you know someone who is a police officer. Otherwise, you cannot obtain the passport. Finally, I found a police person who we know and got it done. After this, we contacted a consulting agency for overseas studies; they helped me apply to study in the U.S. The visa application was fine.

The late reopening of test sites significantly impacted students' travel plans, with some experiencing delays of up to a year. Yan expressed concerns about safety and health, stating, "The most challenging aspect was COVID-19. Compared with those in China, the public health policies in China are inadequate. I worry about contracting COVID-19 and the implications for returning to China."

Another student mentioned, "Keeping myself from getting sick was challenging, especially with limited test places and seats for the TOEFL. The visa application process was fine, but I had to travel to another city due to a flood in my own city."

Owing to ongoing quarantine policies in China and limited flights, students were unable to visit their families. This resulted in significantly higher ticket prices. Rose said, "I cannot visit my parents due to China's quarantine policy and the high cost of air tickets." Xiao added, "I did not return to China for two years, and even when I did, finding tickets was still difficult.

Mixed Experiences After Arrival

Upon arriving at campus, the students reported various experiences. Xiao and Rose faced immediate challenges, particularly with the use of English. Rose share:

> I felt loneliness and didn't know what to do when I was by myself. I also struggled to find female friends, which made me feel sad. Language is a significant barrier for me, and I found that others' English skills were not much better.

Xiao expressed similar sentiments: "I felt challenged and was unsure about my major during the first year. I was confused and didn't know what direction to take."

In contrast, other students initially had positive experiences. Yan remarked, "Things here are attractive and interesting. I felt good about this place." Support from the Intensive English Program (IEP) was beneficial for some students' initial adjustments. Xiao noted, "I followed the advice from my academic advisor. I thought the IEP advisor's guidance was more helpful than that of my academic advisor [professor]. Billy also appreciated the support: "Instructors took me on campus visits, which helped me understand life here. This was very helpful." Yan found that the program provided various activities and options: "[the program offered] more activities and choices. I could try different things."

Differences in Education Systems

The differences between the education systems in China and those in U.S. Chinese education are often focused on direct teaching, textbooks, and memorization, whereas U.S. education emphasizes student-centered learning, guided discovery, projects, and group work. Most students found these differences challenging, except for Yan, who felt well prepared. Yan commented, "The international school I attended prepared me well for studying here. I adjusted easily, though I found spoken English challenging, but not written or reading English. My English proficiency was better."

Billy described his experience: "I work hard in the IEP, and I find the curriculum challenging. The instructors are demanding. Additionally, I need to wear a hearing aid, which adds to my challenges." Rose also faced difficulties and noted that the pandemic affected her motivation:

> I am only studying English in the IEP now. I have some challenges, but not enormous. The pandemic has influenced my motivation to study, and I rate my academic pressure as 4 on a scale of 1--10.

The transition to online classes was another source of difficulty. Xiao explained, "Online classes were challenging, especially for experiments. My first semester was fine with face-to-face classes, but after the COVID-19 pandemic started and online classes began, it became difficult."

Xiao rated his academic pressure as moderate, approximately 6--7 on a scale of 1--10, and linked it primarily to English usage: "Writing in English, such as lab reports, was challenging owing to difficulties with finding materials and formats." However, Xiao acknowledged that his international school background was beneficial in some way:

> My experience in international high school helped me adjust here because I was familiar with the knowledge and study methods. Some classes, such as biology and chemistry, were challenging, as we did not perform many experiments in high school science classes.

Yan was the only student who felt relatively comfortable: "The curriculum is more relaxed, and I have more personal free time. The study methods are similar to those in my international high school, so I do not feel much stress in studying."

Inadequacy of International School Preparation

Despite the expectation that students from international schools would be better prepared for studying overseas, the findings of the current study suggest otherwise. Most of the students, with the exception of Rose, had attended international programs and were preparing for overseas education. It was anticipated that their English proficiency and readiness for an American education system would be stronger. However, contrary to this expectation, the students experienced significant challenges in adjusting to the American education system.

This observation aligns with the first author's previous experiences with consulting in China. This study highlights a critical gap in the effectiveness of international school education in preparing students for the demands of studying abroad. The participants' struggles indicate that the international schools did not adequately equip them for the academic and cultural transitions they faced.

English proficiency, which is a crucial factor in overseas studies, was found to be a significant issue. The inadequacy in English education at international schools appears to have left these students less prepared than anticipated. This finding underscores the need for a more comprehensive approach to English language instruction and preparation for international education.

Inadequate English Preparation and Performance

Most students reported significant challenges with their English skills, which created barriers to their academic success. They expressed difficulties in listening, speaking, and writing in English, which affected their overall performance in class.

Rose noted that their preparation for studying abroad was inadequate and focused primarily on TOEFL preparation rather than comprehensive English language skills. Rose shared, "However, the preparation was not sufficient, only focusing on TOEFL. Classes are now divided into reading, listening, and writing. I find English writing particularly challenging, especially citations. The most difficult part for me is listening; reading and speaking are also challenging."

Yan highlighted a similar struggle: "I am not good at spoken English. I had little practice in high school and passed the TOEFL with the help of a private tutorial in China." Xiao echoed this sentiment, saying, "English writing in my first year was challenging, especially with my lab reports."

The students reported spending extra time on assignments, such as compositions, which led to long hours and intensive workloads. This intensive work contributed to their academic stress. Only Yan experienced relatively few problems with adjustment, which was attributed to the similarities between the curriculum and study methods at his international high school and those at his current institution.

These experiences underscore a significant relationship between prior English preparation and later academic performance. The lack of comprehensive English language training before arriving in the U.S. appears to have affected the students' ability to adapt effectively to their academic environment.

Cultural and Living Adjustments

All the students reported facing significant adjustment issues related to living on campus and adapting to different cultures and ways of life. Billy expressed difficulties with cultural differences and logistical issues: "Different cultures in the U.S. Still adjusting to it, such as direct communication here and some perceptions about me as a foreign student. I must eat on campus, and on Saturdays, the student cafeteria is not open. It is not convenient."

In contrast, Yan reported a smoother adjustment: "I am fine adjusting here. I feel comfortable staying with Chinese people only. I am optimistic and easy to feel happy." However, Yan's experience was not shared by the others.

Food was a major issue for many students. They struggled with local American cuisine, and two students mentioned difficulties with shopping and using the payment system. Yan noted, "I am not used to the payment system here. China was more convenient with WeChat (using cell phones)." The students found that the electronic currency system in China, which is widely adopted, made transactions more convenient than did the U.S. system.

Social integration poses another challenge. Many students reported a lack of local friends and difficulties in making connections with domestic students. Rose said, "Cultural and language differences are barriers for me to adjust here. I hang out with my Chinese friends; it helps me adjust to life here. I have tried to make friends with local students, but it is not easy, and it takes a long time." Xiao shared, "'I live on campus, but I do not socialize with others. I only socialized with my roommate. They were also in the IEP." Yan mentioned, "I am more of an introvert. Not interested in making friends with Americans and strangers."

The use of English emerged as a barrier to effective communication and relationship-building. Many students primarily interacted with fellow Chinese students, limiting their exposure to the broader campus community. Some students mentioned feelings of loneliness and homesickness, which were exacerbated by the inability to return to China during long holidays due to COVID-19. Yan shared, "I miss home, especially when my grandfather passed away recently; I cannot go back." Yan also expressed a preference for staying home and avoiding social activities: "I would like to stay home and do not like to go outside. I will stay here during the winter break; I worry that it will be boring. I do not reach out to make friends here yet."

Despite these challenges, students were gradually learning to cope with and adapt to their new environment. Xiao noted, "I learned how to call a taxi, take a bus, and how to buy things. Public transportation here is not as good or easy as it is in China."

Limited Self-care and Coping Strategies

The students faced significant stress while studying in a new environment, but they reported limited use of effective coping strategies. Some students sought support from teachers or counselors with mixed results. Xiao noted, "IEP advisors helped me a lot through team advising." In contrast, Billy mentioned, "I tried to ask teachers for help, but the effects were minimal. My listening skills cannot improve quickly, and this is an English environment." Rose shared her approach to coping with stress:

> I force myself to go to sleep when I feel stressed. I tend to avoid thinking about it. I just put myself into my studies and keep busy, even though I know it's not a good solution.

Rose also mentioned personal struggles: "I have dating problems, but I cannot resolve them. The more I think about them, the more confused and troubled I become. Therefore, I try to forget about them." Recently, Rose started exploring Buddhism as a form of stress relief: "I'm trying to forget all of these issues through Buddhism."

Billy and Rose sought professional help from counselors. Rose said, "I see a counselor once or twice, but preparing for sessions creates additional pressure. I'm not sure if I should continue, as I feel my problems are unresolved." In contrast, Xiao found some relief through support from friends and family:

> I learned from other students who had more experience. I also talked to my parents and friends. My parents, particularly my father, who is a biology professor, have helped me a lot through virtual meetings.

Yan, however, chose not to seek help from others and reported feeling isolated: "I prefer to stay home and do not like to go outside. I will stay here during the winter break, which I worry will be boring." Yan admitted, "I have not reached out to make friends here yet."

Xiao also mentioned a preference for handling issues independently: "I like to deal with problems by myself and do not want to seek help from professionals like counselors."

With respect to self-care, few students had established effective strategies or knew how to balance their lives. Most students focused primarily on their studies and socialized mainly with other Chinese international students, avoiding campus activities. This limited engagement with broader campus life suggests a lack of effective self-care practices and social integration strategies.

DISCUSSION

The findings from this study underscore the multifaceted challenges international students face during their transition to study in the U.S., especially under the strains of the COVID-19 pandemic. The pandemic significantly affected students' experiences, from delays in passport and visa processes to difficulties with online classes and high travel costs. These issues compound students' stress and disrupt their academic and personal lives.

This study confirms previous research on the pandemic's impact on loneliness, isolation, and emotional struggles (Fischer & Whatley, n.d.; Kerr, 2022; Maleku et al., 2021; Serafini et al., 2020; Song et al., 2021; Xiong et al., 2022), highlighting how COVID-19 exacerbated existing challenges for international students.

Self-Regulation and Coping Strategies

The findings align with the self-regulation model (Miller & Brown, 1991; Chen & Lin, 2018), demonstrating the importance of self-regulation in managing stress. However, the students struggled with effective coping strategies. Many reported using avoidance or minimal strategies, reflecting low self-regulation skills.

This study provides new evidence that self-regulation directly affects academic stress, with a negative and significant relationship during the COVID-19 pandemic. Furthermore, this study elucidates the relationship between stress and self-regulation, corroborating the findings of previous studies (Brock, 2016; Chen & Lin, 2020) conducted prior to the pandemic.

This study revealed a lack of self-care coping strategies among the students. The limited use of coping strategies, such as seeking professional help or engaging in self-care, points to the need for better self-regulation and coping strategies and improved support systems and coping resources for international students.

Motivation and Academic Adjustment

Students were motivated by the desire for better education and career opportunities in the U.S., aligning with King and Baily's (2021) findings. This motivation could help the students continue to complete their program. However, given their limited English ability and ability to enrol in an IEP, their immediate goal was to achieve this goal in the IEP and move on to a degree program. One of the students did not join the IEP, his English was better, and he was directly admitted to a degree program. Despite this motivation, challenges such as limited English proficiency and adjustments to the American education system have hindered their academic progress.

The study revealed that students from international schools in China faced difficulties due to inadequate preparation, contradicting the assumption that international schools provide sufficient readiness for U.S. education. This also confirms the first author's consultation experiences in China. He has seen a mixed quality of international schools there. Some international schools use Chinese as the teaching medium, although they believe that their classes are in English. These schools should use English as their teaching language for their students.

Cultural and Social Adjustment

Students encounter various adjustment issues related to cultural differences, food, transportation, and social integration. Most chose to socialize mainly with other Chinese students, which limited their overall integration into the campus community. This confirms similar findings for international students (Huang et al, 2024; Presbitero, 2016; Yuan et al. 2024). Furthermore, this socializing pattern exacerbates the stress experienced by the CIS, as two individuals reported seeking counseling for their emotional distress and related issues.

The lack of engagement with broader campus activities and the preference for staying within their comfort zones underscore the need for initiatives that promote social integration and cultural adaptation (Li et al., 2010; Cao et al., 2017; Rienties et al., 2011). It appears that the IEP helped the ICS in some way by providing social and cultural activities. International student advisors can work collaboratively with the IEP or similar programs to develop and offer culturally enriching programs, social events, and activities.

Racial Discrimination, Stress, and Social Connectedness

While students did not report significant experiences of racial discrimination, the potential for such issues should not be ignored. Encouraging international students to engage with the broader campus community can mitigate perceived discrimination and reduce stress (Wei et al., 2012; Wong et al., 2014). Wei et al. (2012) reported that high social connectedness in the ethnic community weakened the strength of the association with perceived racial discrimination. However, social connectedness in mainstream society is significantly associated with less perceived general stress, less perceived racial discrimination, and less posttraumatic stress symptoms. This suggests that student affairs professionals should encourage international students to be involved in the campus community with more students, not just those associated with Chinese students, as was the case in the current study.

Wong et al. (2014) reported that among international Asian students who had high levels of masculine identity, their perceived racial discrimination was positively related to their subjective masculinity stress. Additionally, subjective masculinity stress was found to have mediating effects on the relationship between perceived racial discrimination and psychological distress.

Policy and Service Recommendations

Pre-Arrival Preparation: Schools in students' countries of origin should enhance English language training and provide a better understanding of the U.S. education system.

Support Services: IEPs should continue to play a critical role in improving English proficiency and bridging cultural gaps. They should also offer more comprehensive support during the transition and adjustment phases. This could help enhance students' social integration into the new community (Presbitero, 2016)

Addressing Travel Barriers: Governments and airlines should work toward reducing visa restrictions and high travel costs to ease the burden on international students.

In summary, this study highlights the complex challenges faced by international students, exacerbated by the COVID-19 pandemic. It emphasizes the need for improved prearrival preparation, enhanced support services, and effective coping strategies to better support students in their academic and personal adjustment. Addressing these issues is crucial for fostering a more supportive and inclusive environment for international students.

Limitations

The findings offer valuable perspectives on how CISs deal with stress and manage their behavior during the COVID-19 pandemic. However, this study has several shortcomings. First, the study relied solely on interview data, which may not capture the full spectrum of experiences or behaviors. Future studies may incorporate alternative data collection methods, such as surveys and observations, to gather a broader range of information. Surveys could provide quantitative data to validate qualitative insights from interviews, and observations could offer a contextual understanding of students' interactions and behaviors. Second, only CISs were included in the study, which may not reflect the experiences of other international students. Additionally, the majority of CISs in this study was enrolled in a one-year intensive program designed specifically for students with limited English proficiency. Future research should incorporate a diverse sample of international students from various countries and with a range of English proficiency levels to enable a comprehensive comparison and analysis of their experiences. This would provide a more comprehensive view of the challenges faced by different groups and help identify universal and culturally specific issues. Third, because the study was limited to a single public university, it did not consider the variety of experiences that students from other learning environments would have had. In the future, the research should be expanded to include multiple universities with varied characteristics (e.g., private vs. public, large vs. small) to capture a wider range of student experiences. This would help determine if the findings are unique to a particular institution or applicable more broadly. Finally, because the study was performed during a certain pandemic, it might not fully represent how international students handle changing circumstances in the post-pandemic world. Longitudinal studies are recommended to examine how students' experiences and coping strategies evolve over time, particularly as the pandemic situation changes. This could provide insights into how resilient students are in the face of ongoing or future crises.

CONCLUSIONS

This study presents preliminary evidence of the impact of COVID-19 on CISs participating in intense English programs, as well as an explanation of their adjustments. This finding highlights the link between perceived stress and self-regulation in this population. Future studies may duplicate or broaden the current study to include other international students, such as those admitted on a regular basis from different countries of origin.

REFERENCES

Abdullah, D., Abd Aziz, M. I., & Mohd Ibrahim, A. L. (2013). A "research" into international student-related research: (Re)visualizing our stand? *Higher Education*, *67*(3), 235–253. https://doi.org/10.1007/s10734-013-9647-3

Arabzadeh, M., Nikdel, F., Kadivar, P., Kavousian, J., & Hashemi, K. (2012). The relationship of self-regulation and self-efficacy with academic stress in university students. *International Journal of Education and Psychology in the Community*, *2*(2), 102-113. https://proxying.lib.ncsu.edu/index.php/login?url=https://www-proquest-com.prox.lib.ncs u.edu/scholarly journals/relationship-self-regulation-efficacy-with/docview/2220696486/se-2

Balkis, M., and Duru, E. (2016). Procrastination, self-regulation failure, academic life satisfaction, and active well-being: underregulation or misregulation form. *European Journal of Psychological Education. 31*, 439–459. https://doi: 10.1007/s10212-015-0266-5

Brock, C.I. (2016). The relationship between self-regulation and stress, sleep, and behavioral health. *CMC Senior Theses*. Paper 1370. http://scholarship.claremont.edu/cmc_theses/1370

Cao, C., Zhu, C., & Meng, Q. (2017). Predicting Chinese international students' acculturation strategies from sociodemographic variables and social ties. *Asian Journal of Social Psychology*, *20*(2), 85–96. https://doi.org/10.1111/ajsp.12171

Carey, K. B., Neal, D. J., & Collins, S. E. (2004). A psychometric analysis of the self-regulation questionnaire. *Addictive Behaviors*, *29*(2), 253–260. https://doi.org/10.1016/j.addbeh.2003.08.001

Chai, D. S., Van, H. T. M., Wang, C., & W., Lee, J., & Wang, J. (2020). What do international students need? The role of family and community supports for adjustment, engagement, and organizational citizenship behavior. *Journal of International Students*, *10*(3), 571–589. https://doi.org/10.32674/jis.v10i3.1235

Chen Y. H., Lin Y. J. (2018). Validation of the short self-regulation questionnaire for Taiwanese college students (TSSRQ). *Frontiers in Psychology*, 9: 259. https://doi: 10.3389/fpsyg.2018.00259

Creswell, J. W. (2014). Research design: Qualitative, quantitative and mixed methods approaches (4th ed.). p.245-253, Thousand Oaks, CA: Sage.

Fallows, J. (2020). *2020 time capsule #5: The 'Chinese Virus'.* The Atlantic. Retrieved December 9, 2022, from

https://www.theatlantic.com/notes/2020/03/2020-time-capsule-5-the-chinese-virus/60826 0/.

Etkin, J. (2018). Understand self-regulation in education. *BU Journal of Graduate Studies in*

Education, *10*(1), 35–39. https://eric.ed.gov/?id=EJ1230272

Fischer, H., & Whatley, M. (n.d.). *COVID-19 impact research brief: International students at community colleges.* Retrieved August 5, 2021 from https://www.nafsa.org/sites/default/files/media/document/covid-19-impact-research.pdf

Gibbs, G. R. (2007). Analyzing qualitative data. In U. Flick (Ed). *The Sage qualitative research skit.* Sage.

Huang, Q., Qin, D. B., Liu, J., & Park, H.-J. (2024). Challenges and resilience of first-year Chinese international students on academic probation. *Journal of International Students*, *14*(1), 134–151. https://doi.org/10.32674/jis.v14i2.5282

Institute of International Education. (n.d.). *Economic impact of international students.* Opendoors. Retrieved September 5, 2022 from https://www.iie.org/Research-and-Insights/Open-Doors/Economic-Impact-of-International-Students

Institute of International Education. (2023). *Fast facts 2023*. Opendoors.
https://opendoorsdata.org/fast_facts/fast-facts-2023/

Kerr, R. (2022). *A second "pandemic": How COVID-19 has impacted international student mental health in North Carolina* [Capstone Collection]. https://digitalcollections.sit.edu/capstones/3262/

King, C. S. T., & Bailey, K. S. (2021). Intercultural communication and US higher education: How US students and faculty can improve. *International Journal of Intercultural Relations*, *82*, 278–287. https://doi.org/10.1016/j.ijintrel.2021.04.007

Li, G., Chen, W., & Duanmu, J. L. (2010). Determinants of international students' Academic Performance: A comparison between Chinese and other international students. *Journal of Studies in International Education, 14*(4), 389–405. https://doi.org/10.1177/1028315309331490

Lorenzetti, D., Lorenzetti, L., Nowell, L., Jacobsen, M., Clancy, T., Freeman, G., & Oddone Paolucci, E. (2023). Exploring international graduate students' experiences, challenges, and peer relationships: Impacts on academic and emotional well-being. *Journal of International Students*, *13*(4), 22–41. https://doi.org/10.32674/jis.v14i2.5186

Luo, R., Tamis-LeMonda, C. S., & Song, L. (2013). Chinese parents' goals and practices in early childhood. *Early Childhood Research Quarterly, 28,* 843–857.

Maleku, A., Kim, Y. K., Kirsch, J., Um, M. Y., Haran, H., Yu, M., & Moon, S. S. (2021). The hidden minority: Discrimination and mental health among international students in the US during the COVID-19 pandemic. *Health & Social Care in the Community*, *30*(5). https://doi.org/10.1111/hsc.13683

Mattern, J., & Bauer, J. (2014). Does teachers' cognitive self-regulation increase their occupational well-being? The structure and role of self-regulation in the teaching context. *Teaching and Teacher Education*, *43*, 58–68. https://doi.org/10.1016/j.tate.2014.05.004

Miller, W. R., and Brown, J. M. (1991). "Self-regulation as a conceptual basis for the prevention and treatment of addictive behaviors," in *Self-Control and Addictive Behaviors*, eds N. Heather, W. R. Miller, and J. Greeley (Sydney, NSW: Maxwell Macmillan Publishing), 3–79.

NAFSA: Association of International Educators. (2022). *The United States of America benefits from international students*. Retrieved December 9, 2022, from https://www.nafsa.org/sites/default/files/media/document/EconValue-2022.pdf.

Paul, N., Han, J., & Usher, E. L. (2023). "Doing college" amidst COVID-19: A comparative study exploring differences in the psychological experiences of international and domestic students in the U.S. *Journal of International Students*, *13*(4), 240–260. https://doi.org/10.32674/jis.v13i4.4923

Pinquart, M. (2016). Associations of parenting styles and dimensions with academic achievement in children and adolescents: a metaanalysis. *Educational Psychology Review, 28*, 475–493.

Presbitero, A. (2016). Culture shock and reverse culture shock: The moderating role of cultural intelligence in international students' adaptation. *International Journal of Intercultural Relations*, *53*, 28–38. https://doi.org/10.1016/j.ijintrel.2016.05.004

Rienties, B., Beausaert, S., Grohnert, T., Niemantsverdriet, S., & Kommers, P. (2011). Understanding academic performance of international students: The role of ethnicity, academic and social integration. *Higher Education, 63*(6), 685–700. https://doi.org/10.1007/s10734-011-9468-1

Serafini, G., Parmigiani, B., Amerio, A., Aguglia, A., Sher, L., & Amore, M. (2020). The psychological impact of COVID-19 on the mental health in the general population. *QJM: An International Journal of Medicine, 113*(8), 531–537. https://doi.org/10.1093/qjmed/hcaa201

Shen, J. J., Cheah, C. S. L., & Yu, J. (2018). Asian American and European American emerging adults' perceived parenting styles and self-regulation ability. *Asian American Journal of Psychology, 9,* 140–148.

Singh, S., and Sharma, N. R. (2018). Self-regulation as a correlate of psychological well-being.

Indian J. Health Wellb. 9(3), 441–444. Retrieved from https://www.i-scholar.in/index.php/ijhw/article/view/181481

Song, B., Zhao, Y., & Zhu, J. (2021). COVID-19-related traumatic effects and psychological reactions among international students. *Journal of Epidemiology and Global Health, 11*(1). https://doi.org/10.2991/jegh.k.201016.001

Tesch, R. (1990). *Qualitative research: Analysis types and software tools.* Falmer.

Wei, M., Want, K. T., P. Heppner, & Du, Y. (2012). Ethnic and mainstream social connectedness, perceived racial discrimination, and posttraumatic stress symptoms. *Journal of Counseling Psychology, 59(3),* 486-493.

Wong, Y. J. , Tsai, P., Liu, T., & Zhu, Q. (2014). Male Asian international students' perceived racial discrimination, masculine identity, and subjective masculinity stress. *Journal of Counseling Psychology, 61(4),* 560-569.

Xiong, Y., Rose Parasath, P., Zhang, Q., & Jeon, L. (2022). International students' perceived discrimination and psychological distress during the COVID-19 pandemic. *Journal of American college health,* 1–12. Advance online publication. https://doi.org/10.1080/07448481.2022.2059376

Yuan, X., Yang, Y., & McGill, C. (2023). The impact of academic advising activities on international students' sense of belonging. *Journal of International Students, 14*(1), 424–448. https://doi.org/10.32674/jis.v14i3.5227

Zhai, Y., & Du, X. (2020). Mental health care for international Chinese students affected by the COVID-19 outbreak. *The Lancet Psychiatry, 7*(4), e22. https://doi.org/10.1016/S2215-0366(20)30089-4

Zhang, J. (2022). Analysis of the psychological state of college students in the postpandemic period and adjustment strategies. *The 2022 3rd International Conference on Mental Health, Education and Human Development (MHEHD 2022).* https://doi.org/10.2991/assehr.k.220704.145

Zhang, Q., Xiong, Y., Rose Prasath, P., & Byun, S. (2023). The relationship between international students' perceived discrimination and self-reported overall health during COVID-19: Indirect associations through positive emotions and perceived social support. *Journal of International Students, 14*(1), 119–133. https://doi.org/10.32674/jis.v14i1.5368

Zhao, Y. (2020). Psychological impacts of the COVID-19 outbreak on Chinese international students: Examining prevalence and associated factors. *World*

Journal of Educational Research, *7*(3), 45-58. https://doi.org/10.22158/wjer.v7n3p45

Bios

SIU-MAN RAYMOND TING, PhD, Professor of Counseling and Director of Graduate Program in the Department of Educational Research, Leadership, Policy and Human Development at North Carolina State University. His research interest focuses on student success, career development, international students, STEM education, and online education. Email: ting@ncsu.edu.

ZHIQI LIU is a 3rd-year doctoral student in Counseling and Counselor Education at North Carolina State University. Her research focuses on international students' career readiness and multicultural competence among college counselors. Email: zliu78@ncsu.edu.

www.ingramcontent.com/pod-product-compliance
Lightning Source LLC
LaVergne TN
LVHW050540160826
845677LV00011B/2110

* 9 7 9 8 2 3 0 2 0 7 4 1 2 *